Elizabeth Regina

Elizabeth Regina

THE AGE
OF TRIUMPH
1588-1603

ALISON PLOWDEN

M

©Alison Plowden 1980
ISBN 0 333 23174 0
First published 1980 in America
First published in Great Britain 1980 by
MACMILLAN LONDON LIMITED
4 Little Essex Street London WC2R 3LF
and Basingstoke
Associated Companies in Delhi, Dublin,
Hong Kong, Johannesburg, Lagos, Melbourne,
New York, Singapore and Tokyo

Contents

List of Illustrations

Following page 90.

1. Queen Elizabeth in procession. By courtesy of Mr Simon Wingfield Digby, Sherborne Castle.

2. (*Top*) Lord Burghley and Robert Cecil. By courtesy of The Marquess of Salisbury.
(*Bottom left*) Anthony Bacon. Reproduced from The Gorhambury Collection by permission of The Earl of Verulam.
(*Bottom right*) Francis Bacon. By courtesy of National Portrait Gallery, London.

3. (*Top*) Essex House in the Strand. By courtesy of Mansell Collection.
(*Bottom*) Robert Devereux, Earl of Essex. By courtesy of National Portrait Gallery, London.

4. Nonesuch Palace. By courtesy of Mansell Collection.

5. English Attack on Cadiz, 1596. By courtesy of National Maritime Museum, London.

6. Lord Admiral Charles Howard of Effingham. By courtesy of National Maritime Museum, London.

7. (*Top left*) Sir Walter Raleigh, 1588. By courtesy of National Portrait Gallery, London.
(*Top right*) Sir Richard Grenville. By courtesy of National Portrait Gallery, London.
(*Bottom left*) Sir John Norris. By courtesy of Lord Sackville.

Elizabeth Regina

Early before the day doth spring,
Let us awake my Muse and sing:
It is no time to slumber,
So many joys this time doth bring,
As time will fail to number.

But whereto shall we bend our layes?
Even up to Heaven, againe to raise
The Maid, which thence descended:
Hath brought againe the golden days,
And all the world amended.

Rudeness itself she dothe repine,
Even like an Alchemist divine,
Gross times of iron turning
Into the purest forme of gold:
Not to corrupt, till heaven waxe old,
And be refined with burning.

John Davies,
Hymns of Astrea

Prologue
The Year Eighty-Eight

The Spanish fleet did float in narrow seas,
And bend her ships against the English shore,
With so great rage as nothing could appease,
And with such strength as never seen before.

It was late in the afternoon of Friday, 19 June 1588 when Captain Thomas Fleming brought the bark *Golden Hind* scudding under full sail into Plymouth Sound. The Lord Admiral Charles Howard and a group of his senior officers were out on the Hoe relaxing over an after-dinner game of bowls when Fleming came panting up to report that the Spanish Armada had been sighted that morning off the Scillies and Sir Francis Drake, so the story goes, remarked that there was time enough to finish the game and beat the Spaniards too. The story may well be true. The wind was blowing from the south-west and at three o'clock the tide had begun flooding into the Sound. Until the ebb, round about ten in the evening, the English battle fleet was effectively immobilised and there would have been plenty of time to finish a leisurely game of bowls.

But all through that night Plymouth harbour seethed with activity as the crews sweated at their gruelling task of towing the heavy warships out on the ebb tide, and by daybreak the bulk of the fleet was riding at anchor behind Rame Head. All through that night, too, the beacon fires flung the news from hill-top to hill-top – leaping along the south coast from the Lizard to Beachy Head, up to Bristol and South Wales, across the Sussex Downs to the Surrey hills and the heights of Hampstead and into the Midland shires:

> *Till Belvoir's lordly terraces the sign to Lincoln sent,*
> *And Lincoln sent the message on, o'er the wild vale of Trent;*
> *Till Skiddaw saw the fire that burnt on Gaunt's embattled pile,*
> *And the red glare on Skiddaw roused the burghers of Carlisle.*

The long nervous wait was over and England was as ready as she would ever be to meet the onslaught of Spain. Sir Walter Raleigh and his cousin Richard Grenville commanded in the vulnerable West Country and Sir John Norris, responsible for coastal defences from Dorset to Kent, had detached three thousand men to guard the Isle of Wight, regarded as another key point. In Essex, which would be in the front line if the Duke of Parma's army, now embarking at Dunkirk, succeeded in making the crossing, the Earl of Leicester was gathering fourteen thousand foot and two thousand horse; while in Kent Lord Hunsdon had raised another eight thousand. The inland counties were also doing their bit, if a little reluctantly – the imminence of danger by seaborne invasion was naturally harder to impress on men who had never seen the sea. But Sir Henry Cromwell on a visit to London was so struck by the sense of urgency round the capital, by the sight of guarded ferries and crossroads and of men drilling with musket and caliver on every open space, that he wrote home to Huntingdon in a strenuous effort to convey the immediacy of the crisis and ordering all captains and leading gentlemen to stay at their posts, ready to march at an hour's warning.

A notably easy-going and unmilitaristic nation was doing its best and no one questioned the courage and resolution of the islanders as they prepared that long-ago summer to defend their lives and liberty, their homes and their religion. Equally, no one with any military experience could doubt that an encounter between Parma's Black-beards – hard-bitten veterans of a dozen bloody campaigns commanded by the best general in Europe – and Queen Elizabeth's un-trained, sketchily equipped citizen army would result in anything but a massacre. The business must be settled at sea, or the country would go down in fire and slaughter, famine, pestilence and persecution. Fortunately, the seamen, although fully conscious of the awesome nature of their responsibility, had every confidence in their ability to hinder the enemy's quiet passage into England. Francis Drake, writing to the Queen from Plymouth in April, assured Her Majesty that he had not in his lifetime 'known better men and possessed with gallanter minds than the people which are here gathered together, voluntarily to put their hands and hearts to the finishing of this great piece of work'. The navy, in fact, was itching to get to grips with the Armada.

The two fleets first sighted one another west of the Eddystone about three o'clock in the afternoon of Saturday 20 July and during that night the English succeeded in recovering the weather gauge. In other words, they stood out to sea across the enemy's bows and, by a very nice piece of seamanship indeed, worked their way round to the seaward and windward flank of the advancing Spaniards. So, on the morning of Sunday the 21st, began the pursuit up the Channel. At the outset both sides had received some unpleasant surprises. The Spaniards by the realisation that they were opposed by ships faster and more weatherly than any they had seen before, and the English by the sheer size of the Armada and the great defensive strength of its crescent-shaped formation. Even with their superior fire-power and manoeuvrability, they knew that unless they could break that formation, it would be impossible to do it serious damage.

On the following day the Armada lost two capital ships, though neither as a result of enemy action. One blew up after a fire started in the magazine. The other lost her rudder and had to be abandoned. On Tuesday the wind veered. The English fleet temporarily lost the advantage of the weather gauge and a somewhat confused battle was joined off Portland Bill, the English trying to weather the Armada's seaward wing, the Spaniards trying to grapple and board their irritatingly nimble adversaries. Meanwhile, Martin Frobisher in the *Triumph,* the biggest ship in either fleet, together with five middle-sized London merchantmen, had become separated from the main body of the fleet on the shoreward side and was being attacked by Don Hugo de Moncada's galleasses – a hybrid form of sailing ship cum galley. Whether Frobisher was really in difficulties or was attempting to lure the galleasses into a trap has never been made clear but, as the wind veered again to the south, Howard in the *Ark Royal,* followed by the *Elizabeth Jonas,* the *Galleon of Leicester,* the *Golden Lion,* the *Victory,* the *Mary Rose,* the *Dreadnought* and the *Swallow,* stormed down to the rescue, pouring broadside after broadside into the *San Martin de Portugal,* the Spanish admiral's flagship, as he went. 'At which assault', reported Howard, 'after wonderful sharp conflict, the Spaniards were forced to give way and to flock together like sheep.'

On Wednesday there was a lull. The English had been using up their ammunition at an unprecedented rate and were obliged to send urgently to Portsmouth 'for a new supply of such provisions'. Howard was not particularly pleased by the way things were going. Whenever the fleets had come to blows the English had had the advantage, but the Armada was now well on its way towards the rendezvous with Parma, still maintaining strict formation and still relatively intact. But on board the *San Martin,* the Duke of Medina Sidonia also had his problems. He, too, was running short of ammunition and was increasingly worried by the fact that so far he had been unable to make any contact with the Duke of Parma.

On Thursday there was another indecisive skirmish off the Isle of Wight and on Saturday 27 July the Armada suddenly dropped anchor off Calais. The English promptly followed suit and for the next twenty-four hours the two fleets lay within culverin shot of each other. Medina Sidonia had made up his mind not to go any further until he had heard from Parma and at once dispatched an urgent message to Dunkirk asking for forty or fifty flyboats to be sent without delay, 'as with this aid', he wrote, 'I shall be able to resist the enemy's fleet until Your Excellency can come out with the rest and we can go together and take some port where the Armada may enter in safety.' No one, it seemed, had yet explained to Medina Sidonia that the only flyboats operational in the neighbourhood of Dunkirk were the Sea Beggars, tough little craft of the embryonic Dutch navy commanded by Justin of Nassau, which had come down from the Scheldt Estuary and were now efficiently blockading the Flemish coast. The Spanish fighting ships drew twenty-five to thirty feet of water, which they would not find at Dunkirk, or Nieuport, the other port of embarkation, and as long as Justin continued to keep Parma's army penned up in its shallow, sandy harbours, the all important junction of the invasion force and its escort was – short of a miracle – going to be impossible.

Meanwhile, Charles Howard had been joined by the squadron of thirty-odd ships left to guard the mouth of the Thames, and that Saturday night the whole English navy, a hundred and fifty sail great and small was assembled in the Straits of Dover. No one seems to have told Howard that the Dutch were in position and, hag-ridden by the fear that Parma might turn up at any moment, he was determined to lose no time in flushing the Armada out of Calais Roads. The obvious way to do this was with fireships and about midnight on Sunday, eight small craft 'going in a front, having the wind and tide with them, and their ordnance being charged' were set on fire and let loose.

Fire was, of course, one of the greatest dangers a wooden sailing
ship had to fear, and panic swept through the crowded anchorage as
the Armada cut its cables and scrambled out to sea in the darkness.
The fireships, although they did no actual damage, had achieved
something which the English fleet had not yet been able to do and
had broken up the Spaniards' formidable crescent formation. All the
same, and due in large part to the stubborn courage and leadership
of the Duke of Medina Sidonia, the scattered ships rallied, collected
themselves and by Monday morning were ready to do battle once
more.

Sir William Winter, second in command of the squadron which
had been waiting off the North Foreland, told Francis Walsingham
that 'about nine of the clock in the morning we fetched near unto
them being then thwart of Gravelines, and they went into the proportion of a half-moon. The fight continued until six of the clock at
night, in the which time the Spanish army bare away north-north-
east as much as they could; keeping company one with another, I
assure Your Honour, in very good order.' This was the fiercest fight
and the nearest thing to a set battle which had taken place since the
Armada had entered the Channel, but although the Spaniards had,
for the first time, taken a real beating, Charles Howard was still not
very happy. Sending an anxious plea to Walsingham for more victuals and munition, he wrote: 'Ever since morning we have chased them
in fight until this evening late and distressed them much; but their
fleet consisteth of mighty ships and great strength'. And he added a
postscript. 'Their force is wonderful great and strong; and yet we
pluck their feathers little and little.' Francis Drake was rather more
optimistic. 'God hath given us so good a day in forcing the enemy
so far to leeward as I hope to God the Prince of Parma and the Duke
of Medina Sidonia shall not shake hands this few days.'

God was certainly playing his part and, as Francis Drake always
firmly believed, he was apparently a Protestant God, for during that
night the wind blew hard from the northwest, driving the unhappy
Armada remorselessly towards the shoals and banks of the Dutch
coast. The *San Mateo* and the *San Felipe* went aground on the banks off
Nieuport and Ostend to be snapped up by the Sea Beggars, and by
dawn on Tuesday, 30 July it seemed as if the whole fleet must be
pounded to death on the Zeeland Sands while the English looked on
from a safe distance. Then, suddenly, the wind veered again and next
day Drake wrote exultantly to Walsingham: 'We have the army of
Spain before us and mind, with the grace of God, to wrestle a pull
with him. There was never anything pleased me better than the
seeing the enemy flying with a southerly wind to northwards. God

grant you have a good eye to the Duke of Parma; for with the grace of God, if we live, I doubt it not but ere long so to handle the matter with the Duke of Sidonia as he shall wish himself back at St Mary Port among his orange trees.' As they set off in pursuit, still worried by shortages of food and ammunition, neither Drake nor Howard yet realised that they had seen the last of the Invincible Armada.

During those momentous ten days which were to settle the fate of western Christendom, Queen Elizabeth, 'not a whit dismayed', was in London, taking no notice of the specially picked force of two thousand men who were guarding her precious person and showing an alarming inclination to go down to the south coast and meet the enemy in person. It was largely to divert her Majesty's mind from such an unsuitable excursion that the Earl of Leicester had suggested she should pay a visit to his camp at Tilbury and so 'comfort' the army concentrated to the east of the capital, 'at Stratford, East Ham and the villages thereabout'. Elizabeth took the idea up eagerly. In fact, by this time the crisis was over and the battered Armada was being driven into the North Sea, but William Camden wrote: 'Whereas most men thought they would tack about again and come back, the Queen with a masculine spirit came and took a view of her Army and Camp at Tilbury, and riding about through the ranks of armed men drawn up on both sides of her, with a leader's truncheon in her hand, sometimes with a martial pace, another while gently like a woman, incredible it is how much she encouraged the hearts of her captains and soldiers by her presence and speech to them.'

The visit was a roaring success. The Queen had come down the Thames by barge to Tilbury, where she was received by Leicester and his officers, and greeted by a salvo of cannon fired from the fort. She then got into her coach and set off to inspect the camp to a martial accompaniment of drums and fifes. A contemporary versifier, who rushed into print with a very long (and very bad) poem entitled *Elizabetha Triumphans,* probably captured the spirit of the occasion as well as anybody:

> *Our peerless Queen doth by her soldiers pass,*
> *And shows herself unto her subjects there,*
> *She thanks them oft for their (of duty) pains,*
> *And they, again, on knees, do pray for her;*
> *They couch their pikes, and bow their ensigns down,*
> *When as their sacred royal Queen passed by.*

Leicester's belief that the Queen's presence would be good for morale was undoubtedly fully justified.

The soldiers which placed were far off
From that same way through which she passed along,
Did hollo oft, 'The Lord preserve our Queen!'
He happy was that could but see her coach . . .
Thrice happy they who saw her stately self,
Who, Juno-like, drawn by her proudest birds,
Passed along through quarters of the camp.

Elizabeth spent the night at a nearby manor house, and next day came back to Tilbury to see a mock battle and to review her troops. Bare-headed and wearing a breastplate, she rode along the lines of men escorted only by the Earl of Leicester, the Earl of Ormonde, bearing the sword of state, and a page who carried her white-plumed helmet. She had dismissed her bodyguard for, as she was presently to say, she did not desire to live to distrust her faithful and loving people. Such fear was for tyrants. She had always so behaved herself that, under God, she placed her chiefest strength and safeguard in the loyal hearts and goodwill of her subjects.

Her dazzled and adoring amateur army did not see a thin, middle-aged woman with bad teeth and wearing a bright red wig perched on the back of an enormous white gelding. Instead they saw the personification of every goddess of classical mythology they had ever heard about, every heroine from their favourite reading, the Bible. They saw Judith and Deborah, Diana the Huntress and the Queen of the Amazons all rolled into one. But they also saw their own beloved and familiar Queen.

Her stateliness was so with love-show joined,
As all there then did jointly love and fear.
They joyed in that they see their Ruler's love:
But feared lest that in aught they should offend
Against herself, the Goddess of the land.

It was in this hectic emotional atmosphere that Elizabeth made her famous Tilbury Speech. She had not come among them for her 'recreation and disport' she told the soldiers, 'but being resolved, in the midst and heat of the battle, to live or die amongst you all, to lay down for my God, and for my kingdom, and for my people, my honour and my blood, even in the dust. I know I have the body of a weak and feeble woman, but I have the heart and stomach of a king, and of a king of England too, and think foul scorn that Parma or Spain, or any prince of Europe should dare to invade the borders of my realm; to which, rather than any dishonour shall grow by me, I will myself take up arms, I myself will be your general, judge and rewarder of every one of your virtues in the field. I know already for your forwardness you have deserved rewards and crowns; and we do assure you, in the word of a prince, they shall be duly paid you.'

Small wonder that her audience rose to her with 'a mighty shout' and when the Queen had gone back to London, a little disappointed perhaps that she had not after all been called upon to take up arms herself, Leicester wrote to the Earl of Shrewsbury: 'Our gracious mistress hath been here with me to see her camp and people, which so enflamed the hearts of her good subjects, as I think the weakest person among them is able to match the proudest Spaniard that dares land in England.'

The year '88 which, it had long been prophesied, would see many 'most wonderful and very extraordinary accidents', had seen a small island, only half an island in fact, triumphantly defy and repulse the assault of the greatest power in Europe and may surely be said to mark the high noon of the Elizabethan epic. It had also marked the consummation of a unique love affair between ruler and people. But no nation can live for long in such a white-hot passion of love and pride, and even as Elizabeth Tudor rode through the camp at Tilbury her world was changing. Economic pressures and other pressures and aspirations, as yet barely recognised or understood, of a society still emerging from an age of old certainties and dogmas were building up beneath seemingly solid ground, until – within the lifetimes of children already toddling in Armada summer – they were to erupt in a manner which effectively killed the old certainties for ever.

I
A Most Renowned Virgin Queen

Sacred, imperial, and holy is her seat,
Shining with wisdom, love, and mightiness:
Nature that everything imperfect made,
Fortune that never yet was constant found,
Time that defaceth every golden show,
Dare not decay, remove, or her impair;
Both nature, time, and fortune, all agree,
To bless and serve her royal majesty.

A little before noon on Sunday, 24 November 1588, the head of a very grand procession indeed emerged from the courtyard of Somerset House, turned right into the Strand and set off past St Clement Danes and Essex House towards Temple Bar and the City. It was an awesome spectacle, for the greatest names in the land were on their way to church to give thanks to the Almighty for their recent glorious deliverance from invasion and conquest by the mighty power of Spain.

Everybody who was anybody was in town that Sunday morning. Behind the heralds and the trumpeters and the gentlemen ushers rode the nobility, the privy councillors, the judges and bishops and all the great officers of state, the scribes and the men of war, all the brilliance and dignity, all the glamour and gallantry and professional expertise of the Elizabethan establishment: old Lord Burghley and sombre Secretary Walsingham; the Lord High Admiral Howard of Effingham and Lord Chancellor Christopher Hatton; Hunsdon and Pembroke, Knollys and Egerton; that dazzling all-rounder Sir Walter Raleigh and Archbishop Whitgift, the Queen's 'little black husband'.

After the Queen's men came the Queen herself, surrounded by the gentlemen pensioners and riding in an open chariot throne drawn by two white horses. Four pillars at the back end of this contraption supported a canopy 'on the top whereof was made a crown imperial', while in front two smaller pillars accommodated a lion and a dragon. Next came the Master of the Horse, the young Earl of Essex, leading the royal palfrey, and a contingent of ladies of honour with the yeomen of the guard in their gorgeous red and gold liveries, halberds in their hands, brought up the rear.

At Temple Bar the city musicians were in position over the gateway, ready to strike up a welcoming tune, and the Lord Mayor and his brethren, the scarlet-robed Aldermen, waited to greet Her Majesty and escort her through Fleet Street and up Ludgate Hill to St Paul's. According to long-established custom, the way was lined by the city companies in their livery hoods and wearing their best clothes, all standing in order behind railings draped with blue cloth and all 'saluting her highness as she proceeded along'. Lesser mortals seized what points of vantage they could from which to cheer the Queen and gape at the grand folk in her train.

The procession reached Paul's Church between the hours of twelve and one, and was received at the great West Door by the Bishop of London with more than fifty other members of the clergy drawn up in support, all in their richest copes and vestments. Descending from her chariot, the Queen at once fell on her knees and there and then 'made her hearty prayers to God' before being conducted down the long west aisle of the cathedral, where the banners captured from the Armada ships hung on display, while the litany was chanted before her. She then crossed the transept and took her place in the gallery in the north wall of the choir, facing the open air pulpit cross, to hear the Bishop of Salisbury preach a sermon 'wherein none other argument was handled but that praise, honour and glory might be rendered unto God, and that God's name might be extolled by thanksgiving'. Elizabeth did not normally share her subjects' inordinate enthusiasm for sermons, but on this occasion she listened with gracious attention to the eloquent Dr Pierce and when he had finished she herself addressed the assembled congregation, 'most Christianly' exhorting them to give thanks – the people responding with a great shout, wishing her a long and happy life to the confusion of her enemies. Her obligations to a benevolent deity having been thus handsomely discharged, the Queen processed back through the church the way she had come and went to dine in state at the bishop's palace.

This solemn ceremony marked the climax of a series of public holidays, thanksgiving services, sermons, bonfires and other victory celebrations; but although the nation rejoiced, there was little euphoria and less complacency. The thousands who thronged the churches that autumn had needed no urging to give thanks to God as they reflected soberly on the providential nature of their escape from the King of Spain's invincible Armada, and no thinking person believed that this would be the end of the matter. Certainly the Queen did not. One crisis, perhaps the greatest, had been met and overcome, but as she brought a highly satisfactory day to its close, repeating her triumphal journey through the city streets back to Somerset House, the November dusk ablaze with a 'great light of torches', she harboured no illusions about the nature of the hazards which lay ahead.

Elizabeth Tudor was fifty-five now (the same age as her father had been when he died) and had just celebrated the thirtieth anniversary of her accession. By the standards of her day she was already well past middle-age, but if she was daunted by the prospect of beginning a new career as a war-leader so late in life, she gave no sign of it in the presence of her loving people. To a casual glance that spare, wiry figure and high-nosed profile had altered amazingly little over the past thirty years and the Queen's carefully cultivated public image was still, convincingly, that of a woman in her prime. She had once nearly died of smallpox and on at least two occasions since had been ill enough to cause serious anxiety, but she had always possessed great recuperative powers and in her mid-fifties her general health seems to have been excellent; even the ulcer on her ankle which had troubled her on and off for nearly ten years had healed at last. Physically she was as active as ever, dancing six or seven galliards in a morning and walking and riding with undiminished energy; while anyone rash enough to suppose that her mental powers might have begun to decline quickly discovered his mistake. She had kept up her lifelong habit of devoting some part of almost every day to study or serious reading and, as her godson, John Harington, records: 'Her highness was wont to sooth her ruffled temper with reading every morning, when she had been stirred to passion at the council, or other matters had overthrown her gracious disposition. She did much admire Seneca's wholesome advisings when the soul's quiet is flown away, and I saw much of her translating thereof.'

Unfortunately, the soothing properties of Seneca were not always efficacious. When stirred to passion, her Highness was still quite capable of filling the air with good round oaths and was subject on occasion 'to be vehemently transported with anger'. Elizabeth in a rage could be heard several rooms away and she was not above throwing things, or boxing the ears of the nearest maid of honour. 'When she smiled', wrote Harington, 'it was a pure sunshine that every one did choose to bask in; but anon came a storm from a sudden gathering of clouds, and the thunder fell, in wondrous manner, on all alike.' The Queen's bark, however, was usually worse than her bite and these tension-relieving explosions were always kept in the family. No outsider ever saw her other than graciously smiling or regally dignified.

But if, in 1588, Queen Elizabeth appeared to be at the peak of her form – tough, vigorous and autocratic, her appetite for the pleasures and problems of life seemingly unquenchable – time had not dealt so kindly with her contemporaries. Lord Burghley, now in his late sixties, was still in harness but increasingly burdened by the weight of his years and infirmities. Francis Walsingham was a sick man and most of the older generation of councillors and courtiers were nearing the end of their careers. Death, indeed, had already torn one gaping hole in that charmed circle of intimates whom the Queen honoured with pet names, and the procession to St Paul's had been the first great pageant of the reign in which the flamboyant figure of Robert Dudley, Earl of Leicester, had not figured prominently.

Leicester, as commander-in-chief of the home forces, had spent a strenuous summer helping to organise England's land defence and, although he was much the same age as the Queen, he hadn't worn as well as his mistress. Paunchy and red-faced, his white hair receding fast, little trace remained of the dark, slightly sinister good looks which had once earned him the opprobrious label of the Gypsy. When the invasion scare was finally over and his headquarters at Tilbury had been dismantled, the Earl came back to London and was present at a grand military review held at Whitehall on 26 August, watching with the Queen from a window while his young stepson ran two tilts against the Earl of Cumberland. Next day he left for the country, intending to take the waters at Buxton. He stopped en route at Rycote Manor near Oxford, home of the Norris family where he and Elizabeth had often stayed together in the past, and from there he scribbled one of his affectionate little notes to the Queen. A week later he was dead, 'of a continual fever'.

In the excitement of the time, the disappearance of this great landmark of the Elizabethan scene went unmourned and almost unnoticed by the general public. Leicester had never been liked. 'He was esteemed a most accomplished courtier', observed William Camden, 'a cunning time-server and respecter of his own advantages . . . But whilst he preferred power and greatness, which is subject to be envied, before solid virtue, his detracting emulators found large matter to speak reproachfully of him, and even when he was in his most flourishing condition spared not disgracefully to defame him by libels, not without mixture of some untruths. In a word, people talked openly in his commendation, but privately he was ill spoken of by the greater part.'

People, of course, had always resented his special relationship with the Queen (in some quarters he was still blamed for her failure to get married), and he'd recently become a prime target of the Catholic propaganda machine. *Leicester's Commonwealth,* the familiar title of a book published anonymously in Antwerp in 1584, had not only raked up the old scandal of his first wife's death but accused its victim, in exuberant and imaginative detail, of pretty well every iniquity known to man – from fornication and covetousness to murder and treachery. In spite of official attempts to suppress it, this little masterpiece of character assassination enjoyed an immediate runaway success with that numerous section of the community who'd always suspected the Earl of being a bad lot and were only too happy to see their prejudices confirmed in print. So much so that, at least according to the chronicler John Stow, 'all men, so far as they durst, rejoiced no less outwardly at his death than for the victory lately obtained against the Spaniard'.

For the Queen it was a grievous loss and Camden noted that she took it much to heart. Elizabeth had first known Robert Dudley when they were both children and ever since she came to the throne he had been one of her closest and most constant companions, her 'brother and best friend', and more than that, it had often been whispered. One of the Spanish government's secret agents in London picked up a story that the Queen was so grieved that she had shut herself up in her chamber for several days, refusing to speak to anyone, until finally Lord Burghley and some of the other councillors were obliged to have the doors broken open. This report is not confirmed by any other source, and sounds both improbable and uncharacteristic. Elizabeth had learnt to conceal her innermost feelings before she was out of her teens, and as she grew older she 'either patiently endured or politely dissembled' her greatest griefs of mind and body. Besides this, September 1588, when the magnitude of the victory lately obtained against the Spaniard was just beginning to dawn on her subjects, was emphatically not the moment for the Queen to parade a private sorrow which would be shared by no one. But she kept that note from Rycote. Fifteen years later it was found in the little coffer which always stood at her bedside. Across it she had written: 'His last letter.'

Meanwhile, Robert Dudley's death had created a vacancy on the committee of England's most exclusive club and some people thought this would work to the advantage of Sir Christopher Hatton, another close friend of longstanding and the only member of Elizabeth's inner circle who had stayed single for her sake. But although she never forgot old friends, the Queen had already found another Robert in Leicester's twenty-year-old stepson, Robert Devereux, second Earl of Essex. In many ways the choice was an obvious one. Nobly-born, brilliant and beautiful, Essex was plainly marked out to become a leader of the rising generation and, as such, one whom an ageing sovereign would be wise to keep under her eye and attached to her interest. Apart from that, Elizabeth was fond of the boy, who had undoubted claims on her favour. Fatherless from the age of nine (the first earl having died on royal service in Ireland), young Robert had been one of the Queen's wards and his mother, born Lettice Knollys, was the Queen's cousin.

Essex made his debut at Court when he was sixteen, under the sponsorship of his stepfather, and the following year he went with Leicester to the Netherlands to see something of the world and gain some martial experience. He did well in the fighting round Zutphen, where Philip Sidney received his deathwound, and Sidney, that beau ideal of Elizabethan youth, bequeathed his best sword to his 'beloved and much honoured Lord, the Earl of Essex'.

When Essex returned to England in December 1586, he had just passed his nineteenth birthday and the shy adolescent had developed into a mettlesome young blood, impatient to make a name for himself. He certainly made an immediate impact on the social scene for, as well as his striking good looks and impressive connexions, he was fortunate enough to be endowed with the gift of pleasing, 'a kind of urbanity or innate courtesy', which captivated the Queen and won him a popularity enjoyed by few other public figures of the time; the Londoners in particular taking him to their hearts and gazing with sentimental approval on this 'new adopted son' of royal grace.

Elizabeth was seldom given to sentiment and even more rarely visited by maternal yearnings, but she never lost her eye for an attractive man and Essex, with his engaging youthfulness, his cozening ways and eager devotion, offered a welcome addition to her court.

Soon his tall, red-headed figure was seen everywhere at her side, and when her insomnia was troublesome she would keep him with her into the small hours, chatting or playing cards. He was, of course, still far too raw and inexperienced to be trusted with any serious responsibility, but he possessed breeding, courage and style, all attributes which the Queen looked for in her young men, and there seemed no reason to doubt that he would go far.

Even in these early days, though, Essex had his ups and downs, and in July 1587 he first betrayed a glimpse of the paranoid tendencies which would end by destroying him. During the course of her summer progress that year, the Queen paid a short visit to the Earl of Warwick, Leicester's elder brother, and Lady Warwick rather unwisely insisted on including Essex's sister Dorothy in her houseparty. Four years earlier Dorothy Devereux had made a runaway marriage in somewhat unsavoury circumstances to a man of considerably inferior rank and, as a result, had become *persona non grata* at Court.

The Warwicks were old and privileged friends, and kind Lady Warwick was no doubt counting on the Queen's fondness for Essex to smooth over any unpleasantness. But Elizabeth refused to meet Lady Dorothy and gave orders that she was to stay in her own room, a slight which Essex had no hesitation in blaming on the evil machinations of Walter Raleigh, whom he regarded as his most dangerous rival. After supper that evening he attacked the Queen for putting such a disgrace on his sister and himself 'only to please that knave Raleigh'. How could he give himself to the service of a mistress who stood in awe of such a man, he demanded, and proceeded to pour out a tirade of abuse against Raleigh – the scene gaining an added flavour from the fact that Sir Walter, in his capacity as Captain of the Guard, was on duty at the door and could hear everything that was said. The Queen was annoyed. She refused to listen to a word against Raleigh and the quarrel rapidly degenerated into a lively exchange of personalities, Elizabeth making some pungent comments on the manners and morals of her young friend's female relatives in general and his mother in particular. (She had reluctantly forgiven Leicester for marrying the widowed Countess of Essex, but she never forgave her cousin Lettice.)

Essex shouted that he would not endure to see his house disgraced and his sister should no longer remain to disquiet Her Majesty. As for himself, he 'had no joy to be in any place', but nothing would induce him to stay where his affection was spurned for a wretch like Raleigh. Unimpressed, the Queen turned her back on him to resume her interrupted conversation with Lady Warwick and, though it was almost midnight by this time, Essex stormed away to rout his sister out of bed. Since some kind of grand gesture was now clearly called for, he made up his mind to return to the Netherlands and embrace a soldier's career. He would probably be killed and then people would be sorry! As it happened, of course, he got no further than the port of Sandwich before a royal messenger caught up with him and fetched him back – an eventuality he had doubtless been banking on.

In his own account of this rather foolish episode, Essex told a friend that he had been driven to act as he did by 'the extreme unkind dealing with me', a phrase which was to become his constant refrain, although, in fact, the Queen showed remarkable forbearance towards his tantrums. In November she finally yielded to the persuasions of the Earl of Leicester and bestowed his long-held and prestigious office of Master of the Horse on his stepson. The following year Essex was appointed cavalry commander of the army concentrated round Tilbury and created a Knight of the Garter – meteoric progress for a youth not yet twenty-one.

He continued to make his presence felt about the Court, where his obsessive jealousy of anyone who seemed to threaten his position as *jeune premier* led him to pick a quarrel with Charles Blount, another likely young man whose prowess in the tiltyard had attracted favourable notice. Essex got the worst of the duel fought in Marylebone Park and when the Queen heard of his discomfiture she snorted that, by God's death, it was high time someone took him down and taught him better manners or there would be no rule with him! One way and another, her red-haired protégé looked like becoming something of a problem child, but Elizabeth was not unduly perturbed. She liked a man to show some spirit and, in any case, she had more important matters on her mind just then.

After Lord Howard of Effingham finally abandoned his pursuit of the Spanish fleet off the Firth of Forth early in August, there had been a period of uncertainty, almost of anticlimax. Although it had been harassed in the Channel and badly mauled in the engagement off Gravelines, the Armada still represented a formidable fighting unit and for weeks Europe seethed with rumour and speculation. The Spaniards had put into a Scottish haven to refit and were only waiting for a favourable wind to return to the attack. There had been a great battle off the Scottish coast with at least fifteen English galleons sunk. The survivors had taken refuge in the Thames estuary and Drake (in European eyes Francis Drake *was* the English navy) had been wounded, killed, taken prisoner, had fled and vanished in the smoke. More level-headed and better-informed observers, notably the Venetians, were of the opinion that the Armada, driven north-wards into hostile, dangerous waters and already seriously short of provisions and ammunition, would have been in no condition to fight any sort of battle. On the contrary, it would probably be as much as it could do to salvage the remains of the fleet by sailing home round Ireland and, as the reports which presently began to filter across the Irish Sea made plain, it had indeed been a desperate business of *sauve qui peut*.

The realisation that King Philip's long-heralded crusade against the heretical islanders had ended in total and humiliating failure may have taken some time to penetrate, but when it did finally sink in Queen Elizabeth's international prestige rocketed. The King of France, who had his own reasons for welcoming a Spanish defeat, did not hesitate to praise 'the valour, spirit and prudence' of the Queen of England, declaring that her recent achievement 'would compare with the greatest feats of the most illustrious men of past times'. Alone and unaided she had repulsed the attack of so puissant a force as Spain and triumphed over a fleet which had been the wonder of the world. The Venetian ambassador in Paris commented that the English had now proved they were the skilled mariners rumour re-ported them to be, for while they had always been on the enemy's flank they had not lost a single ship. The Queen, for her part, had kept her nerve throughout and had neglected nothing necessary for the occasion. 'Her acuteness in resolving on her action', continued Giovanni Mocenigo admiringly, 'her courage in carrying it out, show her high-spirited desire of glory, and her resolve to save her country and herself.' Even the Pope, who seldom missed an opportunity to annoy the King of Spain, lavished praises on the Queen. What a matchless woman she was! Were she only a Catholic she would be his best beloved. While as for Drake – what courage! What a great captain!

Now, of course, everyone was waiting to see what the Queen, and Francis Drake, would do next, for now, if ever, was surely the mo-ment for a counter-attack – perhaps another of those brilliant smash-and-grab operations which had become synonymous with the name of El Draque. The Venetian ambassador in Spain, in a despatch date-lined Madrid, 22 October, remarked that no small trouble would arise if Drake were to take to the sea and sail to meet the Peruvian fleet, or make a descent on the shores of Spain, where he would find no obstacle to his depredations. He might even destroy a part of those Armada ships which had managed to survive the dreadful journey home and were now lying scattered and helpless in various places along the coast, many of them quite unguarded and some in harbours which had no forts.

The idea of meeting the Peruvian fleet had already occurred to Elizabeth, and as early as the end of August she had summoned Drake to Court to discuss 'the desire that her majesty had for the intercepting of the king's treasure from the Indies'. In normal circumstances Drake would have required no encouragement to set off on a treasure hunt but, as he felt obliged to point out, after their hectic summer the Queen's ships were all in urgent need of refitting, and since the American silver fleet usually arrived round about the end of September there would scarcely be enough time to get a suitable force ready for sea. This was perfectly true. It was also true that Francis Drake, now standing at the peak of his remarkable career, had a rather more ambitious exploit in mind.

Ever since 1580, when the King of Spain had annexed the kingdom of Portugal, together with the wealth of its eastern empire and its first-rate ocean-going navy, the possibility of embarrassing him by supporting the rival claimant to the Portuguese throne had been explored by various people on more than one occasion. The dispossessed Dom Antonio, Prior of Crato and bastard nephew of the last native king of Portugal (or, as some unkind persons maintained, bastard son of a Lisbon merchant), had spent the greater part of his exile in England – a sad little man with a straggling beard who, like most exiles, painted an optimistic picture of the strength of his party at home and was lavish with promises to anyone who seemed even remotely interested in his cause. Drake, acutely conscious of the strategic importance of Lisbon, had always been interested in Dom Antonio's cause and in conference with the Queen he put forward a plan for a landing in Portugal based on the capture of Lisbon, whose population, if Dom Antonio was to be believed, would rise as one man to welcome its rightful king.

In his designs on the Portuguese mainland, Drake found a powerful ally in Sir John Norris, veteran of the war in the Netherlands and generally regarded as England's most distinguished professional soldier. Black John Norris and his comrades could see in the prospect of an expedition to Portugal those opportunities for profit and glory so conspicuously absent from the apparently endless slogging-match being fought over the dismal wastes of Flanders, Brabant and Zeeland, and they very naturally threw the whole weight of their influence behind it. The seizure of Lisbon would also open up the chances of putting into operation another plan long-cherished by the sailors, especially John Hawkins, for establishing a permanent presence in the Azores, those vital off-shore islands belonging to the Portuguese crown, which lay across the sea routes from both America and the East. Such a project had not been feasible while a Spanish navy commanded the whole western coastline of the Peninsula, but things were different now.

England's reply to the Armada – at least according to the scheme devised by her men of war and laid before the Queen and Council during the first fortnight of September 1588 – was thus to be a two-pronged assault on what might be described as the soft under-belly of the Spanish empire. The advantages of having a friendly government in Portugal hardly needed to be spelt out. Even if the expedition did no more than spark off a popular revolt – and there was some independent evidence to suggest that the Portuguese were growing increasingly restive under the heavy-handed rule of King Philip's viceroy – it should still be enough to force the King to divert men and materials from the Netherlands, that other scene of popular revolt against his rule, and with any luck keep him occupied at home for a considerable time to come. As for the other half of the proposed enterprise, the Venetian ambassador in Madrid told the Doge and Senate in December that 'those who understand declare that if Drake were to go now to the Azores, he would not only ruin the whole of the India traffic but could quite easily make himself master of those islands; especially as the garrison is said to be dissatisfied; and if the Azores were captured that would be the end of the Indies, for all ships have to touch there'. And if Philip could be cut off from the life-giving stream of silver flowing in from the mines of Central America, then he might indeed be rendered permanently harmless, the king of figs and oranges wistfully envisaged by Sir Walter Raleigh.

In theory, and as persuasively presented by Drake and Norris, it looked a good plan – just the sort of bold offensive stroke which the hawks around the Queen had been urging on her for years. It was certainly an audacious plan – rather too audacious perhaps for a small country with no standing army and little recent experience as a military power. It would also depend heavily on imponderables like the weather and the attitude of the Portuguese people. But the Queen could see as well as anyone that here was an opportunity which might never come her way again and she was ready to have a go – surprisingly ready in the context of the European situation as a whole. The trouble, of course, was money. It would cost a great deal of money to finance an undertaking on this scale and Elizabeth quite simply did not have the necessary cash at her disposal.

In the autumn of 1584 she had possessed reserves of 'chested treasure' amounting to three hundred thousand pounds, reserves prudently set aside for a rainy day while the going was good. But the cost of military aid for the Dutch rebels had, over the past three years, added up to nearly four hundred thousand pounds and the cost of defending England against the Armada had come to more than two hundred thousand. Since the ordinary revenues of the Crown, even when supplemented by Parliamentary grants, were nothing like enough to meet outgoings of this kind, the Queen had been obliged to draw heavily on her savings and by the autumn of 1588 they had dwindled to a mere fifty-five thousand pounds which, at current rates of expenditure, would barely see her through another six months. Nor was there any prospect of current rates of expenditure being reduced in the foreseeable future. True, it should now be possible to cut down on home defence, but the navy would soon be pressing for a new ship-building programme and the Queen dared not pull out of the Netherlands, where Philip's formidable lieutenant the Duke of Parma still commanded the army which had been intended for the invasion of England.

Everyone who knew anything about such matters knew that all the skill and courage of the English mariners, all the superior manoeuvrability and fire-power of their ships, might very easily have gone for nothing if, after the battle of Gravelines, the Armada had had the use of a deep-water port in which to refit and revictual; a port where it could have rendezvoused with Parma before carrying out its primary task of convoying his bargeloads of seasoned troops across the Channel. So long as Parma remained in Flanders it would continue to be vital to secure the mouth of the Scheldt estuary against any future armadas and that meant continued aid for the Calvinist Dutch of Holland and Zeeland. It also meant that the towns of Flushing and Brill, Ostend and Bergen-op-Zoom must remain in friendly hands whatever the cost.

There were other inescapable calls on the Queen of England's purse. Money was needed for Ireland and for Scotland, where it was important to keep King James in a good temper by paying his pension regularly. Moreover, events in France strongly suggested that Elizabeth might soon find herself having to subsidize her friends in that country as well. One way and another, she was beginning to be seriously worried about the financial situation and had started to explore the possibility of raising a foreign loan. No wonder she'd been so interested in ambushing Philip's treasure fleet – the quickest and most satisfactory form of foreign borrowing that could have been devised.

Drake and Norris quite understood the Queen's predicament and they had accordingly worked out an ingenious scheme by which rather more than two-thirds of the cost of the Portugal Expedition, as it came to be known, would be put up by private shareholders. If the Queen would contribute twenty thousand pounds and six of her 'second sort' of ships victualled for three months, plus a train of siege artillery for dealing with the defences of Lisbon, then Drake and Norris Incorporated undertook to raise forty thousand pounds and twenty or so armed merchant ships to make up the fleet. They further promised that if Elizabeth would appoint a treasurer and pay five thousand pounds into the kitty straight away, she would not be asked for another penny piece until the other 'adventurers' had given sureties for the whole of their forty thousand. The two commanders were to have the Queen's commission to recruit six thousand men for foreign service, while the remainder, two to three thousand in the original estimates, would be borrowed from the force of seven thousand more or less trained and experienced troops maintained by the Crown in the Netherlands under the terms of the Anglo-Dutch treaty of 1585. The Dutch would also be asked to provide transports, more siege guns and gunpowder.

The practice of waging war by joint stock company may seem fantastic (and it did seem both fantastic and immoral to a whole generation of nineteenth century historians), but the logical Elizabethans could see nothing unreasonable in appealing to the business instincts of the Queen's wealthier subjects who, while they would have jibbed at paying higher taxes, could easily be persuaded to invest in a project which offered the chance of a handsome return. In any case, it was certainly the only method by which such an operation could have been financed in the time available.

It was not, of course, an ideal method – the most obvious snag being the fact that, when the two conflicted, commanders with their backers' interests to consider would naturally be more inclined to concentrate on taking prizes than on purely strategic objectives, and this was a snag which the Portugal Expedition encountered in its very early stages. The Queen and Council were still examining the small print of the prospectus when news began to come in from Spain that the battered survivors of the Armada, fifty or more capital ships, were limping home, not to Lisbon or the other western ports where the expedition could have finished them off at leisure, but to the nearest available refuges, Santander and San Sebastian deep in the Bay of Biscay. This was an unfortunate complication. It would be difficult and perhaps dangerous for Drake to have to take his fleet so far to leeward and then out again on the long windward beat to Cape

Finisterre, but to Elizabeth the destruction of those ships was a matter of paramount importance and altered her whole concept of the enterprise.

The Queen has often in the past been accused of lacking any grasp of generalship, and of consistently impeding her gallant soldiers and sailors by her cheeseparing habits, her reluctance to take risks and her inability to make up her mind. This is an old canard, only recently beginning to be contradicted by modern scholarship, and one which arose, at least in part, from the fact that Elizabeth's war aims were always rather different from those of her gallant soldiers and sailors. Unlike Walter Raleigh and his fire-eating friends, the Queen had no particular desire to see Philip's great empire 'beaten in pieces', an eventuality likely to create as many problems as it solved. What she wanted – had always wanted – was to see the Netherlands restored to its old dominion status and given a measure of religious toleration, while remaining under the protection and sovereignty of Spain. She wanted an agreed share of trade with the New World for English merchants and, above all, relief from the constant burdensome dread of Spanish aggression. In short, she wanted a sensible, unexciting settlement of a foolish and wasteful quarrel.

Elizabeth may not have been a tactical expert, but she brought to the conduct of the war the same shrewd judgement and long experience of men and affairs which served her so well in other directions, and every instinct told her that the quickest way – probably, indeed, the only way – of forcing Philip to the negotiating table would be to destroy his naval strength once and for all. The King was a stubborn man and every report coming in from abroad spoke of his resolute determination to avenge his honour and go on serving God's cause. He meant to rebuild his shattered fleet – if necessary he would sell the very candlesticks on his dinner table – and return to the attack at the earliest possible moment. Those fifty odd ships in the Biscayan ports therefore represented both an invaluable asset and a unique opportunity. With all his resources, it had taken Philip the best part of seven years to assemble his first Armada. He'd lost half of it in the Enterprise of England and if the remaining half could be destroyed while it still lay immobilised, unrigged, unmanned, unarmed and defenceless, he might very well never be able to assemble another. For with no Spanish navy to interfere, it should be a comparatively simple matter not only to cut off the King's American revenues but also the supplies of grain and munitions, timber and cordage coming in from France, the Netherlands and the Baltic – at least until he was ready to see sense and start talking.

This is certainly how it looked to the Queen of England, and all the available evidence suggests that, if she had been in a position to call the tune, she would have scrapped the plan to restore Dom Antonio, which was bound to be a chancy business at best, and instead gone straight for the enemy's jugular vein. Unfortunately, though, the Queen was paying less than half the piper's wages and could hardly expect Drake and Norris to abandon their cherished Portuguese adventure altogether, but she did make it very clear that Lisbon was now to be regarded as no more than a sideshow. The expedition was to go first to the ports of Guipuzcoa, Galicia and Biscay and do their best endeavour either to take or destroy all the ships of any importance they found there. Only then might they go on to Lisbon and intercept the shipping in the Tagus, but they were not to attempt a landing unless they had real grounds for believing that Dom Antonio's supporters were as numerous 'and stand so well affected towards him as he pretendeth, and that there will be a party of the Portugal nation that will be ready to aid the king and join with his forces against the Spaniard'. Elizabeth was clearly worried that Drake was placing too much reliance on his protégé's optimistic assurances and might run himself and his fleet into a trap. If all went well at Lisbon, they might stay just long enough to see the new king settled in and then go on to their other important task in the Azores; but, in her Instructions, the Queen again emphasised that 'before you attempt anything either in Portugal or the said Islands, our express pleasure and commandment is you shall first distress the ships of war in Guipuzcoa, Biscay and Galicia'.

The expedition had intended to sail in February 1589 – it was important that the troops drawn from the Netherlands should be back in time for the summer campaigning season and every month that passed gave Philip more time to repair and refit his ships of war – but a series of misunderstandings with the Dutch, always notoriously touchy and difficult to deal with, caused several weeks delay. Then the drafts from overseas were held up by freezing weather at the ports and after that the fleet itself was penned up in Plymouth Sound for a full month by persistent southwesterly winds, so that it was mid-April before they finally got away. By this time the Queen had been let in for considerably greater expense than she'd budgeted for (more than double the expense as it turned out), and the size of the expeditionary force had swollen to very nearly double the original estimate, which, of course, had played havoc with the logistical calculations.

The vast majority of these extra mouths so improvidently taken on

the strength by Drake and Norris were 'gentlemen and divers companies of voluntary soldiers offering to be employed in this action' –
among them being no less a person than the Earl of Essex, who had
defied the Queen's prohibition and slipped away from Court to join
Sir Roger Williams on board the *Swiftsure*. Like the rest of the volunteers, Essex was motivated by a mixture of enthusiasm, restlessness
and greed, but in his case acute financial difficulties added an extra
spur. 'If I should speed well, I will adventure to be rich', he wrote in
one of the letters he left behind in his desk; 'if not, I will never live
to see the end of my poverty.' This chance to recoup his fortunes and
perhaps win some useful glory into the bargain had seemed too good
to miss; but Elizabeth was furious and some historians, with a lack
of perception only matched by their vulgarity of mind, have accused
her of being more concerned with missing the company of her fancy
man than over the shoddy provisioning of her army.

Such a flagrant disregard of her wishes by one so close to her was
naturally hurtful – 'our great favours bestowed on you without des-
erts, hath drawn you thus to neglect and forget your duty; for other
constructions we cannot make of these your strange actions' – but to
a woman engaged in a lifelong struggle to stay on top in a world
which took male superiority for granted, open insubordination of
this kind had far more serious implications. In any case, for a nobleman of Essex's standing, who also held a responsible office in the
Household, to go absent without leave and attempt to depart the
realm without the sovereign's licence, was an insult to the Crown
which no self-respecting monarch could have overlooked.

The Queen therefore fired a threatening salvo across the bows of
her generals down in Plymouth. Sir Roger Williams was to be relieved of his command forthwith and placed under close arrest until
her further pleasure was known, as they would answer for the contrary at their peril; 'for as we have authority to rule, so we look to
be obeyed, and to have obedience directly and surely continued unto
us'. If Essex had now come into their company, he was to be sent back
to London at once, 'all dilatory excuse set apart'; and a posse headed
by the truant's grandfather was despatched to the West Country. But
this time Essex did not mean to be caught. Making the journey in a
record thirty-six hours, he had gone straight to Falmouth where
Roger Williams, a bloody-minded little Welshman generally believed to be the original of Shakespeare's Captain Fluellen, was waiting for him, and the *Swiftsure* promptly put to sea.

The fact that the second-in-command of the land forces of such
an important undertaking apparently thought nothing of taking himself, his noble stowaway and one of the Queen's ships off on a private

marauding expedition down the coast of Spain, only rejoining the main body at Lisbon when things looked like getting interesting, illustrates as clearly as anything can the extraordinary difficulty of imposing any sort of effective central control. Indeed, the whole history of the Portugal Expedition is an illustration of the government's inability to control the rugged individualism of its servants, for when the fleet did at last set sail it made not for San Sebastian or Santander, where forty Armada galleons were still slowly refitting, but for Corunna – or the Groyne as the English called it – Drake having got wind of a valuable prize in the vicinity. In fact, they found the harbour almost deserted. One warship and some half-dozen other assorted vessels were destroyed and the army stormed and sacked the lower town, spreading alarm and despondency in the surrounding countryside and seizing a large quantity of stores. (Any complaints about shortage of victuals after Corunna can only have been due to slackness and inefficiency on the part of the officers.) All this could, or should, have been accomplished in a couple of days but Norris and the sappers, for reasons best known to themselves, proceeded to waste a precious fortnight in a fruitless attempt to take the fortified upper town, while the rest of the army predictably got drunk on the local wine and went down with the local dysentery. Then, after the troops had finally been re-embarked on 8 May, the expedition set course straight for Lisbon.

The excuses subsequently offered for this piece of disobedience included unfavourable winds (always a useful one at sea) and lack of heavy guns to deal with shore batteries (the promised siege train never having materialised). But Elizabeth had already heard from William Knollys, who'd been with the fleet as far as Corunna, that there had been eight days fair wind for the Bay of Biscay prior to the descent on the Groyne and she was not impressed, remarking sourly that Drake and Norris 'went to places more for profit than for service'.

The Queen was, in fact, far from satisfied by the way things were going and she wrote to her commanders reminding them that: 'before your departure hence you did at sundry times so far forth promise as with oaths to assure us and some of our council that your first and principal action should be to take and distress the king of Spain's navy and ships in ports where they lay, which if ye did not, ye affirmed that ye were content to be reputed as traitors'. These were strong words, and Elizabeth ended by urging both men not to be 'transported with an haviour of vainglory which will obfuscate the eyes of your judgement'.

Whether it was vainglory or, more likely, the profit motive which obfuscated the judgement of Drake and Norris, there are strong reasons for assuming that they had always privately considered Lisbon as their main objective and, oaths regardless, had never intended to make more than a token gesture in the Biscayan area. After all, if they pulled off the more spectacular part of their mission, nobody was going to remember those semi-derelict galleons at Santander.

Nevertheless, when the expedition arrived off Cascaes at the mouth of the Tagus, it muffed its best and probably only real chance of success by a mixture of irresolution, faulty intelligence and plain ineptitude. The Spanish governor, having received ample warning of the English approach, had naturally used the time to take what precautions he could; but Cardinal Archduke Albert, with barely seven thousand troops, many of them unreliable Portuguese, under his command, might have found it hard to withstand a determined assault undertaken jointly by the fleet and the army, and bold action might also have encouraged the Portuguese to come out for Dom Antonio. Instead, it was decided to land the army at Peniche, nearly fifty miles north of Lisbon, presumably with the idea of carrying out a reconnaissance in force, while Drake took the fleet back to Cascaes, promising to meet Norris in the Tagus.

This loss of contact was to prove disastrous. The army encountered no opposition to speak of on its march down the coast but, apart from a handful of barefoot peasants and a gentleman bringing a basket of cherries, it gathered no support to speak of either. The heat, the aftermath of their excesses at Corunna and a virulent form of Portuguese tummy was playing havoc among the inexperienced amateur troops and by the time they reached the outskirts of Lisbon, Norris had only about six thousand men fit for duty. He had no artillery, such heavy guns as there were being still on the ships, there was obviously not going to be any internal revolt and, worst of all, Drake had not come upriver in support. No general could have risked an attack in such circumstances and on 29 May, despite Dom Antonio's pleas, Norris began to retreat to Cascaes. It was a grievous disappointment all round and nobody had made their fortunes. Plunder had been forbidden as long as there was any hope of the Portuguese playing their part, although, as one of those present observed wistfully, 'had we made enemies of the suburbs of Lisbon, we had been the richest army that ever went out of England'. According to John Norris's brother Edward, the soldiers found a wonderful store of riches in merchandise, spices and victuals, 'but for lack of carriage they were forced to leave all behind them'.

It was at Cascaes at the beginning of June that the expedition had

its first and only stroke of luck when Drake at last picked up the prize
he'd been hoping to take at Corunna – sixty ships from the Baltic
ports, some laden with grain and marine stores, and others in ballast,
intended, so it was thought, to reinforce King Philip's 'decayed navy'.
This was better than nothing, but it was nothing like enough, and
after six largely wasted weeks the expedition still had to justify itself.
On 5 June it was decided to abandon Lisbon. The prizes were sent
home with the worst of the dysentery cases, and the Earl of Essex,
having distinguished himself by a few flamboyant and perfectly
useless gestures, such as wading ashore shoulder high through the
waves at Peniche and offering his personal challenge to the gates of
Lisbon, condescended to go with them. The fleet then set course for
the Azores, but a strong southerly gale intervened and they never
even sighted the Islands, let alone any treasure ships. Blown back on
to the coast of Spain, Drake landed at Vigo and sacked the town,
finding a great store of wine 'but not any thing else'. By now there
were only about two thousand men in a fit state to fight; the ships,
including the Queen's *Revenge,* were feeling the strain, and time was
running out. Drake, with twenty of the best ships, made a last desperate effort to reach the Azores, but once again the weather turned
nasty with southerly gales and storms. The great Portugal Expedition
scattered before them and by the beginning of July the last stragglers
had come trailing dejectedly and rather bad-temperedly back to
Plymouth.

II

God's Handmaiden

All English hearts rejoyce and sing,
That feares the Lord and loves our Queene;
Yield thanks to God, our heavenly King,
Who hytherto her guide hath been.
With faithfull hartes, O God! we crave
Long life on earth her grace may have!

By no stretch of the imagination could the Portugal Expedition be regarded as a success. 'That miserable action' thought the rear-admiral, William Fenner, and John Norris was afraid that her Majesty would 'mislike the event of our journey', although, as he rather plaintively pointed out, 'if the enemy had done so much upon us, his party would have made bonfires in most parts of Christendom'. It was true that, if nothing else, the expedition had shown up the weakness of Spain's defences, demonstrating English ability to descend on the coast of the peninsula more or less as they pleased. Colonel Anthony Wingfield, hastening into print with his account of the Portugal Voyage, could boast that they had 'won a town by escalade, battered and assaulted another, overthrown a mighty prince's power in the field, landed our army in three several places of his kingdom, marched seven days in the heart of his country, lien three nights in the suburbs of his principal city, beaten his forces into the gates thereof, and possessed two of his frontier forts'.

According to the Venetian ambassador, the events of May and June 1589 had caused Philip great anxiety, 'not so much on account of the loss he suffers as for the insult which he feels that he has received in the fact that a woman, mistress of only half an island, with the help of a corsair and a common soldier, should have ventured on so arduous an enterprise, and dared to molest so powerful a sovereign'. But while the King undoubtedly smarted at this further humiliation – a complete black-out on news from Corunna and Lisbon was imposed in Madrid – the fact remained that little or no permanent damage had been done, and in August Tomaso Contarini could tell the Doge that a Spanish fleet of forty great and twenty smaller ships, although seriously undermanned, had left Santander for Corunna. In the same despatch he reported the safe arrival at the Azores of five ships of the India fleet, including one especially rich vessel from the Moluccan Spice Islands, and towards the end of November word came from the Duke of Medina Sidonia that the American treasure ships, belated but unscathed, were anchored at Seville. A literally golden opportunity of bringing the war to an end had gone and was not likely to recur.

In the circumstances, the Queen of England kept her temper remarkably well. In public she was gracious, assuring Drake and Norris 'for both your comforts that we do most thankfully accept of your service and do acknowledge that there hath been as much performed by you as true valour and good conduction could yield'. Essex, needless to say, had already been forgiven. In spite of everything, Elizabeth found it very difficult to stay angry with him for long and even Roger Williams escaped further castigation – England possessed few enough experienced professionals in the military field. But while the Queen had too much common sense to indulge in useless recrimination, or to undermine the nation's confidence in its heroes, the expensive failure of the Portugal Expedition – especially its failure to go to Santander – continued to rankle and it was probably not entirely coincidental that Sir Francis Drake spent the next five years on the beach.

No more large-scale operations on the Spanish mainland were contemplated, at least for the time being. Instead, the English reverted to that element where they were most at home, the sea, and to the game they played so much better than anyone else. Before the war – or, more accurately, in the days when it was still possible and politic to pretend the war did not exist – the name of the game had been piracy, a matter for private enterprise surreptitiously abetted by the Crown. Now things were different. The sea-dogs had turned respectable and the Crown was asserting its right to confiscate the cargoes of neutral vessels trading with Spain. This was a new concept of war at sea and led to a flood of protests from such irritated neutrals as Denmark, Poland and Germany. But the Queen held firm. 'Her Majesty thinketh and knoweth . . . that whenever any doth directly help her enemy with succours of any victual, armour or any kind of munition to enable his ships to maintain themselves, she may lawfully interrupt the same.'

The Channel blockade was, of course, an official matter, the concern of a naval squadron stationed in the Downs with instructions to stop and search any vessel whose master failed to produce a pass issued by the Lord Admiral. Out in the Atlantic, though, off the Azores and westward to the Spanish Main along King Philip's colonial trade routes there was still plenty of room for the individual privateer, and privateering was the growth industry of the eighties and nineties. Most of it, and most of the profits, passed into the hands of syndicates of hard-headed businessmen in London, Bristol and Plymouth dealing in prize cargoes of relatively prosaic commodities like hides and sugar, ginger and cochineal; but the age-old romantic lure of the treasure hunt, the unquenchable hope of one day seizing some great carrack stuffed with gold and jewels, silks, ivory and spices such as would make a man rich beyond his dreams, operated powerfully on all sorts and conditions of the Queen's subjects. Outstanding among them were men like Walter Raleigh and the Earl of Cumberland, both of whom financed and led their own expeditions, but nearly all the leading figures at Court put money into privateering ventures – even the sober Robert Cecil was not immune to the prevailing fever. Some people, notably the merchant bankers of the City of London, did very nicely out of privateering, which in a good year brought in prizes worth up to £300,000, and the seaport towns of the south and west prospered on the pickings; but many a likely lad ran off to sea to make his fortune only to die miserably far from home of typhus or scurvy or some other nastiness, and many an optimistic gentleman ruined himself and his family trying to get in on the act.

The Queen herself was often a shareholder in prize-hunting forays, more than once going into partnership with the Earl of Cumberland, and in 1590 a dozen royal ships, commanded by Martin Frobisher in the *Revenge* and John Hawkins in the *Mary Rose,* spent the summer in Spanish waters lying in wait for the American flota. Their presence created something of a panic, especially among the merchants of Lisbon and Seville; while from the colonial administrators in Puerto Rico and Havana, where privateers had already picked up a couple of silver ships, came anguished complaints that the English were daring them at their very doors. The English, reported a Dutch observer in the Azores, are become lords and masters of the sea and need care for no one. As it turned out, Frobisher and Hawkins enjoyed a negative success. They saw nothing of the treasure fleet for the simple reason that Philip had been driven to cancel that year's sailing, a confession of weakness which resulted in widespread failures among the Italian banking houses, a mutiny by Parma's unpaid troops in the Netherlands and still further delay in Spain's naval recovery.

Meanwhile, the focus of the land war was shifting. In July 1589 the last of the Valois kings was assassinated, an event which set alarm bells ringing in London. Henry III may never have been a conspicuous success either as a man or a monarch, but he had always somehow contrived to resist the pressures of the reactionary pro-Spanish elements around him and to preserve a tenuous link of friendship with Elizabeth. His death seemed likely to lead to a renewal of the civil wars which had ravaged France intermittently over the past forty years and, worse, to Spanish intervention; for the heir to the throne was the Huguenot leader, Henry of Navarre, and the prospect of a Protestant king would surely push the fanatics of the Catholic ultra party into extreme measures. The Catholic League was heavily subsidised by Spain and a Leaguer victory, with the consequent addition of France to Philip's clientage, was not something which the Queen of England could regard with equanimity. Henry of Navarre, an experienced, hard-bitten warrior, could be relied on to fight for his rights, but unfortunately he was also stony broke. Without money from somewhere soon, he would be unable to continue the struggle for Paris and the north, where the League was strongest, and would probably be forced to withdraw south of the Loire, leaving the Channel coast and the Channel ports open to England's enemies.

So, when a special envoy from the new king appeared at Court in August with an urgent appeal for assistance, Elizabeth responded with uncharacteristic promptitude and on 7 September the sum of twenty thousand pounds in cash was handed over at the Lord Treasurer's house in Covent Garden. Henry could scarcely believe his eyes. When the Queen's gold reached him, he is reported, credibly enough, to have said that he'd never seen so much money in his life. It was nothing like enough, of course, and within a year the loan had trebled. In the autumn of 1589 a small expeditionary force under the command of Peregrine Bertie, Lord Willoughby, embarked at the port of Rye to spend three uncomfortable months campaigning with Henry's forces. Other contingents were to follow, and over the next five years Elizabeth spent getting on for four hundred thousand pounds altogether in aid to the King of France. In 1589, too, she'd had to find an extra six thousand for the King of Scotland to help him put down his Catholic rebels and set up house for his Protestant Danish bride.

Old Lord Burghley reflected the difficulty his generation sometimes experienced in adjusting to a situation which had transformed England's ancestral enemies into her most valued allies when he wrote to the Earl of Shrewsbury: 'My lord, the state of the world is marvellously changed, when we true Englishmen have cause for our own quietness to wish good success to a French king and a King of Scots.' Burghley, who seldom missed an opportunity to moralise, added, 'this is the work of God for our good, for which the Queen and us all, are most deeply bound to acknowledge his miraculous goodness, for no wit of man could otherwise have wrought it'.

For her part, the Queen may well have wished the Almighty could so have arranged matters that her friends were not invariably penniless. By 1590 the last of her peace-time savings had gone and already she was being driven to such distasteful expedients as extracting forced loans, or 'benevolences', from her wealthier subjects and selling off crown lands – £125,000 worth in 1590 alone. It was financial necessity which drove her to call another Parliament in the autumn of 1588. The session should have opened in November, but some sharp-eyed individual pointed out that the last instalment of the subsidy voted in 1587 was still being collected and to ask, as the government would have to do, for another grant of double the size before payment of the old was complete would scarcely be tactful. The assembly had therefore been postponed until February.

The Queen got her double subsidy. These were exceptional times – the House of Commons could see that – and, being a responsible, patriotic body of men, they had no wish to appear ungenerous. Only Henry Jackman, member for Calne in Wiltshire, seems to have spoken against the supply bill. In his view the danger of invasion, 'the principal and almost only persuader for the bill', was no longer imminent, 'the teeth and jaws of our mightiest and most malicious enemy having been so lately broken'. Higher taxation, on top of the recent burden imposed on the counties by home defence and having to contribute to the loan now being raised, would, he argued, breed discontent among the people and, worse, create a dangerous precedent 'both to ourselves and our posterity'.

The member for Calne may have gathered little open support, but he undoubtedly voiced the private misgivings of many of his colleagues, who clung to the old-fashioned belief that taxation should be no more than an occasional nuisance imposed to meet extraordinary expenditure in time of national emergency. The mediaeval habit of regarding government officials as the sovereign's personal servants and all the ordinary costs of government as the sovereign's personal responsibility died very hard; but in an increasingly complicated and expensive world, such pleasantly domesticated notions of public finance were becoming less and less realistic.

The Queen's income was derived principally from the revenues of the crown lands, supplemented by the monarchy's traditional perquisites of feudal and customs dues, by judicial fines and, since the Reformation, by ecclesiastical tribute which had formerly been diverted to Rome. Even when every source was squeezed dry it never amounted to more than £300,000 a year and, despite the famous Elizabethan parsimony, was becoming barely adequate for peacetime needs, let alone a continuing war situation. Elizabeth was close-fisted because she had to be, but there were economies she could not make. In an intensely status-conscious age, when a man's or an institution's potency was largely measured by his or its outward show, the Queen was obliged to maintain a suitably magnificent establishment or run the risk of being under-valued, and in an age of personal monarchy the Crown inevitably represented the fountain-head of all patronage. Ambitious men looking for jobs, impecunious peers hoping for hand-outs (the Queen wasn't the only one with appearances to keep up), businessmen on the make, social climbers impatient for honours, everyone with an axe to grind, a career to advance or a favour to seek gravitated towards the Court, and they could not all be disappointed. Everyone naturally expected to pay for a word in the right ear, and palace functionaries living on subsistence wages grew fat on the never-ending queues of petitioners who haunted the corridors and anterooms of power.

Of course it was a bad and a ramshackle system, wide open to every kind of abuse and cause of much of the corruption which spread like a cancer through the body politic. But although the Queen complained bitterly and often that she was surrounded by beggars and although the problem of making ends meet grew steadily more acute, she was as much a prisoner of the system as any of her subjects. As much as any member of the House of Commons she recoiled from the idea of increased taxation, and this was not just because taxation was unpopular. The more the Crown had to depend on Parliament for money, the more insistently that body would de-

mand a say in matters which the Queen regarded as being none of
their business and the harder it would be to maintain discipline.
Elizabeth had in the past fought and won several pitched battles with
the Commons in defence of her prerogative, but that was before the
financial situation had become so threatening.

In 1589 the Commons came up with two private members' bills
designed to redress various long-standing grievances against the mal-
practices of the royal purveyors and officials of the Court of Exchequer, but the Queen rejected them both. If the purveyors, officers of
her own household, and the officers of her own court of her own
revenues had been acting unlawfully, then 'her Majesty was of herself both able and willing to see due reformation' and would do so
without assistance from anybody. Least of all, she indicated crossly,
did she require assistance from those busy young gentlemen in the
Commons who appeared to suffer from an uncontrollable itch to
meddle in her private affairs.

The Commons of 1589 was a somewhat less obstreperous assemblage than some of its predecessors, but it was not to be put off with
a mere royal scolding. A committee was set up and recommended
that in 'humble and dutiful wise' this House should 'exhibit unto her
Majesty the causes and reasons' which moved them to proceed with
the two disputed bills. Such a course, it was felt, would best stand
with the liberties and honour of the Commons, and the Speaker was
instructed to make 'most humble petition and suit . . . that her
Majesty would vouchsafe her most gracious favour' in the matter.
Elizabeth agreed to receive a small deputation and, so the Speaker
presently reported to the House, received it with 'most comfortable
and gracious speeches . . . of her Highness's great and inestimable
loving care towards her loving subjects; yea, more than of her own
self, or than any of them have of themselves'.

All this, of course, was part of the recognised ritual of communica-
tion between Queen and Parliament played out in public, while the
serious business of negotiation went on behind the scenes. The result
of this particular bout was made known on 17 March, when the
Speaker announced her Majesty's pleasure that four members of the
Commons should be appointed to confer with a committee of Privy
Councillors and Household officials over the drawing up of a new set
of regulations to govern the purveyors in the discharge of their
thankless task of provisioning the Court. A similar procedure seems
to have been adopted with regard to the Court of Exchequer, with
four MPs being invited to join a royal commission of enquiry in a
consultative capacity. It was a typical Elizabethan compromise,

which safeguarded the Queen's prerogative while, at the same time, allowing Parliament some outlet for its reforming zeal and giving the Commons at least an illusion of participation. Compromise in matters of this kind was, in fact, becoming increasingly necessary if the Tudor constitution was to have any chance of survival in a society rapidly outgrowing its paternalistic confines.

But in spite of the trouble it sometimes gave her, Elizabeth never really doubted her ability to manage the House of Commons. Infinitely more dangerous, in her opinion, were those who sought to use the Commons as an instrument in their campaign to undermine the authority of the Crown in the name of religious reform. When the Elizabethan Religious Settlement, as embodied in the Act of Uniformity of 1559, was first reached, there had been an influential body of opinion, both inside and outside Parliament, which would have liked to see a more radical, that is a more Protestant, church in England, more closely modelled on John Calvin's Genevan empire. On the other hand, the Queen, to whom all forms of Calvinism were anathema, would have preferred a settlement nearer the idiosyncratic form of Anglo-Catholicism evolved by her father and in which she herself had been brought up. In 1559 it had been necessary to make some concessions to radical sensibilities, but the Act of Uniformity marked the absolute limit to which Elizabeth was prepared to go and, as presently became clear, this was one of the issues over which she was emphatically not prepared to compromise.

Despite their sovereign lady's disappointing lack of godly zeal, the radical or Puritan party never gave up hope of securing further reform and purging the Church of England of the last remaining vestiges of Romish idolatry, of such symbols and practices as the wearing of surplices, the use of the ring in marriage and the sign of the cross at baptism, the churching of women and kneeling at communion. Although never more than a minority, they were nevertheless a formidable minority, utterly committed to the righteousness of their cause and able to count on powerful support in high places – Francis Walsingham, Francis Knollys, the Earl of Leicester and Lord Burghley were all known to sympathise with some at least of their aims.

During the seventies and early eighties Puritan strength and organisation grew steadily within the Church itself, leading to the formation of the so-called Classical movement with groups of progressive clergy meeting together in private in *classes* and synods for prayer, for self-examination under the stimulus of brotherly censure, for exposition of the Scriptures and the discussion of problems of common interest. This may sound harmless enough, and the objectives of many of those attending such gatherings were unexceptionable in themselves: the remedying of certain all too obvious abuses in the administration of the Anglican Church, the attainment of a higher standard of morals and education in the ministry, and a striving after greater 'purity' in religion generally. But the leaders of the movement, men like John Field and Thomas Cartwright, were planning a revolution. Adepts at the revolutionary arts of propaganda, of exploiting legitimate grievances and of infiltration, they were, in short, attempting to set up a 'shadow' church, 'the embryo of the Presbyterian Discipline lying as yet in the wombe of Episcopacy', intended to penetrate the established order from within and, in due course, quietly to take it over.

Under the 'Presbyterian Discipline' each individual church would be governed by a consistory of ministers and lay elders, whose duties included the supervision of the rank and file by means of domiciliary visits. Then came the *classis,* meeting every six weeks or so and composed of the ministers and elders from twelve neighbouring parishes. Above the *classis* was the provincial synod, representing twelve *classes* and meeting twice a year and finally, at the apex of the pyramid, the national synod. Experience of non-conformist sects abroad, notably the Huguenots in France, had proved this to be an extremely effective method of organising a subversive minority, capable of imposing strict control over its own members and of exerting pressure out of all proportion to its actual strength.

The greatest threat to the episcopal church and, by implication, to the State itself, lay in the fact that English Puritanism – unlike English Catholicism of the same period – was essentially a grass-roots movement and its leaders were able to appear as sincere, dedicated and highminded patriots. Indeed they *were* burningly sincere, dedicated and high-minded patriots – that was just what made them so dangerous; that and their skilful exploitation of those external circumstances working in their favour. Many moderate Anglicans, uneasily aware of corruption and 'worldliness' within the Church, were eager to see some measure of reform. Many loyal and muddle-headed Englishmen saw the left-wing preacher thundering from his pulpit as a diligent watch-dog barking against the Popish wolf and therefore worthy of encouragement.

The Queen, with her infallible instinct for such matters, saw deeper. Elizabeth detested doctrinaire zealots of any complexion, but while she could often sympathise with the predicament of her Catholic subjects, torn as they were between allegiance to their sovereign and their faith, she had no sympathy whatever with Puritanism. She realised, even if no one else did, that the logical end of the system advocated by the radical party would be a theocracy, leading to intolerable innovation and unspeakable tyranny. It would inevitably mean the end of royal supremacy as established by her father and would result in the subjection of the monarchy to a parcel of insolent, Bible punching upstarts, all claiming a direct line to the Almighty and licensed to pry into the private affairs of their betters. Elizabeth's autocratic Tudor soul revolted at the very idea; nor had she forgotten Calvin's teaching that subjects had a positive duty to overthrow and spit upon an ungodly prince. Jerusalem, or Geneva, she indicated flatly would be built in England over her dead body and throughout her reign she fought tenaciously to keep the stealthy encroachment of Puritanism at bay.

It was frequently an uphill struggle – many people, including members of her own Privy Council, wondering audibly why the Queen should be so hard on loyal followers of God's Word at a time when the papist beast was ravening at her door. Surely such doughty opponents of the common enemy might be forgiven a little harmless non-conformity? Unimpressed, Elizabeth demanded the suppression of all unauthorised prayer meetings and nagged the bishops to be on their guard, but it was not until 1583 that she acquired a really trustworthy lieutenant. John Whitgift, the new Archbishop of Canterbury, was a man after the Queen's own heart – a tough disciplinarian who fully shared her views on left-wing clergy and set about the business of rooting them out with more enthusiasm than tact.

The fury roused by the Archbishop's activities offered disconcerting proof of the strength and efficient organisation of the radical movement. *Classes* met excitedly behind locked doors to discuss tactics and the Privy Council was deluged with petitions and complaints. The Archbishop himself became the target of a concerted and bitter attack – tyrant, pope and knave were only some of the epithets flung at him – and even Lord Burghley felt bound to reproach him for proceedings which savoured of 'the Romish Inquisition'. Whitgift, a dour, obstinate individual, as convinced of the righteousness of his cause as any Puritan, had a scornfully dismissive way with criticism which alienated moderate as well as extreme opinion, and England was not to have a more generally hated ecclesiastic until the primacy of the unhappy Laud. Only a generation separated them – William Laud was a boy of ten when John Whitgift was enthroned at Canterbury – but Whitgift was the more fortunate, both in his generation and his patron. The Queen made it clear that she backed her Archbishop's hard-line policy absolutely and, to ram the point home, she admitted him to the Privy Council. He was, significantly, the first and only Elizabethan cleric to be so honoured.

But while Whitgift continued to pursue the Puritans through the Church courts, the real battle was fought out in the House of Commons, where the radical element had always been strongly represented. The Parliament of 1584 met in an atmosphere of rabid anti-Catholicism. Recent events such as the assassination of William of Orange, the discovery of the Throckmorton Plot and the continuing infiltration of the dreaded Jesuit missionaries had all helped to raise Protestant temperatures to sizzling point, and the stage could surely not have been better set for a left-wing assault. As a preliminary step, the Puritans did what they could to ensure the return of 'godly' members to the Nether House, and the conference or *classis* of Dedham in Essex urged that 'some of best credit and most forward for the Gospel' in every county should go up to London to further 'the cause of the Church'. This idea was evidently taken up, for it was noticed that groups of earnest furtherers of the Gospel 'were all day at the door of Parliament and some part of the night in the chambers of Parliament-men, effectually soliciting their business with them'. But no business, however effectually solicited, was going to get very far in the face of the Queen's implacable opposition to any Parliamentary interference in the government of the Church, and her implacable hostility towards the Puritan faction.

At the end of February 1585 she told a select gathering of councillors and bishops about private information received from abroad 'that the Papists were of hope to prevail again in England, for that her Protestants themselves misliked her. "And indeed, so they do", quoth she, "for I have heard that some of them of late have said that I was of no religion – neither hot nor cold, but such a one as one day would give God the vomit." ' Papists and Puritans were united in one opinion at least, Elizabeth declared, 'for neither of them would have me to be Queen of England'; but, she added bitterly, there was an Italian proverb which said: 'From mine enemy let me defend myself; from a pretensed friend, good Lord deliver me.'

A few days after this outburst the Speaker was summoned abruptly to Greenwich and ordered to inform the Commons that there was to be no more meddling with Church affairs, 'neither in reformation of religion or of discipline', no tampering with the Prayer Book and no more disrespectful attacks on the bishops. The Queen, let no one forget it, was, next under God of course, Supreme Governor of the Church with full power and authority to reform any disorder in the same. She hoped no one doubted that as she had the power, so she had the goodwill 'to examine and redress whatsoever may be found amiss'. But 'resolutely she will receive no motion of innovation, nor alter or change any law whereby the religion or church of England standeth established at this day'. She had maintained the Church of England for twenty-seven years. She meant in like state, by God's grace, to continue it and leave it behind her.

This was plain speaking beyond any possibility of mistake and the Commons, who had been happily occupied in drawing up a shopping-list of reforms designed both to make a Church safe for Puritans and clip the wings of proud prelates like Dr Whitgift, 'found themselves so greatly moved and so deeply wounded as they could not devise which way to cure themselves again'. It seemed that either they must come into direct collision with their gracious sovereign – a course still unthinkable to many – or else 'suffer the liberties of their House to be infringed'. Again there was much discussion of tactics carried on 'in private sort', in the houses of left-wing sympathisers, in the upper rooms of taverns and quiet corners of the Palace of Westminster itself.

Several bright ideas emerged from these conclaves. Those in favour of confrontation pressed for the dismissal of the Speaker, 'for that he durst enterprise to go to the Queen without the privity of the House'; while others wanted one of their number to stand up and publicly 'refuse' her Majesty's commandment. More prudent spirits 'wished rather that some way might be wrought underhand that should as forcibly restore the liberty of the House as any violent action openly used'. In the end, old habits of deference to the sovereign and, indeed, of affection and respect, overcame the stirrings of revolution and it was agreed to make a gesture rather than a stand. A bill was therefore introduced for 'the better execution' of a statute dating from the thirteenth year of the reign which regulated admission to the ministry. As this concerned religion (and contained a controversial clause providing for the trial of a would-be pastor's suitability by a panel of twelve laymen) it was certainly defying the royal prohibition; but it could also have been argued that the Commons were only seeking to strengthen an existing law. In the event, the Queen, having successfully frustrated the main attack, wisely turned a blind eye, and the bill was quietly killed off in the Lords.

Another battle had been won, but Elizabeth was undoubtedly worried and upset by the Puritan agitation and in her speech at the end of the session she returned to the subject of religion, 'the ground on which all other matters ought to take root'. 'I am supposed to have many studies', she told the assembled Lords and Commons, 'but most philosophical. I must yield this to be true: that I suppose few, that be no professors, have read more.' Yet in her library God's book was not the most seldom read and anyone who doubted the sincerity of her faith did her too much wrong. 'For, if I were not persuaded that mine were the true way of God's will, God forbid I should live to prescribe it to you.' She saw many overbold with God Almighty, making too many subtle scannings of His blessed will, as lawyers did with human testaments. The presumption was so great that she could not suffer it. She would neither encourage Romanists ('what adversaries they be to mine estate is sufficiently known') nor tolerate new-fangledness, but do her best to guide both by God's holy true rule.

So far, in spite of everything, the Puritans had achieved little or nothing – except perhaps to draw attention to themselves – but they had no intention of abandoning the struggle. In the year and a half which elapsed before the next parliamentary session, the party machine was hard at work completing a major survey intended to provide supporting evidence for their complaints about the deplorable state of the clergy. This, it was hoped, would shock moderate public opinion and win support for the cause from conscientious laymen everywhere, but especially from those influential 'gentlemen of worship' in the shires and counties who had livings in their gift. The survey gleefully identified parish priests who were 'suspected of whoredome' and others 'scarce able to read', one who was an idle ruffian, another 'taken in adultery' and yet another who was 'a common gamester and pot-companion'.

These judgements were not notable for their Christian charity, but there's no doubt that standards generally were pretty low. Many parishes, especially the smaller rural ones, were too poor to attract able men and, in any case, there were not enough able men to go round. The shortage of educated, preaching clergy did not worry the Queen unduly. There was nothing like a little learning for giving a parson ideas above his station, and she was well aware that the most eloquent and persuasive preachers were most liable to be ardent Puritans. To her way of thinking, it was quite enough for the parish priest to be an honest man, capable of administering the sacraments as laid down in the Prayer Book and of reading homilies to the people. On the other hand, scandals in the ministry were obviously undesirable. They damaged the Church, making it vulnerable to attack from both left and right, and the bishops were therefore sharply admonished by their Supreme Governor to look well to their charges or face dismissal.

The hard-pressed Dr. Whitgift and his bishops did their best. Articles passed by Convocation in 1585 laid down stricter rules about the qualifications to be required from candidates for ordination, and a genuine effort was being made to crack down on the more glaring instances of laxity and corruption. But the root-and-branch radicals – like root-and-branch radicals of every age – were not interested in moderate reform, except, of course, for propaganda purposes. What they wanted was a clean sweep – the abolition of 'the titles and names of Antichrist – as Lord's Grace, Lord Bishop, Dean, Archdeacon'. 'Let cathedral churches be utterly destroyed' urged one trigger-happy member of the brotherhood, for they were 'very dens of thieves, where the time and place of God's service, preaching and prayer is most filthily abused: in piping with organs; in singing, ringing and trolling of the Psalms . . . with squeaking of chanting choristers.' If these sinks of iniquity, together with all the lazy, loitering lubbards, dumb dogs, destroying drones and unskilful, sacrificing priests who frequented them, were done away with, then their revenues could be used for the maintenance of a learned ministry.

When Parliament met again in November 1586 the godly brethren, stimulated by the prospect of wholesale iconoclasm, girded their loins and once more descended on the capital. The first weeks of the session were, however, monopolised by the momentous business of winding up the earthly affairs of Mary Queen of Scots, and the reformers were obliged to wait until nearly the end of February 1587 before launching a fresh assault. Then, despite a warning that the Commons were especially commanded by her Majesty to take heed 'that none care be given or time afforded the wearisome solicitation of those that commonly be called Puritans, wherewithal the late Parliaments have been exceedingly importuned', Anthony Cope, one of the Puritan members, rose to move the reading of a 'Bill and a Book'.

The Speaker, guessing something of what was coming, tried vainly to intervene, but the organised left wing was ready to talk down any opposition. Several members spoke in favour of Cope's motion, among them Job Throckmorton – a red-hot radical and not to be confused with the Throckmorton of the Catholic plot. In a brilliant piece of special pleading he argued that the surest way for the safety, long life and prosperity of the Queen's majesty – chief cause of all their consultations – was 'to begin at the house of God and to prefer the reformation of Jerusalem before all the fleeting felicities of this mortal life', and went on to protest against the use of 'puritanism' as an opprobrious epithet. 'To bewail the distresses of God's children, it is puritanism. To reprove a man for swearing, it is puritanism. To banish an adulterer out of the house, it is puritanism. To make humble suit to her Majesty and the High Court of Parliament for a learned ministry, it is puritanism . . . I fear me we shall come shortly to this, that to do God and her Majesty good service shall be counted puritanism.'

Throckmorton and his friends carried the day, but godly zeal and brevity seldom go together and the Commons rose very late, agreeing to read Mr Cope's bill in the morning. They should have known better. Elizabeth, still suffering from the violent emotional reaction caused by the Queen of Scots' execution and in a mood to be exasperated by this latest manifestation of Puritan arrogance, acted overnight, ordering the Bill and the Book to be sent to her at Greenwich. Neither was calculated to reassure. The bill, after a long preamble, contained two clauses, one authorising the use of the Book which was, of course, a version of the Genevan Prayer Book incorporating a Presbyterian form of discipline. The second would, in effect, have abolished the Anglican Church, declaring all existing laws, customs, statutes, ordinances and constitutions concerning it to be 'utterly void and of none effect'!

While the Commons waited for the inevitable thunderclaps of royal wrath they continued defiantly to debate the state of the Church, and Peter Wentworth, another leading radical, delivered himself of a resounding series of demands for freedom of Parliamentary speech and action – demands which, if conceded, would have speedily hamstrung the monarchy and put an end to the ancient system of government by the sovereign in council. In the words of Professor Neale, greatest modern authority on the Elizabethan era, 'through the plottings of the godly brotherhood and their organised group of Parliamentary agents, Queen Elizabeth was menaced with revolution in Church and State'.

Queen Elizabeth, as might be expected, reacted vigorously. She knew all about the organised lobbying of members of Parliament and the semi-secret conferences being held by the Puritan members and their supporters. Extra-mural activities of this kind were not protected by privilege; they were, in fact, not far removed from conspiracy, and Wentworth, Cope and three others were arrested and committed to the Tower. At the same time, the government launched a counter-attack spear-headed by Sir Christopher Hatton. The Queen, he announced, had suppressed the Bill and the Book and there was to be no more argument about it but, in her 'concern for their contentment', she was prepared to tell the Commons why. Hatton then went on to spell out just what the consequences of extremist action would be. Did the House, he enquired, really want to alter the whole form and order of the familiar church service? Did it really want to do away with the Book of Common Prayer, which a whole generation of Englishmen had been brought up to think 'both good and godly'? In the Calvinist version, with its overwhelming emphasis on the sermon and extempore prayer, 'all or the most part is left to the minister's spirit' and the unlettered would be deprived of the comfort of well-known and loved incantations.

Turning from the spiritual to the material, Hatton wanted to know how the new order was to be financed. Every parish, he reminded his audience, even the poorest, would have to support at least one pastor and two deacons, 'besides I know not how many elders'. Leaving aside the question of where all these wise and godly men were to be found, they would certainly have to be paid for. The bishops and the cathedral churches might be despoiled, but that would not be enough. Sooner rather than later the surrender of the abbey lands and other church possessions filched at the Reformation, and on which so many family fortunes had been founded, would be demanded by the presbyteries. And what of the Queen? Her royal supremacy would be 'wholly abrogated by this Bill and Book' and without first fruits, tenths and clerical subsidies her revenues would be seriously depleted. The Crown was still bound to defend the realm, so how was the deficiency to be made up if not out of taxpayers' pockets? Worse than this, the Queen would be made subject to censure and even excommunication by the pastors, doctors and elders.

Hatton was followed by Sir Walter Mildmay, himself known to have Puritan sympathies, and Thomas Egerton, the Solicitor General, who between them completed the work of demolition, of isolating and exposing the extremist minority as 'men of small judgement and experience'. Remorselessly they listed the Acts of Parliament, including those aimed at the Catholic recusants, which would disappear, and pointed to the legal confusion which would result from the dismantling of the Church courts. What, for example, would happen to wills and testaments, to contracts of marriage and questions of bastardy and inheritance?

The House of Commons might tend towards radicalism in its religious opinions and thus be liable to become carried away by Puritan eloquence, but the knights and burgesses, the lawyers and landowners and businessmen who made up its solid, conservative, self-interested bulk were nobody's fools. Elizabeth had reckoned that if they could once be shocked into realising how their loyalty, their patriotism and their genuine concern for the Protestant faith were being exploited by the irresponsible few, they would draw back – and she was quite right. There was some grumbling in the ranks, some talk of petitioning the Queen to release the imprisoned members, some threats of a sit-down strike; but at the same time it was clear that the crisis was over, that the militant left wing had been defeated by a shrewdly calculated mixture of coercion and reasoned argument. The five members remained in gaol until the end of the session, and it was a sobered assembly which finally dispersed on 23 March.

The Puritan or Presbyterian movement had not been destroyed – surreptitious mini-Genevas continued to flourish in the Midlands, East Anglia and the London area – but after 1587 it lost its power base in Parliament, something it was not to regain in the Queen's lifetime. The movement suffered other set-backs in the last years of the eighties. The death of John Field, its brilliant organising secretary, in March 1588 was a serious loss and, as no other leader of comparable ability came forward to take his place, the cohesion and unity of purpose which had made the left wing so formidable earlier in the decade began to break down. Disappointment and frustration, too, betrayed some members of the fraternity into a grave error of judgement.

Puritans as well as Catholics had always made use of the secret printing press in their propaganda campaigns and in the autumn of 1588 the first of the Martin Marprelate tracts appeared on the streets. These remarkable productions – there were seven of them altogether – caused a sensation. Written in a vein of broad, sarcastic humour they lampooned the unfortunate bishops, both individually and collectively. They were irreverent, witty and clever and good for a cheap laugh – everybody was reading them and sniggering over them – but in the long run they were a mistake. Serious minded people were alienated by their levity and they went a long way towards disenchanting the more moderate Puritans, especially those in high places. 'As they shoot at bishops now', remarked the Earl of Hertford, 'so they will do at the nobility also, if they be suffered'; and Lord Burghley noted that 'care is to be taken to suppress all the turbulent Precisians who do violently seek to change the external government of the Church'.

The authorities were doing their utmost to suppress Martin Marprelate and in the summer of 1589 an accident to the cart transporting the secret press from Warrington to Manchester led to its capture.

Several arrests were made and, although Martin's identity was never established, a lot of useful information had come into the government's hands during the course of its enquiries. As a result, by 1590 the Presbyterian underground was in disarray and its leaders in custody.

1590 was also a satisfactory year from the Queen's point of view in that it marked a welcome lull in foreign hostilities. Henry IV's victory over the Catholic League at Ivry in March had won him a temporary respite and no English troops were required to fight in France. The two sovereigns, however, kept in close touch. Elizabeth wrote regularly to her 'dearest brother' – in spite of what he was costing her, the King of France was a friend worth having – and the French ambassador received some distinguishing marks of royal attention. In August he was invited to Oatlands for a few days hunting and the Queen herself killed a deer for him, and in November a new envoy, the Vicomte de Turenne, was guest of honour at the Accession Day tilt.

In typically English fashion the custom of observing 17 November, the anniversary of the Queen's accession, as a public holiday seems to have originated out of a chance incident, possibly at Oxford in 1570. It may well have started even earlier. No one really seems to know for certain. What is certain is that by the fifteen-eighties Queen's Day had become a major national festival, and after 1588 the celebrations spread over to 19 November which happened to be St Elizabeth's Day. Up and down the country the occasion was marked by bonfires and feasting, by pageants and shows and pealing bells and, of course, sermons. It made a pleasant and harmless substitute for all the feast and saints' days which had disappeared from the calendar with the Roman Church – a day when the good Protestant people of England could joyfully triumph for purely Protestant reasons. 'The sacred seventeenth day' had, in fact, been gradually built up into a day of official rejoicing and thanksgiving, an annual opportunity for reminding the lieges of the manifold blessings they enjoyed under the beneficent rule of their gracious Queen: the pious and virtuous maiden who had delivered them from the tyranny and cruelty of the Bishop of Rome; the wise and merciful princess who had brought them peace at home, freedom and true religion.

> *The noblest Queen*
> *That ever was seen*
> *In England doth reign this day.*

Now let us pray,
And keep holy-day
The seventeenth day November;
For joy of her Grace,
In every place,
Let us great praise render.

In the more unsophisticated provinces, the emphasis was on the Queen in her role of God's handmaiden; the scriptural heroine, the English Judith and Deborah and, although this could scarcely be admitted, a surrogate Virgin Mary. At Court, where the festivities centred around the Accession Day tournament, the cult took on a heavily romantic, neo-classical, neo-mediaeval bias with Elizabeth cast as Astraea, virgin goddess of justice, as Cynthia 'the Ladie of the Sea', as Diana, Belphoebe and Gloriana, the Faerie Queene – a semi-divine object of courtly love before whom the knights, drawn mainly from the ranks of the Gentlemen Pensioners and the younger nobility, came to render homage and devotion.

The tournament normally took place in the tiltyard at Whitehall, roughly the area occupied today by Horse Guards Parade, and the knights made their entrances in a variety of elaborate and expensive disguises. Some arrived riding in chariots drawn by strange beasts, by men, or apparently self-propelled, and from which they would vault in full armour on to their chargers. Others, less confident of their horsemanship, entered already mounted. There were Black Knights, Wandering Knights, a Blind Knight from the Americas whose sight miraculously returned in the Queen's presence, Melancholy Knights, Unknown Knights, even Clownish Knights, all attended by retinues of servants, squires and lance-bearers suitably got up as wild men, or Indian princes, or sailors or shepherds according to the chosen theme. Each carried a shield on which his *impresa,* or device, was depicted and the more loaded with symbolism and allusion the more successful it was considered.

Often the allusion was topical. In 1590 the Earl of Essex appeared 'all in sable sad' and escorted by a funeral cortege. This was a reference to his recent disgrace with the Queen, for the previous April Essex had married Frances, daughter of Francis Walsingham and widow of Sir Philip Sidney. Apart from her well-known dislike of seeing any member of her court get married, Elizabeth had been particularly annoyed on this occasion because the wedding had taken place without her knowledge and because she considered the alliance an unworthy one – Essex was, after all, rather a special case. However, since the Earl was wise enough not to parade his bride, being pleased 'for her Majesty's better satisfaction' that she should live very retired in her mother's house, and since young Lady Essex showed no sign of wishing to put herself forward, the storm had blown over quite quickly. Essex was now noticed to be 'in good favour' again, and on 19 November he and the Earl of Cumberland and Lord Burgh 'did challenge all comers, six courses apiece, which was very honourably performed'.

Although jousting or tilting – two armoured knights charging one another at full gallop on either side of a parallel barrier with the object of shattering the opponent's lance – was no longer quite the rugged and realistic combat exercise it had once been, it still required enough athleticism and speed of reaction to make it primarily a young man's sport, and the 1590 tilt was marked by the retirement of the Queen's Champion. Sir Henry Lee had stage-managed the Accession Day tilts for the past ten years and had been largely responsible for making them into an entertainment worthy of Gloriana and her Court, but now at fifty-seven he felt the time had come to make way for a successor. The retiring Champion made his entry

> . . . in rich embroidery
> And costly caparisons charged with crowns
> O'ershadowed with a withered running vine

and when the tilting was over presented a charming tableau before the Queen: 'a Pavilion, made of white Taffeta, being in proportion like unto the sacred Temple of the Virgins Vestal' and seeming to consist upon pillars of porphyry, 'arched like unto a Church'. Inside this confection of the scene-painter's art were many lamps burning and an altar covered with cloth of gold on which had been laid out a selection of expensive gifts, 'which after by three Virgins were presented unto her Majesty'. The offering was accompanied by sweet music and the lutenist Robert Hales sang Dowland's setting of 'His golden locks time hath to silver turn'd'.

> His helmet now shall make a hive for bees,
> And, lovers' sonnets turn'd to holy psalms,
> A man at arms must now serve on his knees,
> And feed on prayers, which are age his alms.
> > But though from court to cottage he depart,
> > His saint is sure of his unspotted heart.

And when he saddest sits in homely cell,
He'll teach his swains this carol for a song,
Blest be the hearts that wish my sovereign well,
Curst be the souls that think her any wrong.
Goddess, allow this aged man his right,
To be your bedesman now, that was your knight.

The new Champion was George Clifford, Earl of Cumberland, but Henry Lee continued to help with staging the tournament – his knowledge and long experience of such matters were too valuable to waste – and he made positively his last appearance at James I's Accession Day tilt in March 1604. Nor can it be said that the old man turned entirely to a diet of prayers, for during the nineties he became the protector of the beautiful but notorious Anne Vavasour, who lived with him as his mistress at his country house in Oxfordshire.

Queen's Day was observed until the end of the reign and 'fair England's knights' continued to don their archaic panoply and play their obsolete game of chivalry

In honour of their mistress' holiday
A gracious sport, fitting that golden time.

At Court, where the occasion had taken on the character of a royal command performance and become an important event in the social calendar, there was naturally a strong element of axe-grinding as knight vied with knight to put on the most impressive show and offer the most exquisite compliment to majesty. In the country at large, everyone, equally naturally, welcomed the excuse to have a party and a break in the grinding routine of daily life. But celebration of 'the sacred seventeenth day' as the birthday of England's happiness, which had risen out of a spontaneous wave of indignant patriotism in the late sixties and early seventies, could not have flourished on into the more sober nineties if it had not continued to provide a necessary outlet for genuine emotion. Nor, despite the obvious self-interest and the deliberate official encouragement, could the cult of the Queen have existed in a rough, tough, individualistic society if it had not been rooted in genuine 'affectionate love'.

The glorification and idealisation of an ageing, over-dressed woman into a peculiar amalgam of biblical saint and classical goddess may seem excessive, even perhaps a trifle ridiculous, but to the Elizabethans, nurtured as they were on the Bible and the classics, it was entirely logical. The Queen's actual physical appearance had nothing to do with the matter, for by the fifteen-eighties Elizabeth had become an almost mystical symbol. She *was* Protestant England, a legitimate focus for swelling national pride. Besides this, in an age of upheaval and insecurity, when all sorts of unsettling new ideas were working their way to the surface, the Queen represented continuity, an instinctive confidence that as long as she reigned the Protestant God would continue to look after his own.

> *In her days every man shall eat in safety*
> *Under his own vine what he plants; and sing*
> *The merry songs of peace to all his neighbours.*

When she had gone, what then?

III
Fair Stood the Wind
for France

Seated between the Old World and the New,
A land there is no other land may touch,
Where reigns a Queen in peace and honour true;
Stories or fables do describe no such.
Never did Atlas such a burden bear,
As she, in holding up the world opprest;
Supplying with her virtue everywhere
Weakness of friends, errors of servants best.

Although the new decade had opened relatively quietly on the European front, Henry IV's early successes and Queen Elizabeth's intervention on his behalf were having the inevitable effect of driving the French Catholic party still further into the Spanish camp. In January 1590 the Catholic League – a powerful right-wing confederation of nobles, government officials, cities and, indeed, whole provinces – made a fresh appeal to the King of Spain and, as a result, a new agreement was reached between the champions of orthodoxy. Philip assumed the title of Protector of the Crown of France and was promised possession of certain towns, plus the exclusive and unrestricted use of all ports and harbours under the League's control. In return, Spain would provide the League with increased financial and military aid in its struggle to dislodge the heretic king. Spanish troops now began to move in from the Netherlands and that summer an army under the command of the great Duke of Parma himself marched down through Picardy, forcing Henry to abandon his siege of Paris. In the early autumn, three thousand Spaniards landed on the coast of Brittany and proceeded to occupy the town of Hennebon, which overlooks the modern naval base of Lorient. Rumour exaggerated the size of this invasion and for a while there were serious fears that Parma in the north and Don Juan d'Aguila in Brittany would join hands and between them seize the whole of the Channel coast from Brest to Calais. So, when the Vicomte de Turenne arrived in London in November, he found a ready audience for his master's urgent requests for help.

Elizabeth placed very little reliance on Henry's solemn undertakings to repay the money she was lending him, nor did she really expect that he would keep his promise to double the size of any army she sent to Brittany. In fact, she didn't trust him further than she could see him and it was this distrust which, paradoxically, made her continued involvement unavoidable. The King of France had half his kingdom still to conquer and, for all his fair words, the defence of the Channel ports looked like remaining pretty low on his list of priorities for some time to come; but to the English the security of those ports was vital, especially now that Spain had begun to rebuild her naval strength. Clearly another expedition would have to be mounted, and on 11 January 1591 Sir John Norris received his commission as General of the Queen's Army in Brittany.

In spite of the apparent urgency of the situation there were the usual delays and difficulties in extracting a nucleus of experienced troops from the Netherlands, the usual anguished complaints about the wretched quality of the new levies – Norris lamenting that one of the West Country contingents was made up of 'the worst men and the worst furnished' he had ever seen, and 'so poor and weak that they will scarce endure the passage by sea'. What with one thing and another it was nearly the end of April before the expedition finally got away, and the beginning of May by the time it landed at Paimpol in northern Brittany.

The campaign turned out to be an indecisive affair. Towards the end of May, Norris, in conjunction with the local royalist leader, the Prince de Dombes, succeeded in capturing the town of Guingamp, but the rest of the summer was frittered away in skirmishing and generally manoeuvring for position – neither of the opposing armies being strong enough to force matters to a conclusion. In spite of constant rumours that reinforcements were on their way from Spain, none came after April, and although the Leaguer Duc de Mercoeur had claimed to be able to offer Philip a choice of the useful seaports of Brest, Morlaix and St Malo, the native Bretons had other ideas. At St Malo the townsfolk took the precaution of occupying the castle, while at Brest and Morlaix they were in a position to exercise a controlling influence over their military governors – the governor of Brest was, in any case, a staunch king's man. England and Spain both retained a toehold in Brittany and Norris's presence was at least helping to keep the Spaniards tied down in the southern part of the province, but otherwise remarkably little had been accomplished.

The Queen was not pleased. Needless to say, Henry had failed to support Norris as promised and, even more aggravating, the Prince de Dombes had been trying to lure the English inland to join him in a campaign in 'the high parts of Brittany' – nothing to do with securing the coast. Elizabeth wrote angrily threatening to withdraw her troops altogether unless the French kept their side of the bargain, but by this time she was committed to yet another cross-Channel adventure.

All through the spring of 1591 the King of France had continued to press his urgent need for reinforcements. He wanted money for German mercenaries to match Parma in Picardy, and he wanted military aid to help him meet the growing threat to Normandy. There was already a small English force in Dieppe under Roger Williams, but Honfleur and Fécamp had recently fallen into the hands of the League and now even Boulogne was in danger. Henry's immediate objective, so he said, was the capture of Rouen and this woke a sympathetic response in London. Rouen, lying as it did on the Seine midway between Paris and the sea, would not only be a valuable strategic base from which to reduce the other northern cities (Lord Burghley considered it even more valuable than Paris), but was also a great commercial centre which would provide a welcome outlet for English continental trade, now almost at a standstill. When, as a further inducement, Henry offered to allow the Queen's agents to collect the royal revenues from Rouen and Le Havre until his debts had been cleared, Elizabeth undertook to raise and equip four thousand men, paid for two months and commanded by no less a personality than the Earl of Essex.

The Queen had consented to this appointment very much against her better judgement, but the pressures on her were hard to withstand. In many ways Essex was the obvious choice. His popularity would help to hold the army together and his prestige would attract the better class of volunteer – an important consideration, as no more veterans could be drawn from the Netherlands. Lord Burghley, who had his own reasons for wanting the favourite temporarily out of the way, supported the idea and Essex himself was wild to go. Ever since the Portugal voyage he'd been growing increasingly bored with the tameness of his courtier's life and impatient for martial glory. Then again, the prospect of charging to the relief of a hard-pressed warrior king, fighting for his throne against all the odds, was exactly cal- culated to appeal to his ardently romantic nature – all the more so since the warrior king in question was taking every opportunity to curry favour with him. Essex had been deeply disappointed at miss- ing the campaign in Brittany. Now he pestered the Queen to send him to France. On three occasions, so he told the King, he had knelt before her for as much as two hours at a time. Elizabeth surrendered, but her misgivings remained. Essex was still only twenty-three with no experience of high command. It seemed only too probable that he would do something silly, and she warned Henry that he would need the bridle rather than the spur.

Having got what he wanted, the new Lord General was in high spirits and quite untroubled by self-doubt. 'I am commanded into France for the establishing of the brave King in quiet possession of Normandy' he wrote to a friend, and was soon happily immersed in the delightful business of raising a troop of horse from among his own cronies and dependents. On 24 June letters went out to the counties ordering a levy of 3,400 men which, with the six hundred already in Dieppe, would make up the promised four thousand. The Lords Lieutenant had special instructions to pick only the best type of recruit, as many as possible from the train bands or militia, and the officers, too, were carefully chosen to include many of the new, younger men like John Wingfield and Thomas Baskerville who were making soldiering their profession.

The army which sailed for France at the end of July was probably the finest and best equipped of all the Elizabethan expeditionary forces, though one observer remarked that he had never known so gallant a troop go out of England with so many young and untrained commanders. In fact, the misfortunes which were to overtake the gallant troop cannot be blamed entirely on the youth of its captains and the inexperience of its general. When the English disembarked they found that Henry, so far from being ready and waiting to begin the siege of Rouen, was not even in Normandy. Instead he was still engaged a good hundred miles to the east at Noyon and the German mercenaries, paid for by the Queen, had not yet arrived. After spend- ing a fortnight hanging about waiting for news, Essex left the army camped round Dieppe and, with only a small cavalry escort, set out on a hazardous cross-country journey through Leaguer-held territory to meet Henry near Compiègne. He entered the city to the sound of trumpets, resplendent in orange-tawny velvet and gold lace, and if the shabby King and his grim, battle-hardened companions found the spectacle a trifle comic, they were careful not to show it.

On the contrary, Henry set himself out to charm Queen Elizabeth's youthful Lieutenant. Apart from his renowned fighting qualities, the King of France was famous for his affability and his easy-going, friendly ways. Everyone who came into contact with him felt the attraction of his warm, out-going personality and the impressionable Essex quickly succumbed. He spent three delightful days as the King's guest and it was agreed that the bulk of the royalist forces, under the veteran Marshal Biron, should start for Rouen at once, Henry promising to follow just as soon as the Germans put in an appearance.

Meanwhile, Essex had to get back to base and the return trip turned out to be quite an adventurous one. He and his party had to make a wide detour and do some hard riding to evade a strong Leaguer force out looking for them, and when they reached Pont de l'Arche, a town held for the King, it was thought advisable to send for the rest of the army. Thus reinforced, Essex could not resist the temptation to try and entice the governor of Rouen to come out and fight. Unhappily, in the resultant skirmish his younger brother, Walter, was killed and Essex himself, who had gone down with a nasty attack of fever, had to be carried back to camp in a litter.

His discomfiture was presently increased by a scolding from the Queen. Having had no news of her problem child for nearly three weeks Elizabeth was already querulous with anxiety, and when she heard what he'd been up to, she exploded. The Lieutenant and General of her forces had no business to go gallivanting round France without her knowledge or permission. He had risked his own life by his irresponsible behaviour and endangered the army, first by leaving it without proper leadership and then exposing it uselessly. This was bad enough and confirmed all her forebodings about the unsuitability of the appointment. But what infuriated the Queen more than anything was the delay in getting to grips with the purpose of the expedition, caused by the King's failure to keep his solemn promise 'to join with us to the besieging of Rouen'. She was not appeased by explanations or excuses; nor was her temper improved when Marshal Biron, arriving in the vicinity of the city on 12 September, decided that the neighbouring towns of Gournay and Caudebec must be taken first.

The English assisted at the assault on Gournay, Essex joining the ranks and trailing a pike like any common soldier. No doubt he enjoyed himself, but he got another angry telling-off from London. He was again hazarding his life in a childish desire for vainglory, denigrating his high office and, by implication, the sovereign who had bestowed it on him.

Elizabeth had, by this time, more than half convinced herself that Essex and the King of France were ganging up on her. She suspected Henry of openly mocking her, of accepting her help while, at the same time, cynically disregarding her wishes and her instinctive reaction was to order the immediate withdrawal of all her troops, leaving the French to stew in their own juice. Only the knowledge that if she abandoned him now, Henry, a king without a crown making wars without money, would almost certainly go under, leaving Spain to fill the vacuum, prevented her from taking this satisfying form of revenge. Reluctantly she agreed that, provided the siege of Rouen was really about to begin at last, the army in Normandy might stay for another month or forty days beyond its original two months' contract – but on the clear understanding that Henry would be responsible for paying its wages. Essex she was determined to recall. He'd made it only too plain that he couldn't be trusted to conduct himself with the restraint and decorum required of a senior commander, and Elizabeth was sufficiently fond of him genuinely not to want to see him lose his life in some stupid piece of bravado.

Essex, for his part, was equally determined not to be dragged away just as things were getting interesting. He went over to England early in October and got a cold reception. 'I see your Majesty is constant to ruin me', he wrote sadly. In the end he spent a week with the Queen at Oatlands and managed to talk her into a more reasonable frame of mind. Back at Dieppe in the middle of the month he was writing in typical Essex vein: 'I will humbly beseech your Majesty that no cause but a great action of your own may draw me out of your sight, for the two windows of your privy chamber shall be the poles of my sphere where, as long as your Maj. will please to have me, I am fixed and immovable. When your Maj. thinks that heaven too good for me, I will not fall like a star, but be consumed like a vapour by the same sun that drew me up to such a height. While your Maj. gives me leave to say I love you, my fortune is as my affection, unmatchable. If ever you deny me that liberty, you may end my life, but never shake my constancy, for were the sweetness of your nature turned into the greatest bitterness that could be, it is not in your power, great Queen as you are, to make me love you less. Therefore, for the honour of your sex, show yourself constant in kindness . . .'

By the same post the newly returned Lord General sent the Council a report on the state of the army, which he had found 'in great disorder'. The soldiers in the camp at Arques were now officially in the pay of the King of France and, since this meant no pay, they were reacting in the traditional manner by foraging over the surrounding countryside, looting and burning as they went. According to Essex, 'the King's ministers do not give them that which they promised me, because they say our men spoil the King's subjects and live well upon the country' but, as the King himself freely admitted to Queen Elizabeth's ambassador, he had not five hundred crowns in his treasury. 'The state of France is most miserable and lamentable', reported Sir Henry Unton. The necessities of the poor King, it seemed, were such that he even wanted bread to eat. 'If I were not an eyewitness hereof, I could not believe it', declared the ambassador impressively.

Unless and until the King could take Rouen there would be no money to meet his obligations to the English or anyone else, but it was not just the fact that their pay was in arrears – a common enough condition of sixteenth century armies – which had demoralised the Queen's soldiers. When it came to actual fighting, as they had already proved in the Netherlands, even the raw levies could hold their own in any company. What they could not stand was boredom. The gentlemen volunteers simply went home and there was a steady trickle of desertion from the ranks, but mostly they got drunk and went on the rampage, or went sick. Sickness – always the largest single cause of wastage – was taking an increasing toll from men stagnating in the insanitary compounds round Dieppe, so that by the end of October, when the siege did at long last look like beginning in earnest, fewer than fifteen hundred effectives remained out of the original four thousand.

Elizabeth still sharply resented the 'public affront' she considered she had received from the King of France. 'Be not displeased', she wrote to him in November, 'if I tell you roundly, that if you thus treat your friends, who . . . are serving you at a most important time, they will fail you hereafter at your greatest need.' However, now that Henry and his Germans had finally put in an appearance, the Queen, grumbling steadily that some people seemed to forget she had a realm of her own to provide for and had neither 'the eastern nor the western Indies' at her disposal, did what she could to ensure their success. A small detachment of pioneers and a thousand veterans from the Netherlands were sent to Normandy and the English army, much to its relief, was taken back into the pay of the blessed Queen. But in spite of these last ditch efforts the siege made little progress, dragging inconclusively through the winter and early spring until the Duke of Parma, making another of his lightning forays from the north, revictualled and reinforced the Rouen garrison and once again forced the King to withdraw.

Essex had gone home by this time. He had handed over his greatly reduced command to Roger Williams early in January and sailed for England, disenchanted, at least temporarily, with a military career. Nor was he the only person to be disillusioned about the French war. In its initial stages the Normandy campaign, wakening as it did romantic echoes of past glories, had made a particular appeal to the Queen's subjects. In March 1592 Lord Strange's company of actors capitalised on the public mood with a production of *Henry VI*, the work of a new writer, a civil young fellow by the name of William Shakespeare, who was just beginning to make his way in the profession. Enthusiasm, though, was already waning, and as time went on the authorities found it more and more difficult to raise suitable recruits for service overseas.

Between the years 1591 and 1595 Elizabeth somehow contrived to maintain a military presence strung out along the European coastline from Brittany in the south to Zeeland in the north. Apart from the heavy financial burden this entailed, the drain on the manpower of a small nation was not inconsiderable – bearing in mind that the mortality rate from dysentery, typhus, malaria and other forms of disease (not to mention all those who died of quite minor wounds for lack of the most basic medical care) was seldom far short of fifty per cent. Of the twenty thousand men who went to France between 1589 and 1595 no more than half returned.

The government, unhappily aware of the shortcomings of a system which had begun to lose its usefulness before the end of the Hundred Years' War, made various well-intentioned efforts to check the worst abuses and improve the lot of the private soldier. But jobbery, vested interest, public indifference, chronic shortage of cash and, perhaps most important, a total absence of corporate spirit among the men of war, were too strong for good intentions and combined to ensure that England's armed forces should continue to be scratch collections of untrained or, at best, half-trained civilians, ill-equipped, badly paid, shockingly fed, sometimes half-naked, and always mercilessly exploited by corrupt captains and profiteering contractors. In the circumstances it is hardly surprising that military service grew increasingly unpopular and the subject of 'great murmuring' by the families and friends of those liable to be called up. Draft dodging was a national pastime and as a result the levies came more and more to consist of the scourings of the slums and gaols who deserted at the first opportunity.

The Queen hated the whole business, the expense, the bare-faced cheating and the waste, but she dared not disengage as long as France remained precariously balanced on the edge of a pro-Spanish take-over, or while reports continued to come in of another great Armada building in the Spanish ports. If even half the rumours were true, it was clear that Philip's navy could no longer be written off as a spent force. Indeed, England had been given an unmistakable hint of her enemy's reviving strength back in August 1591, when

At Flores in the Azores Sir Richard Grenville lay,
And a pinnace, like a fluttered bird, came flying from far away:
'Spanish ships of war at sea! We have sighted fifty-three!'

Grenville in the *Revenge*, with Lord Thomas Howard in the *Defiance* and another half-dozen or so of the Queen's ships, had been cruising off the Azores all summer in the hope once more of catching the treasure fleet on its homeward voyage, and at the end of August they were at Flores taking on provisions and fresh water and cleaning out their filthy ballast. A look-out was being kept to the westward for the American flota but no one, it seems, had been anticipating trouble from the east. So it was fortunate that the Earl of Cumberland should also have been spending the summer in Spanish waters on a semi-private marauding expedition. It was he who had spotted the Spanish fleet putting out from Ferrol and despatched Captain William Middleton in the pinnace *Moonshine* 'both to discover their forces the more as also to give advice to my Lord Thomas of their approach'.

Even with Middleton's warning, the English at Flores were caught at a considerable disadvantage. An epidemic, probably typhus, had been raging in the squadron. There were ninety sick on the *Revenge*, nearly half her crew. The *Bonaventure*, commanded by Robert Cross, had 'not so many in health as could handle her mainsail' and the rest were in little better case. Many of the ships' companies were on shore, either lying sick and helpless or out on foraging expeditions; nor were the ships themselves, after four months at sea, in very fit condition. Some had not yet finished rummaging and were conse-quently 'very light for want of ballast'. Thomas Howard, a cousin of the Lord Admiral Howard of Effingham, may have been no coward but he was no fool either, and it was patently obvious that he was in no position to give battle against such odds. The only sensible course was to get as many of the crews as possible back on board and run for it while there was still time.

Just how much time there actually was is not very clear – certainly no more than twenty-four hours and probably less. But Howard in the flagship, together with the *Bonaventure*, the *Lion*, the *Foresight*, the

Crane and a small miscellaneous flotilla of victuallers and pinnaces, were able to get to windward of the approaching Spaniards and make a reasonably dignified exit. Not so the *Revenge.* She was the last ship to weigh anchor and had left it too late to go with the others. Just what had delayed her is something else which is not very clear. According to Walter Raleigh, Grenville waited 'to recover the men that were upon the island, which otherwise had been lost'.

> . . . *Sir Richard bore in hand all his sick men from the land*
> *Very carefully and slow,*
> *Men of Bideford in Devon,*
> *And we laid them on the ballast down below.*

A later and less sympathetic account says that Sir Richard 'being astern, and imagining this fleet to come from the Indies, and not to be the Armada of which they were informed, would by no means be persuaded by his master or company to cut his cable to follow his Admiral . . . nay, so headstrong, rash and unadvised he was that he offered violence to all that counselled him to the contrary'.

Whatever the truth of the matter, all the authorities agree that the *Revenge* could still have got clear by running before the wind to leeward. 'But Sir Richard utterly refused to turn from the enemy ('For I never turned my back upon Don or devil yet.'), alleging that he would rather choose to die than to dishonour himself, his country, and her Majesty's ship.' It was now about five o'clock on the afternoon of 31 August. General Marcos de Aramburu, leading a squadron of galleons from Castile, was already close enough to exchange fire with the departing Howard and Don Alonso de Bazan, the Spanish Admiral, was coming up fast with the rest of the fleet. At this point the *Revenge* appears to have borne straight down on the enemy, Grenville 'persuading his company that he would pass through the two squadrons in despite of them, and enforce those of Seville to give him way'.

It was the act of a berserker – crazy, magnificent and suicidal. The *Revenge* was almost immediately grappled and boarded, first by the huge *San Felipe* and then by the *San Barnabe,* leader of the Biscayan contingent. Soon she lay surrounded, like a baited bull, 'having never less than two mighty galleons at her side and aboard her'. But, like a baited bull, she put up an epic resistance. The *San Felipe* 'having received the lower tier of the *Revenge* discharged with crossbar shot, shifted herself with all diligence from her sides, utterly misliking her entertainment', says Walter Raleigh. The rest made repeated attempts to board, hoping to force the stubborn Englishman by sheer weight of numbers, but still they were repulsed again and again, 'and at all times beaten back into their own ships or into the seas'. The battle continued intermittently all night:

> *And the sun went down, and the stars came out far*
> *over the summer sea,*
> *But never a moment ceased the fight of the one and*
> *the fifty-three.*
> *Ship after ship, the whole night long, their high-built*
> *galleons came,*
> *Ship after ship, the whole night long, with her battle-*
> *thunder and flame.*

Dawn broke and incredibly the *Revenge* was still there, and still fighting. She had accounted for three of the enemy, two so badly damaged that they presently sank and another with her prow destroyed down to the water; but she herself was in desperate case, with six foot of water in her hold, 'masts all beaten overboard, all her tackle cut asunder, her upper work altogether razed, and in effect . . . but the very foundation or bottom of a ship, nothing being left overhead either for flight or defence'. Powder was down to the last barrel, forty men had been killed and most of the rest hurt, so that the ship – what was left of her – was like a slaughter-house, filled with the blood and bodies of the dead and dying. Grenville had been shot in the head and body, but even in his present extremity this harsh-tempered, violent, quarrelsome man, pig-headed and brave to the edge of insanity, refused to discuss the possibility of surrender. There was for him an infinitely more satisfying way out and one, moreover, which would leave nothing of glory or victory to the Spaniards.

> *'Sink me the ship, Master Gunner – sink her, split*
> *her in twain!*
> *Fall into the hands of God, not into the hands of Spain!'*

The master gunner, 'a most resolute man', was ready and eager for self-immolation, but a majority of the other survivors, feeling reasonably enough that they had earned a chance of life, overbore their leader. Honourable terms were agreed with Alonso de Bazan and Richard Grenville was carried reverentially aboard the Spanish flagship where, a few days later, he died, grumbling passionately, so it is said, about those traitors and dogs in his company who had crossed his will 'and would leave a shameful name for ever'.

Like the defeat of the Armada, the last fight of the *Revenge* is a vital part of the Elizabethan tradition, and with the passage of the centuries (and some assistance from Alfred Tennyson) has become absorbed into the national folk-memory – part of the recurring pattern of standing alone against the powers of darkness and of the peculiar English genius for creating triumph out of defeat.

The episode caused a considerable stir at the time, the Spanish navy naturally making the most of this rare achievement – its first and, as it turned out, only major prize of the war. An English prisoner in Lisbon Castle later recalled how he had seen one of King Philip's great galleons entering the river in her fighting sails, dressed overall with streamers and pennants, and letting fly all her ordnance 'for the taking of Sir Richard Grenville in the *Revenge'.* At the same time, awkward questions were being asked in Madrid as to why the whole of Howard's squadron had not been destroyed, considering the size of the force under Don Alonso de Bazan's command.

In England there was consternation. The *Revenge* was by no means the largest of the Queen's galleons, being rated at five hundred tons and one of the medium-sized, fast, heavily-armed warships built in the fifteen-seventies and eighties during the enlightened rule of Sir John Hawkins at the Navy Board. But she was a famous ship, chosen by Drake for the Armada campaign and specially associated with the glories of 1588. Her loss was therefore a special humiliation, and questions were asked in London about how she had come to be caught in such a compromising situation.

Fortunately for the islanders' self-esteem, God was once more about to demonstrate that he was an Englishman and a Protestant. No sooner had the returning American flota rendezvoused with de Bazan off the Azores than storms and hurricane force winds roared in from the west and north-west with catastrophic results. The Venetian ambassador in Madrid heard that thirty-one merchantmen and three men-of-war were missing, and other accounts put the losses in the two fleets at over seventy. Among the casualties was the battered remains of the *Revenge* which broke up on a cliff near the Island of Terceira. 'So it pleased them', wrote Walter Raleigh grimly, 'to honour the burial of that renowned ship, the *Revenge,* not suffering her to perish alone, for the great honour she achieved in her lifetime.'

The year's consignment of gold and silver from the mines of New Spain had not yet left Havana and so escaped the general holocaust, but even so Spanish shipping and commerce had suffered a major disaster and in the Azores it was being freely said that 'the taking of the *Revenge* was justly revenged upon them, and not by might or force of man, but by the power of God . . . and that he took part with Lutherans and heretics'. A more orthodox school of thought held that the shade of Sir Richard Grenville, being descended into Hell, had raised up all the devils to the revenge of his death.

The following summer, 1592, a privateering venture financed jointly by the Queen, Sir Walter Raleigh and a syndicate of London merchants hit the jackpot when they intercepted a huge Portuguese carrack homeward bound from the Far East. The *Madre de Dios,* at 1600 tons one of the largest ships afloat, was laden with gemstones and spices and rare drugs, with musk and ambergris, silks, calicoes and carpets, porcelain and elephants' teeth, coconuts, hides and ebony – the sort of prize every privateer dreamed of taking – and even after wholesale looting of the cargo on its way back to Plymouth, the principal shareholders netted a very satisfactory return.

But although the capture of the *Madre de Dios* naturally boosted morale, it was an isolated incident and one which helped to conceal a turning point in the war at sea; for the early fifteen-nineties marked the beginning of the end of those carefree days when tiny English squadrons could roam the Spanish shipping lanes at will. 'It is to be observed', wrote William Monson, 'that from the year the *Revenge* was taken . . . there was no summer but the King of Spain furnished a fleet for the guarding of his coasts and securing of his trade.' The King of Spain was, in fact, learning at last to defend himself and to adopt a regular convoy system for his treasure fleets. In spite of a chronic shortage of cash as acute as Elizabeth's own and made worse, as the Venetian ambassador remarked, by 'the delay and uncertainty in the arrival of the ships which ought to bring the silver from the Indies', Philip was persevering with an ambitious ship-building programme. In 1592 he had forty galleons under construction, as well as fast, ocean-going pinnaces to improve his naval communications. He was also taking steps to fortify the American ports of departure and to provide a secure base in the Azores – that vital area on which both East and West Indian routes converged. Privateering went on, of course, and continued to be a sizable thorn in the King's side, but the pickings were becoming progressively less easy – even the masters of the big merchantmen were no longer always playing the game according to the rules. They were beginning to fight their ships and, in most unsportsmanlike fashion, would sometimes prefer to destroy them than see their cargoes fall into English hands.

It wasn't only at sea that things were changing. Francis Walsingham had died in the spring of 1590 and now Hatton, too, was gone, together with lesser names like Walter Mildmay, Thomas Randolph, the Earl of Shrewsbury and Sir James Crofts. Of the old guard at Court and Council only Lord Hunsdon, Francis Knollys and Lord

Burghley were left, so that when the Earl of Essex returned from France in January 1592 the field looked wide open for a promising young man seeking 'domestical greatness' – or almost wide open. Lord Burghley was now seventy-one and a martyr to gout or, more likely, arthritis; but he was still a regular attender at Council meetings and his pre-eminent position as pillar of the state remained unchallengeable.

Of the younger generation, Sir Walter Raleigh, once considered by Essex to be his most serious rival, was to fall disastrously out of favour with the Queen in the coming summer for getting Bess Throckmorton into trouble but, in any case, Elizabeth had never considered him suitable material for high office. Although the Earl had not yet realised it, a far greater threat to the sort of future he was planning for himself existed in the apparently insignificant person of Robert Cecil, Burghley's son by his second wife, the blue-stocking Mildred Cooke. Robert had been a sickly child with a deformed shoulder. He had grown into a slender, delicate-looking, under-sized young man (the Queen called him her Pigmy or, in more mellow mood, her Elf), but there was nothing under-sized about his intellectual capacities or his political ambitions and he enjoyed, of course, the inestimable advantage of being his father's son.

When Francis Walsingham died the Queen had not appointed another Secretary of State, the office and its burdens being shouldered once again by old Burghley on the tacit understanding, so it seems, that his son should take over in due course. In May 1591 Elizabeth paid a formal state visit to Theobalds, the Burghleys' Hertfordshire mansion, staying for ten days at a cost to her hosts of over a thousand pounds. Broad hints were dropped by the family that everyone's workload would be eased if the son of the house were now to receive the Secretaryship; but although the Queen knighted young Robert during her visit and at the beginning of August (the week after Essex sailed for France) admitted him to the Privy Council, she did not, contrary to widespread expectations, make any official appointment. Robert Cecil was still in his twenties – he was about three years older than Robert Devereux – and still learning his trade; the Queen would wait and see how he shaped. But by the time Essex came home, little Cecil, 'his hands full of papers and head full of matter', had become a familiar sight in the corridors of Whitehall and it was an open secret that he was already dealing with most of the routine work of the secretariat.

The protagonists in The War of the Two Roberts, which was to dominate English political life during the second half of the nineties,

had known one another since they were children when Essex, as a
royal ward, had been placed in Lord Burghley's charge and spent
several months in his guardian's household before going up to Cambridge. There is no record of any special relationship, friendly or
otherwise, between the boys at that time – probably Essex felt no
more than slightly contemptuous pity for a youth whose physical
disabilities would surely condemn him to a life of clerking – and,
since they had grown up, their paths had scarcely crossed, the Earl
being fully occupied with his glamorous career as courtier, royal
favourite and military man. Now, though, things were different.
Essex would soon be twenty-five, war had disappointed him of glory
for the second time and he was ready to turn his attention to politics
where, sooner rather than later, he would be bound to come up
against the Cecil family. Already he was inclined to blame Lord
Burghley's influence for the Queen's irascibility during the Rouen
campaign, and he'd been greatly put out at being passed over in the
election for the Chancellorship of Oxford University – a prestigious
office once held by his stepfather. Although the job went to a senior
and well-qualified candidate, Essex characteristically took his rejection as a personal slight. Equally characteristically he suspected the
machinations of enemies and wrote to Robert Cecil, whose support
he had been canvassing: 'Sir R. I have been with the Queen and have
had my answer. How it agrees with your letter you can judge, after
you have spoken with the Queen. Whether you have mistaken the
Queen, or used cunning with me, I know not. I will not condemn you,
but leave you to think if it were your own case, whether you would
not be jealous. Your friend, if I have cause, R. Essex.'

Essex continued to be conspicuous as a courtier but when, in February 1593, he too was sworn a member of the Privy Council, an
enthusiastic friend reported that 'his lordship is become a new man
– clean-forsaking all his youthful tricks, carrying himself with
honourable gravity and singularly liked of both in Parliament and at
Council-table, for his speeches and judgment'. Unquestionably the
Earl possessed both brains and a talent for public life. When not
blinded by paranoia he could put a point of view persuasively and
had all the natural leader's flair for drawing men to his side. But in
matters of statecraft and high politics he remained an amateur. To
compete with such dedicated professionals as Lord Burghley and his
son on anything approaching equal terms Essex needed professional
allies, and before the end of 1592 he had found them.

The Elizabethan establishment was very much a family affair, almost all its leading figures being connected by blood or marriage or
both, and Anthony and Francis Bacon were Lord Burghley's nephews

– the sons of his wife's sister Ann who had married the lawyer
Nicholas Bacon, Queen Elizabeth's first Lord Keeper. Both brothers
possessed trained and brilliant minds. Both had been born into the
highest political and intellectual circles. Both were ambitious, hard-
working and astute. It might reasonably have been supposed that two
such gifted and well-connected young gentlemen would experience
no difficulty in making honourable and lucrative careers for themselves in the service of the state. But that was not how it had worked
out. There was, it seemed, no place for the Bacons in a world domi-
nated by Lord Burghley and the brothers had no hesitation in blaming their otherwise inexplicable lack of progress on the old man's
jealousy and his determination to reserve all the sweets of office for
his son. Simplistic reasoning, and yet the Lord Treasurer's consistent
refusal to advance his nephews' cause was surely rooted in some
fundamental dislike and distrust. No doubt their homosexual pro-
clivities had a good deal to do with it, but Burghley was a shrewd
and experienced judge of human nature and perhaps he sensed something of the cold-hearted, conscienceless self-seeking which lay beneath the brilliance.

By the early fifteen-nineties Francis, now turned thirty and still no
more than a back-bench M.P. practising law at Gray's Inn, had come
to the conclusion that it was more than time to seek another patron.
He turned to the Earl of Essex, that bright and rising star who, so he
later affirmed, he had then held 'to be the fittest instrument to do
good to the state' and, so he might have added, to Francis Bacon. The
two became close friends and when, in February 1592, Anthony
Bacon returned to England after an absence of twelve years spent
mostly in the south of France, the younger brother lost no time in
drawing the elder into his new orbit.

Anthony had never been strong and at thirty-three suffered from
a painful and often crippling disease described as gout, but which
was probably a form of arthritis, something not recognised by sixteenth century medicine. Unlike the more robust Francis, he shrank
from the rough and tumble of public life and sedulously avoided the
Court – any suggestion that he should pay his duty to the Queen
would at once bring on an acute flare-up of his bad leg. Paying his
duty to the Earl of Essex was a very different matter. Anthony had
been captivated at first sight by the 'rare perfections and virtues' of
this handsome, courteous young nobleman and longed for an opportunity to show the Earl how much he honoured and esteemed his
excellent gifts and how earnestly he desired to deserve his good
opinion and love.

The opportunity to serve, in fact, lay ready to hand. During his residence in France Anthony had for some time been one of Francis Walsingham's most valued correspondents, passing on information from the agents who slipped to and fro across the Pyrenees and from merchants whose trading vessels plied between the ports of Spain and south-west France. He was also a personal friend and admirer of King Henry IV and had acquired numerous French contacts, both Protestant and Catholic. Since Walsingham's death the intelligence network so closely associated with his name had passed under the nominal control of Lord Burghley, but without Walsingham's organising genius and passionate commitment to the cause he served, the organisation no longer possessed its former cohesion and sense of purpose.

Here, then, was Anthony's chance. While brother Francis acted as the Earl's political counsellor, let Anthony take over responsibility for foreign affairs and build up his own intelligence service. His invalidism need be no bar to the work of collecting and collating agents' reports, and there could be no doubt as to the usefulness of the service he would be performing. Detailed, reliable information from abroad was always a precious commodity and vital to the successful conduct of affairs. If, with the Bacons' help, Essex could begin to assume the reputation for omniscience which had done so much for Francis Walsingham, it must infallibly raise his prestige with the Queen and give him the right to be regarded as a serious character. For the Bacons, of course, the scheme offered a not to be missed opportunity for attacking the Cecils on their own ground and opened up agreeable prospects of being in a position to display their talents independently of Cecil patronage.

It was therefore unfortunate that Francis should have picked this moment of all others to offend the Queen by opposing the supply bill in the Parliament of 1593. He may, as he subsequently assured his uncle Burghley, have been honestly obeying the voice of his conscience when he maintained that the proposal to collect a treble subsidy in three years would be an intolerable burden on the Queen's subjects, and drew a pathetic picture of gentlemen forced to sell their plate and farmers their brass pots. On the other hand, he may have seen an opportunity to court popularity with his fellow back-benchers in a tussle between the Lords and Commons over the latter's right to initiate taxation which had invoked the sacred name of privilege. Or he may, quite simply, have been unable to resist the temptation to show off and embarrass his cousin Robert who, with old Sir Thomas Heneage, was now responsible for managing government business in the Commons.

But for a man in Francis Bacon's position, the temporary discomfiture of Robert Cecil was a heavy price to pay for royal displeasure. The Earl of Essex and his friends were all too apt to make the expensive mistake of forgetting that England was ruled not by the Cecil family but by Elizabeth Tudor, and the Queen, increasingly harassed with financial problems, would not soon forgive anyone who made difficulties about money. Especially not at a time when, as the Lord Keeper had warned the Commons, the King of Spain 'breathed nothing but bloody revenge' and, with his navy rebuilt largely after the English pattern, was looking more dangerous even than in 1588.

Elizabeth had not been afraid of Philip in 1588 and she was not afraid now. 'For mine own part', she told Parliament at the end of the 1593 session, 'I protest I never feared, and what fear was my heart never knew. For I knew that my cause was ever just; and it standeth upon a sure foundation.' But however just the cause, it must still be defended. This would continue to cost money and money could not, as certain members in their simplicity appeared to believe, be picked out of the air. The Queen was well aware of the anomalies and inequities of a system of assessment which, while consistently failing to tap the country's undoubted wealth (the last double subsidy had yielded no more than £280,000), tended all too often to press hardest on the little man. Nevertheless, pious concern about the burden of taxation must sometimes have been supremely irritating to a pacifically-minded lady struggling to meet the inescapable and ever mounting costs of a war she detested.

None of this irritation could be allowed to appear in public of course, and the Queen's end of session address concluded with 'as great thanks as ever prince gave to loving subjects' for the treble subsidy which, it had finally been agreed, should be collected over a period of four years. Elizabeth had never, in her conscience, been willing to draw from her people more than they would contentedly give and she repeated her customary soothing assurances that her care for their welfare would always take precedence over all other worldly cares whatsoever. She could only hope that she would be able to last out the next four years when another Parliament would have to be patiently cajoled into loosening the purse-strings.

IV
A Maid in an Island

Happy hour, happy day,
That Eliza came this way!
    Great in honour, great in place,
    Greater yet in giving grace,
    Great in wisdom, great in mind,
    But in both above her kind,
    Great in virtue, great in name,
    Yet in power beyond her fame.

Elizabeth was now approaching her sixtieth birthday but her health remained excellent. If anything it had improved – the nerve storms and sudden, violent stomach upsets of earlier decades seem to have disappeared. She worked long hours at her papers, often starting before dawn, and in times of crisis would be shut up in Council until late at night – as she grew older she slept less and less. But she still found time for recreation and the outdoor exercise she loved. Although music and dancing remained her favourite indoor pastimes, she was addicted to bear baiting and enjoyed the theatre. Plays were performed regularly at Court during the season and the Queen was always a good friend to actors, more than once intervening personally to protect their precarious livelihood from disapproving city fathers.

She was still passionately interested in clothes, and when the Bishop of London was tactless enough to preach before her on the vanity of decking the body too finely, her Majesty remarked tartly that if the bishop held more discourse on such matters, 'she would fit him for heaven, but he should walk thither without a staff, and leave his mantle behind him'. Perhaps, observed John Harington, who recorded the incident in his *Brief Notes and Remembrances,* the bishop had never sought her Highness's wardrobe, or he would have chosen another text!

With the possible exception of John Whitgift, Elizabeth had never held a very high opinion of bishops, and she would certainly not have tolerated even a hint of episcopal criticism of her taste in dress. In any case, clothes were an important part of her job, part of the showmanship expected of all sovereigns and, for Elizabeth, part of the business of emphasising her semi-magical *persona* of Virgin-Goddess-Queen. With this in mind, she wore a lot of white and silver, especially in her later years.

Another important part of the job which she kept going almost to the end was the annual summer progress. These famous journeyings not only provided a welcome break from routine, giving the Queen a chance to see something of her kingdom and take the temperature of opinion in the provinces, they were also invaluable as public relations exercises, an opportunity to display the reverse side of the royal image – the gracious, lovable mother-figure. 'In her progress', wrote Edmund Bohun, 'she was the most easy to be approached; private persons and magistrates, men and women, country people and children, came joyfully and without any fear, to wait upon her, and to see her. Her ears were then open to the complaints of the afflicted, and of those that had been in any way injured . . . She took with her own hand and read with the greatest goodness the petitions of the meanest rustics. And she would frequently assure them that she would take a particular care of their affairs; and she would ever be as good as her word . . . She was never seen angry with the most unseasonable, or uncourtly approach: she was never offended with the most impudent or importunate petitioner . . . Nor was there anything in the whole course of her reign that more won the hearts of the people, than this her wonderful facility and condescension, and the strange sweetness and pleasantness with which she entertained all that came to her.'

Elizabeth, in fact, never travelled farther north than Norwich or farther west than Bristol, but given the uncertainty of the times and the logistical problems involved in transporting, accommodating and feeding the Court, this is not such a bad record. Apart from Woodstock, which was only a hunting lodge and in poor repair, all the royal residences were clustered around London, so the Queen naturally expected to be put up at the great houses along her route.

Much has been written about the financial burden this enforced hospitality imposed on her hosts, but for those concerned the prestige conferred by the royal presence more than compensated for any inconvenience or expense. When, in August 1591, the Queen arrived to spend a week as the guest of Lord and Lady Montague at Cowdray, the mistress of the house was so overcome that she shed tears on the royal bosom, exclaiming 'Oh, happy time! Oh, joyful day!' All the same, the information that the houseparty's Sunday breakfast alone accounted for three oxen and a hundred and forty geese does give some indication of the strain which a progress could put on the resources of the favoured neighbourhood.

After leaving Cowdray, the Queen went on to visit Chichester, Portsmouth and Southampton, staying at Petworth and Tichfield. The return journey took in Basing, Odiham and Elvetham, where the Earl of Hertford had solved the accommodation problem by employing three hundred workmen to enlarge his house and erect a temporary encampment in the park. The centrepiece was a large rustic pavilion with a withdrawing room for the Queen at one end and overlooking a specially constructed artificial lake. The outsides of the walls were decorated with green boughs and clusters of ripe hazel nuts, while the inside had been hung with arras, the roof lined with wreaths of ivy leaves and the floor strewn with rushes and sweet herbs. It sounds delightful, but the practical Lord Hertford had also remembered to provide comfortable quarters for the royal footmen and their friends, the Queen's guard and the servants of her house, as well as 'a great common buttery', two extra kitchens, a scullery, a boiling-house for the great boiler and special lodgings for the cook.

Elizabeth was lavishly entertained with all the usual pageants, masques, fireworks, music and flattering verses:

> *Eliza is the fairest queen*
> *That ever trod upon this green;*
> *Eliza's eyes are blessed stars,*
> *Inducing peace, subduing wars;*
> *Eliza's hand is crystal bright,*
> *Her words are balm, her looks are light;*
> *Eliza's breast is that fair hill*
> *Where virtue dwells, and sacred skill!*
> *Oh, blessed be each day and hour,*
> *Where sweet Eliza builds her bower!*

The Queen was used to taking this sort of thing in her stride but there was a pleasant touch of originality in the performance of ten of the Earl's servants, all Somersetshire men, in their shirt-sleeves playing with a handball, 'at bord and cord, as they termed it' five against five on an improvised court under her window. This amused her Majesty so much that 'she graciously deigned to behold their pastime more than an hour and a half'.

In spite of persistent bad weather, the visit was considered to have been a rousing success. At her departure, her Majesty, 'notwithstanding the great rain', stayed her coach to give great thanks to a consort of dripping musicians who were playing her off the premises, at the same time assuring a gratified Earl of Hertford that the beginning, process and end of his entertainment had been so honourable that she would not forget it.

The following year, 1592, Elizabeth got as far as Sudeley in Gloucestershire, returning by way of Oxford for a formal visit to the University and a heavy programme of sermons, dinners, speeches, Latin orations and disputations. By the end of September she was at Rycote, where she could relax in the company of Henry Norris and his black-haired wife Margery, nicknamed Crow, whose four soldier sons were all to give their lives in the royal service.

Elizabeth had known the Norrises since the far-off days of her precarious girlhood and, like most ageing people, she clung to the friends of her own generation who could share her memories, her prejudices, her way of looking at the world. But, in the nature of things, such friends were growing steadily fewer in number. The future was pushing impatiently at the door and the Queen would have to come to terms with it.

In the circumstances, then, it was ironical that the stage should have been set for so exact a recreation of the past, with Robert Cecil ready to fill his father's old office of Secretary and the Earl of Essex, as it appeared, taking the place once occupied by his step-father – the place of royal plaything and companion, chief ornament and organiser of Court ceremonial, military figure-head when such was needed, and general counter-balance to the Cecil interest.

Although certainly aware of the antagonism existing between the younger men, the Queen seems largely to have discounted it. Burghley and Leicester, after all, had never liked or trusted one another but, under her watchful eye, they had learned to work more or less in harness, even grudgingly to respect one another's qualities. In any case, she had to make use of the material available and the fact that the gulf separating Robert Cecil and Robert Devereux proved in the end to be unbridgeable was her misfortune rather than her fault.

The fault, it must be said, rested largely with the Earl of Essex. The Cecil family had not survived for half a century in the political jungle by making unnecessary enemies and Robert Cecil was in very many, if not quite all, ways his father's son. Robert Devereux, though, owed little or nothing to his step-father. Leicester, grandson of a rather shady professional man, had been the Queen's creation, his career and his greatness founded entirely on her favour, while Essex's ancestors had been noble before ever the Tudors emerged from their Welsh mountains. Leicester's dependence on the Queen had been constantly emphasised by his widespread unpopularity, while Essex was the people's darling. Leicester, like his mistress, had grown up in a hard school; he had learned, if reluctantly, to accept the drawbacks of his position and the wisdom of putting his passions in his pocket. Essex, on the other hand, was constitutionally incapable of discretion. 'He can conceal nothing', observed one of his secretaries; 'he carries his love and his hatred on his forehead'.

The Earl's impetuous candour, his artless habit of saying exactly what he thought on any given occasion regardless of consequences, his single-minded, childlike pursuit of whatever happened to be his current objective were, of course, all part of his charm, though scarcely the most desirable characteristics in a would-be serious man of affairs. Had they been due only to the natural insensitivity of youth and inexperience, snags of this kind could most likely have been overcome. But, unhappily, they were rooted in a fundamental instability which grew steadily more apparent and finally wrecked the Queen's hopes of ever moulding Robert Devereux into a viable substitute for that other Robert, now six years in his grave. The peculiar relationship which had existed between Elizabeth and the Earl of Leicester had often been stormy, but it had rested on a sure foundation of genuine mutual regard – it could not otherwise have lasted as it did for more than forty years. By contrast, her relationship with Essex was coming increasingly to be poisoned by an unhealthy mixture of mutual fear and resentment.

The uncomfortable truth was that Elizabeth and Essex could not do without each other. In an unforgiving world, ever watchful for the first sign of weakness, it was essential that Gloriana should be able to display her continued command of the homage of the rising generation, and especially of its most brilliant star. She could not afford to allow any whispers to get about that her powers were failing, that she could no longer control her young men. Considerations such as these, not the foolish infatuation of an elderly woman, explain her nervous irritability when Essex absented himself from Court without leave and her sometimes surprising tolerance of his importunities and bad manners. Essex, too, had to show the world that he, above all others, enjoyed first place in the Queen's affections, that he, above all others, could count on her generosity towards himself and his friends; for, however much he and some of his cronies might be beginning to regret it, the Queen remained the *fons et origo* of power and patronage. No man, however deserving, would get office or preferment without her word.

It was an issue of patronage which led to the first major trial of strength between Elizabeth and Essex. The Earl was naturally beset by scroungers but, to maintain his position, a public man had to be able to reward his servants, either directly out of his own resources, or indirectly by using his influence on their behalf, and Essex was chronically short of private resources. So, when he saw an opportunity to further the career of Francis Bacon, whose devoted behind-the-scenes labours were doing so much to establish him as a political force, he seized on it with the impulsive good-nature which was another of his many charms.

Had Essex stopped to think, even he might have realised how remote were the chances of getting Bacon considered for the forth-coming vacancy of Attorney General. Not merely was the Queen still so annoyed over his tactless behaviour in Parliament that she was refusing to speak to him, but there was already a well-fancied candidate for the post. Edward Coke, the present Solicitor General, was a notoriously rough-tongued, bad-tempered man but, as Speaker of the Commons, he had proved himself a reliable supporter of the Crown; he was nine years older than Bacon and had had far more experience in the courts. (Although the law was Bacon's profession, he seems to have spent remarkably little time actually practising it.) Not surprisingly, the Queen's senior advisers favoured Coke but Essex continued to pester her with his friend's claims throughout the autumn and winter of 1593, apparently unconscious of the fact that he was laying himself open to a humiliating rebuff. When Robert Cecil tried to point out that Bacon would have been better advised to apply for the Solicitorship, a thing that 'might be of easier digestion to the Queen', he refused to see the tacitly offered face-saver. 'Digest me no digestions', he exploded, 'for the Attorneyship is that I must have for Francis; and in that will I spend all my power, might, authority and amity, and with tooth and nail defend and procure the same for him against whomsoever.'

As for Elizabeth, she simply adopted a variation on the stone-walling tactics of which she was such a past mistress. Sometimes she would listen amiably enough to the Earl's vehement advocacy, while repeating her own objections: Bacon's recent offence had been great, he was too young, he lacked experience and Essex himself lacked the necessary judgement to advise her. At other times she would be too busy or too 'wayward' to be approached. Meanwhile the Attorney-ship remained vacant. Only when Essex had at last run out of steam was Edward Coke's appointment quietly put through.

Her reaction to an equally vigorous campaign to get Bacon the despised Solicitorship was 'very reserved', though Essex, who certainly rated A for effort, would not let the matter rest until the Queen, 'in passion', bade him go to bed if he could talk of nothing else. 'Wherefore in passion', wrote Essex, 'I went away, saying while I was with her I could not but solicit for the cause and the man I so much affected, and therefore I would retire myself till I might be more graciously heard . . . Tomorrow I will go hence of purpose, and on Thursday I will write an expostulating letter to her. That night or upon Friday morning I will be here again, and follow on the same course, stirring a discontentment in her.'

This persistent bullying refusal to take no for an answer would have been enough to stir a discontentment in anyone, but all the same, Bacon was probably unlucky not to get the Solicitorship. Burghley and Robert Cecil were both ready to support his candidature and the job would have given him his longed-for chance to prove himself. But Elizabeth, while acknowledging that he had 'a great wit, and an excellent gift of speech, and much other good learning', would not give way. Her decision was no doubt influenced by an intuitive wariness of any man who had once let her down in public, and also very likely by disapproval of Bacon's lifestyle (she would have known all about his money troubles, his mounting debts and the pretty young men who frequented his chambers at Gray's Inn), but the overriding reason for his rejection was almost certainly the closeness of his connexion with Essex. The Queen was by now fully aware that the task of containing the Earl himself within reasonable bounds was going to become increasingly difficult – if once she let him start packing her service with his nominees it might well become impossible. Wise in the ways of men, she harboured no illusions about the true nature of Essex's feelings towards her, or about the sort of threat he could come to represent in the hands of abler, more subtle and more unscrupulous operators than himself.

Elizabeth continued to lavish caresses on her 'wild horse' – not for nothing had she taken *video et taceo* as one of her favourite mottos. At the Twelfth Night revels of 1594, when a play was performed and the dancing went on till one o'clock in the morning, the Queen presided on a high throne, richly adorned, looking, says one observer, 'as beautiful as ever I saw her; and next to her chair the Earl, with whom she often devised in sweet and favourable manner'. The Earl could still apparently get almost anything for himself – in July he got a useful present of four thousand pounds cash together with a sibylline warning to 'look to thyself, good Essex, and be wise to help thyself without giving thy enemies advantage, and my hand shall be readier to help thee than any other' – but it was beginning to be noticeable that he could get nothing for his friends.

Although Essex had been obliged to admit defeat in the matter of Francis Bacon, his own reputation and prestige were growing and he was now an internationally accepted part of the political scene. English envoys abroad, Thomas Bodley at The Hague, Thomas Edmondes in Paris and Robert Bowes in Edinburgh, sent him regular reports, and the King of Scots, who had reason to take a special interest in rising men of power south of the Border, wrote flatteringly friendly letters.

More embarrassing than flattering was the dedication of *A Conference About the Next Succession to the Crown of England* to the Most Noble the Earl of Essex, 'for that no man', wrote the author, 'is in more high and eminent place and dignity at this day in our realm than yourself . . . and consequently no man like to have a greater part or sway in deciding of this great affair than your Honour'.

The *Conference,* a detailed survey of all existing heirs to the throne, both likely and unlikely, was printed in Antwerp in 1594 under the name of R. Doleman, a pseudonym only thinly concealing the identity of the Jesuit priest Robert Parsons, himself a synonym for Satan in English Protestant circles. Apart from this unfortunate circumstance, the succession, whose unsettled condition had overshadowed English politics for so long, remained a strictly taboo topic. The intrepid Peter Wentworth had attempted to raise it at the last session of Parliament and had gone to prison for his pains, and even the privileged Essex showed unmistakable signs of alarm when a copy of this latest production of Father Parsons' controversial pen reached the Queen. Elizabeth, however, chose to take the matter lightly. She had, after all, no cause to suspect Essex of trafficking with the pro-Spanish Catholic exiles (an imprudence he never was tempted to commit), and as a mark of confidence in this regard 'many letters sent to herself from foreign countries were delivered only to my Lord of Essex and he to answer them'.

By this time Essex was, in fact, acting as an unofficial unpaid Foreign Secretary, employing four secretaries to deal with his voluminous correspondence. The organisation set up and supervised by Anthony Bacon was ensuring that a wide range of confidential infor-

mation reached Essex House as well as, if not before, it reached the
Cecils and, just as the Bacons had calculated, was giving their patron
valuable additional status. Sooner or later, though, the rival networks
were bound to come into collision and then someone would get hurt.
The clash came in 1594 and the victim was the unhappy Dr Ruy
Lopez.

Ruy or Rodrigo Lopez, a Portuguese Jew converted to Protestant
Christianity, had been settled in London since 1559 and by the
mid-eighties was established as a successful and fashionable physi-
cian who numbered Francis Walsingham, the Earl of Leicester, the
Earl of Essex and even the Queen herself among his patients. The
origins of his career as a secret agent are obscure, but circumstances
point to the arrival in England of Dom Antonio and his Portuguese
retinue – several of whom Walsingham strongly and quite correctly
suspected of being Spanish spies. The Portuguese doctor would have
been an obvious choice of instrument to penetrate the activities of his
compatriots and in April 1587 one Antonio de Vega was writing to
inform Bernardino de Mendoza, King Philip's ambassador and spy-
master in Paris, that he had gained over Dr Ruy Lopez 'with good
promises' and converted him to his Majesty's service.

De Vega hinted that Dr Lopez would be prepared to dispose of
Dom Antonio, by poison if necessary. But Mendoza was sceptical,
the doctor reluctant to proceed without a written authorisation and
so the matter rested. By 1590, however, Lopez had become heavily
involved in the murky and hazardous world of spy and counter-spy.
Manuel de Andrada, code-named David and one of the most efficient
and energetic of Philip's agents, reported to Mendoza that, if he
received his Majesty's order, Lopez was ready to help negotiate an
arrangement with Spain, and that this was the time. He (Lopez) was
confident that the Queen would concede any terms that were demanded of her, as she was in great alarm. If Andrada were given a
passport allowing him to go to and fro, and Lopez had undertaken
to see to this, then he could come secretly to London where Secretary
Walsingham would speak to him. Lopez hoped that everything might
be speedily settled to the King's satisfaction, but in any case, provided the secret was kept, he promised to continue to pass on the
decisions taken by the Queen's Council and 'everything that happens
of interest to his Majesty'. 'In very truth', Andrada concluded impressively, 'no person can report so well as he can, in consequence
of his great influence with the Queen and Council.'

There seems no reason to doubt that Lopez was acting under instructions – the putting out of 'peace feelers' being a recognised
method of keeping one's adversary off-balance, while at the same

time finding out more about his intentions and current strength. It was, of course, a method recognised by both sides. After speeding 'David' on his way to Madrid, Mendoza recommended that he should be sent backwards and forwards to England under cover of the negotiation, 'so that he may be able to report what is going on there'. But by the time Andrada returned from his mission in the summer of 1591, Walsingham was dead and Lord Burghley seems to have been unconvinced of his value as a double agent. After some strenuous de-briefing, he was released into the custody of Dr Lopez and after about eighteen months went abroad again to gather news 'in the interests of England', but he became very dissatisfied with Burghley's niggardly rate of pay and threatened to take his services elsewhere.

Meanwhile, Lopez continued to be employed by the Cecils to monitor the various rather nebulous intrigues being hatched among the Portuguese expatriates in England and the Spanish vice-regal court at Brussels. Exactly why and when he first incurred the ill-will of the Earl of Essex is not clear, although one account says that he betrayed certain discreditable details about his noble patient's physique – a breach of professional etiquette which was promptly reported back. A more likely explanation is that Essex had got wind of the doctor's connexion with Andrada's trip to Spain, possibly from Antonio Perez, a renegade Spaniard now living in London under the Earl's protection, and therefore began to regard him with suspicion. Messages passing between members of the Portuguese community and incoming letters containing mysterious references to the price of pearls and the proposed purchase of 'a little musk and amber' were intercepted by Essex House, and in January 1594 Lopez was arrested.

Taken before Lord Burghley, Sir Robert Cecil and the Earl of Essex the doctor vehemently protested his innocence and a search of his house in Holborn revealed nothing incriminating, as Robert Cecil hastened to report to the Queen. The result, according to Anthony Standen, a prominent member of the Essex House fraternity, was that when the Earl came to Court a day or so later, the Queen turned on him, calling him 'a rash and temerarious youth' for making unfounded accusations against a poor man whose innocence she knew well enough. Malice and nothing else lay behind the attack on Dr Lopez, and she was particularly displeased because her honour was involved in the matter. But if, as seems likely, Elizabeth was hoping by a display of authority to scotch the scandal at birth and save a useful servant and friend, she had miscalculated badly.

Uncontrollably furious at such a rebuke, delivered in the presence of Cecil and the Lord Admiral, Essex slammed out of her presence and shut himself up in his private cabinet, refusing to emerge until 'atonement' had been made. The Admiral had to go to and fro smoothing things over, while the Earl flung himself into renewed interrogation of the prisoners (two other Portuguese were also in custody) and a fresh examination of the documents, scarcely pausing for food or sleep until he was satisfied that he had a convincing case. On 28 January he scribbled a triumphant note to Anthony Bacon: 'I have discovered a most dangerous and desperate treason. The point of conspiracy was her Majesty's death. The executioner should have been Dr Lopez: the manner poison. This I have so followed, as I will make it appear as clear as noon day.'

Whether or not Dr Lopez had ever crossed the debatable land separating counter-espionage from treason has long been a matter of purely academic interest; but the only evidence that he was 'deeply touched' in a murder plot consisted of 'confessions' wrung from exhausted and terrified prisoners, ready to say anything they thought would please. The one fact appearing as clear as noon day out of the whole malodorous mess was that once the word poison had been mentioned in connexion with the Queen, the unhappy doctor's doom was sealed. Neither Elizabeth nor the Cecils were prepared to risk a confrontation with Essex over such an emotive issue. Lopez was tried and condemned on 28 February in an atmosphere of intense popular excitement and, although there is some evidence to suggest that the Queen made an eleventh hour attempt to rescue him (she did ensure that his widow was provided for), he was executed at Tyburn the following June amid the joyful execrations of a howling mob.

To the general public Dr Lopez was yet another in a long line of would-be assassins threatening the Queen's precious life and his unmasking, while it had provoked a wave of vicious anti-Semitism, was soon forgotten in the more pressing concerns of daily life. To the Queen herself, to Lord Burghley and Robert Cecil the case had worrying implications, for it had provided a disagreeable illustration of the sort of power Essex was now able to exert and of the extraordinary difficulties of dealing with a man whose volcanic temper so often seemed to put him outside the recognised conventions of well-bred behaviour.

At the Accession Day tilts of 1595 Essex presented an elaborate Device written for him by Francis Bacon, and in which he appeared in the guise of the knight Erophilus, torn between the rival attractions of Love and Self-love, or the goddess Philautia. He is tormented by the importunities of 'a melancholy dreaming Hermit', representing Contemplation, 'a mutinous brain-sick Soldier', who is Fame, and 'a busy tedious Secretary', Experience – all persuasive orators for Philautia urging him to adopt their own particular course of life. In the end, Erophilus, through the mouthpiece of his Squire, predictably renounces Philautia and all her enchantments – wandering Hermit, storming Soldier and hollow Statesman – and makes up his mind henceforward to dedicate himself to the service of Love, in other words the Queen. 'For her recreation, he will confer with his muse: for her defence and honour, he will sacrifice his life in her wars, hoping to be embalmed in the sweet odours of her remembrance; to her service will he consecrate all his watchful endeavours; and will ever bear in his heart the picture of her beauty, in his actions of her will, and in his fortune of her grace and favour.'

Elizabeth sat through this somewhat windy performance, which contained several pretty obvious digs at the Cecils and was clearly intended still further to establish the Earl as principal champion of Queen and country in the public mind, but she did not appear unduly impressed. According to one of those present, she went off to bed remarking that 'if she had thought there had been so much said of her, she would not have been there that night'.

But if the Queen took a sceptical view of the quality of Essex's devotion as laid before her in the rhetorical flourishes of Francis Bacon, she was soon going to need his soldierly services, for the international situation was changing and, after a period of stalemate, the war looked like hotting up again.

In the early summer of 1593 Henry IV had made his well-known decision that Paris was worth a mass and in July of that year was formally received into the Catholic Church – a development which, despite her indignantly reproachful reaction, cannot really have come as any very great surprise to the Queen of England. It had been obvious for some time that Henry had little or no chance of ever persuading the French people to unite behind him as long as he remained a Protestant; but his conversion was still a blow to the common cause of European Protestantism, and brought with it the added danger that he might now be tempted to make a separate peace with Spain and repudiate his debts to his English ally. On the credit side, of course, the collapse of the Holy League meant that the King would at last be able to draw the revenues of all those wealthy northern towns which had so stubbornly refused to recognise him, and Elizabeth would at least be relieved of the burden of subsidising him.

As it turned out, Henry did not become self-supporting for nearly two years. With a Catholic sovereign once more on the throne of France, Philip's insubstantial dreams of bringing her permanently under Spanish 'protection' faded, but he was still maintaining a presence in Brittany which, by the early spring of 1594, had begun to

close in on the strategic deep-water port of Brest. This was a threat
Elizabeth could not ignore. 'I think there never happened a more
dangerous enterprise for the state of your Majesty's country', wrote
Sir John Norris, 'than this of the Spaniard to possess Brittany, which
under humble correction I dare presume to say will prove as prejudi-
cial for England as if they had possessed Ireland.'

The Queen quite agreed and that summer a task force of eight
warships and four thousand men, under the joint command of Norris
and Martin Frobisher, sailed from Portsmouth for the Breton coast.
But having raised the siege of Brest and destroyed the Spanish for-
tress at Crozon, the expedition was recalled, the last of the garrison
troops from around Paimpol leaving for home before the end of
February 1595. The eight companies of English soldiers which had
remained in Dieppe after the abortive Normandy campaign had already been withdrawn and although Henry's northern frontiers continued to be menaced by the Spanish army in Belgium, England's
long and wearisome involvement in the French wars was now effectively at an end: a relief to everyone but especially to those who had
always regarded it as an irritating distraction, diverting valuable resources from the proper business of all right-minded Englishmen –
the business of 'offending our capital enemy, the King of Spain'.

Certainly the naval war had languished during the early nineties
and Francis Drake, unemployed since the Portuguese debacle of
1589, was itching to get to sea again—a restless urge which may not
have been unconnected with the fact that the busy Earl of Cumberland, with his annual freebooting excursions to Spanish waters, was
beginning to acquire something of the reputation for derring-do on
the high seas which ten years earlier had been Drake's alone. At any
rate, the most famous freebooter of them all, supported by that other
veteran sea-dog John Hawkins, was now badgering the Queen to let
him loose once more in the Caribbean.

The Queen hesitated and understandably so. At a time when she
still did not know which way the King of France was going to jump,
and was being reliably informed that preparations for the launching
of another Armada were nearing completion, she felt far from convinced of the wisdom of allowing experienced sailors and precious
ships to go off into the blue on what might well prove to be a wild
goose chase. But 'as all actions of this nature promise good hope until
they come to be performed, so did this the more in the opinion of all
men, in respect of the eminence of the two Generals and their great
experience', and in January 1595, after weeks of haggling and discussion, Elizabeth was at last persuaded to agree in principle to invest

in another joint-stock type of expedition to the Spanish Main. But it was June before the arrangements were finalised, and even then serious doubts remained about the advisability of the project. These doubts were strengthened in July, when the remnants of the Spanish forces in Brittany staged a daring commando-style raid on the coast of Cornwall, burning Mousehole, Newlyn and Penzance before vanishing as suddenly as they had come. The raid itself was a flea-bite, but the fact that any Spaniards had actually succeeded in landing caused a disproportionate amount of alarm – especially to the population of Mousehole which decamped in a body.

The Queen was now in two minds whether to cancel the West Indian expedition altogether, or else perhaps combine it with a foray to Portugal and yet another attempt to intercept the returning treasure fleet. Drake and Hawkins objected that they had taken on too many soldiers for a purely naval operation; besides, if the purpose of the voyage were to be altered at this late stage, the Queen, by the terms of her contract, would have to meet all the expenses. If they encountered a Spanish fleet, the two Generals would naturally give battle, but they were not going to waste time hanging round the Azores waiting for the flota – that had been tried unsuccessfully too often. Spanish treasure must be sought at its fountain-head and Drake at least still clung to his old dream of seizing control of the Panamanian Isthmus. In the end, the deciding factor seems to have been a report reaching England that a galleon from the last treasure fleet with a cargo of gold and silver ducats worth £600,000 had been damaged at sea and forced to take refuge at Puerto Rico. The lure of such a prize proved too much for everyone and the fleet – six royal ships, with about a dozen armed merchantmen and others making the total up to twenty-seven – finally sailed from Plymouth at the end of August.

Things began to go wrong almost at once. There was friction between Drake and Hawkins from the start, and they nearly came to an open breach over Drake's obstinate insistence on attempting a landing at Las Palmas. Little was achieved by this, apart from still more delay, while the fleet's presence in the Canaries told the enemy all he needed to know about its ultimate destination. Misfortune struck again at Guadeloupe, when a group of well-armed Spanish frigates captured the *Francis,* a small vessel which had become separated from the main body of the expedition. These frigates, ironically enough, were also on their way to Puerto Rico to convoy the coveted treasure and were able to give the alarm, so that when the English arrived off San Juan on 12 November the city was waiting for them.

Morale on the ships was already low and became lower still when John Hawkins, architect of the Elizabethan navy but now a tired old man of sixty-three who should have been at home by his own fireside, sickened and died as the fleet dropped anchor. The attack on San Juan went ahead as planned, but it failed. The good old days when Spain's colonial outposts had been a happy hunting ground for roving bands of marauders were gone for ever, and in the harsher, more professional climate of the fifteen-nineties harbours like San Juan were protected by forts and shore batteries. Drake didn't give up easily – not with the thought of all that gold in the citadel – but after three days he was obliged to admit defeat, telling his disappointed crews that he would soon bring them to 'twenty places far more wealthy and easier to be gotten'. Accordingly the fleet stood across for the Spanish Main and, after some rather desultory and not especially profitable raiding of coastal settlements, came to the port of Nombre de Dios towards the end of December.

At one time, Nombre de Dios, a notoriously fever-ridden spot, had been the depot for all the gold and silver brought by sea from Peru to Panama and thence on mule-back across the Isthmus for shipment to Spain; but the traffic had been re-routed more than ten years ago to Puerto Bello, a few miles up the coast, and the former Treasure House of the World lay silent and deserted. Drake landed the army, 2,500 men under the command of Thomas Baskerville, but their attempt to force a way through the fifty-odd miles over the mountains to Panama ended in another fiasco. Too much time had been wasted. The governor of Panama City had had too much warning and was fully prepared to defend the passes. The English had no proper guides, the weather was bad, the terrain notoriously rugged and they were running short of food. They floundered on as far as the halfway mark and then gave up, the hardships and losses suffered on the march making many of them swear that they would 'never venture to buy gold at such a price again'.

Baskerville's failure seems to have taken much of the heart out of Drake, and he 'who was wont to rule fortune, now finding his error, and the difference between the present strength of the Indies and what it was when he first knew it, grew melancholy upon this defeat'. Since no one would yet face the prospect of returning empty-handed, it was decided to make for the Bay of Honduras and perhaps attack the settlements on Lake Nicaragua which were popularly and hopefully believed to be roofed and paved with gold. But the fleet got no further than the island of Escudo de Veragua. Sickness was already raging through the ships and now Drake himself, who had always seemed to bear a charmed life, fell victim to an acute form of dysentery. He died delirious on board the *Defiance* during the small hours of 28 January and they buried him at sea off Puerto Bello, saluted by all the cannon in the fleet, 'the trumpets in doleful manner echoing out this lamentation for so great a loss'.

Leaving their beloved General 'slung atween the round shot in Nombre Dios Bay', the expedition sailed sorrowfully for home on 8 February, fighting their way past a Spanish fleet which came out from Cartagena to intercept them. Apart from causing a good deal of alarm in Spain that winter not one of their objectives had been achieved, but they had at least finally learned that the fabled Indies were no longer vulnerable to the sort of casual, scrambling plunder which had won Francis Drake his early fame.

When Spain heard that the terrible El Draque was dead the merchants of Seville, whose profit margins and nervous systems had suffered so severely and so long from the depredations of the great corsair, illuminated their houses and addressed heartfelt thanks to the Almighty. As for King Philip, it was the best piece of news to come his way since the Bartholomew's Day massacre.

In England, and especially in Plymouth and the West Country, there was mourning; but generally speaking the disappearance of so great a figure of the age seems to have made less of an impression than might have been expected. Drake had, of course, been out of the public eye for several years and in the spring of 1596 there were new and stirring doings afoot all along the south coast. Ever since the previous November the military men had been urging the Queen to agree to another major attack on the Spanish mainland. If, as was widely believed, another Armada would be ready to sail by the summer of 1596 this, they argued, was the time for England to abandon her defensive posture and repeat the triumphant beard-singeing exploits of ten years ago.

Elizabeth, as usual, hesitated. She was worried about the Irish situation, where the Earl of Tyrone's revolt looked as if it might be about to turn into something serious, and at home a succession of bad harvests was beginning to cause distress in some parts of the country – hardly the most propitious moment to call for an increased war effort. On the other hand, she could see the point of another pre-emptive strike. She always had seen the point of them, but always found it hard to rid herself of the suspicion that she was being pressurised into taking unacceptable risks with precious, irreplaceable resources – as well as denuding the island of its first and only effective line of defence – in order to satisfy the greed and ambitions of the commanders. However precise and detailed her instructions, she knew from bitter experience that once the fleets and armies had sailed, control, for all practical purposes, was lost and she would be in the hands of the men on the spot. War was the one department where Elizabeth's femininity became a definite and inescapable handicap – not even she could take the field in person – and this was undoubtedly one, if not perhaps the chief, reason why she disliked it so much.

But on this occasion everyone was pressing for action, even old Lord Burghley being cautiously in favour, and on 18 March a commission was signed and sealed naming the Earl of Essex and the Lord Admiral Howard of Effingham as 'lieutenant-generals and governors of her Highness's navy and army' and authorising them to levy five thousand men for service overseas. The expedition was to destroy warships and stores in Spanish ports, to capture and destroy Spanish coastal towns and to seize whatever booty and prizes they could; but there was to be no unnecessary slaughter and no killing of non-combatants. Thomas Howard and Walter Raleigh (just returned from a voyage to the Orinoco and partially restored to favour) were appointed Vice and Rear-Admirals respectively and they, together with Francis Vere and Conyers Clifford representing the army and George Carew as Master of the Ordnance, were to form a Council to advise the two commanders. No action was to be undertaken without their consent, and the Lord Admiral also received private instructions from the Queen to make sure that Essex did not expose himself needlessly to danger. In other words, Charles Howard was to have the unenviable task of keeping his volatile colleague under control. Elizabeth had not forgotten that the last time the Earl had been entrusted with an important command there had been occasions when she did not know what he was doing, what he meant to do, or even where he was.

Preparations for the expedition were going forward smoothly, or at least as smoothly as such preparations ever did go forward, when, at the end of March, came the alarming intelligence that a Spanish force from the Netherlands, commanded by its new general, Archduke Albert of Austria, was at the gates of Calais, and for a time it looked as if the great sea-voyage would be shortened to a hasty cross-Channel rescue operation. Essex hurried down to Dover, where the bombardment could be clearly heard, and waited in a fever of impatience for orders to embark. But if there ever had been a chance of saving Calais, it was lost in the diplomatic sparring between London and Paris. Elizabeth couldn't resist the temptation to capitalize

on this sudden opportunity to regain possession of the last outpost
of England's old continental empire, whose loss back in her sister's
reign had always rankled. The King of France, on the other hand,
openly preferred to see the town in Spanish rather than English
hands; or, as he put it, he would as lief be bitten by a dog as scratched
by a cat. The King, in short, had no difficulty in reading the Queen
of England's mind when he rejected her kind offer of succours for
Calais on condition that it was placed in her hands by way of 'security' thereafter.

The matter was settled in mid-April by the fall of the town and,
although Calais was not a large enough port to be of much use to an
ocean-going fleet, the thought of the enemy ensconced on his very
doorstep was enough to give every Englishman the shivers. To the
military, a swift counter-stroke now seemed more than ever essential
and they were, therefore, driven to distraction by the Queen's apparent perversity during the next few weeks. Just as with Drake and
Hawkins the previous summer, she was 'daily in change of humour'
about the future of the great voyage and at times 'almost resolute to
stay it'. Alternatively, she considered the possibility of sending out
a smaller expedition under the command of 'an inferior officer',
Thomas Howard perhaps, or else of dispensing with a landing force
altogether and letting the fleet go on its own.

Essex who, with the Admiral and Francis Vere, was down at Plymouth working furiously among the accumulating chaos of stores,
ships and soldiers, began rapidly to run out of his never very plentiful
supply of patience. 'The Queen wrangles with our action for no cause
but because it is in hand', he wrote bitterly. 'If this force were going
to France, she would then fear as much the issue there as she doth
in our intended journey. I know I shall never do her service but
against her will.' In his letters to Robert Cecil he complained patheti-
cally about the Queen's coldness and ingratitude, 'I receive no one
word of comfort or favour by letter, message, or any means whatsoever.' He was working harder than any gentleman of his degree had
ever done before to bring some sort of order out of the prevailing
confusion, and to get the army trained and organised; yet he was so
far from receiving any thanks from her Majesty that anyone would
think he had, through 'fault or misfortune', lost her troops. On 12
May he pointed out that he was also being put to considerable personal expense. He had not touched a penny of the Queen's money,
but was having to pay lendings to about five thousand soldiers. 'I
maintain all the poor captains and their officers', he went on, 'I have
a little world eating upon me in my house, am fain to relieve most

of the captains and gentlemen and many of the soldiers that come from the Indies; and yet I complain not of charge, but of want of direction and certainty in your resolutions.'

Elizabeth was, of course, nagged by the new anxiety of the Spanish presence in Calais and disappointed and worried by the failure of the West Indian venture; but the principal factor influencing her 'want of direction and certainty' most likely had to do with the negotiations currently proceeding with the French. On 16 May, after several weeks of tough bargaining, a new offensive and defensive alliance was concluded and signed by King Henry's representatives at Greenwich, and eight days later the Queen's letters authorising the departure of the expedition reached Plymouth. To Essex she had written: 'I make this humble bill of requests to Him that all makes and does, that with his benign hand He will shadow you so, as all harm may light beside you, and all that may be best hap to your share; that your return may make you better, and me gladder. Let your companion, my most faithful Charles, be sure that his name is not left out in this petition. God bless you both, as I would be if I were there, which, whether I wish or not, He alone doth know.'

The fleet sailed from Cawsand Bay on 3 June. It made an impressive and beautiful sight, as even the Spaniards were presently to admit, this great Armada of seventeen royal galleons and about a dozen London men-of-war, reinforced by a strong Dutch contingent which, with transports, victuallers, flyboats, pinnaces and hangers-on, brought the total to around a hundred and fifty ships great and small.

The English were divided into four squadrons, the Lord Admiral leading the first in the *Ark Royal,* then Essex in the *Repulse,* Thomas Howard in the *Merhonour* and Walter Raleigh bringing up the rear in the *Warspite,* each squadron wearing distinguishing colours of crimson, orange tawny, blue and white. Among the soldiers were to be found the usual quota of gentlemen volunteers and 'green-headed youths, covered with feathers, and gold and silver lace', but the standard in general was high, the county levies being stiffened by two thousand veterans from the Netherlands commanded by that first-rate professional, Sir Francis Vere.

All in all, the expedition which set course for the North Cape of Spain in June 1596, a fair north-easterly wind filling its sails and taking with it the Queen's prayers for its good success 'with the least loss of English blood', was certainly the largest and grandest of any that had yet gone to war with King Philip. Whether or not the Protestant deity would listen to his handmaiden and 'speed the victory' remained to be seen.

Queen Elizabeth going in procession to Blackfriars in 1600.
Attributed to Robert Peake the Elder.

Above: Father and son – Lord Burghley and Robert Cecil. *Below:* The brothers – Anthony (*left*) and Francis Bacon (*right*).

Above: Essex House in the Strand – from Hollar's *View of London. Below:* Robert Devereux, Earl of Essex – portrait after Marcus Gheeraerts the Younger.

Nonesuch Palace, Surrey.

English Attack on Cadiz, 1596.

Lord Admiral Charles Howard of Effingham –
portrait by Daniel Mytens.

Above left: Sir Walter Raleigh in 1588. *Above right:* Sir Richard Grenville.
Below left: Sir John Norris. *Below right:* Sir Francis Drake in 1591
portrait by Marcus Gheeraerts the Younger.

Above: Elizabeth I with "Time and Death". *Below:* James I in 1604.

V
Great Eliza's
Glorious Name

Faire branch of Honor, flower of Chevalrie!
That fillest England with thy triumphs fame,
Joy have thou of thy noble victorie,
And endless happinesse of thine own name
That promiseth the same;
That through thy prowesse, and victorious armes,
Thy country may be freed from forraine harmes;
And great Eliza's glorious name may ring
Through all the world, fill'd with thy wide Alarmes,
Which some brave muse may sing
To ages following . . .

After a long run of failures and disappointments, everything went right for the summer expedition of 1596. The weather co-operated, blowing the fleet swiftly southwards, and for once security seems to have been good – many people, both in Spain and on the fleet itself, apparently believing until almost the last moment that it must be making for Lisbon. So, when the English were sighted off the Bay of Cales, or Cadiz, early in the morning of 20 June, surprise was complete.

In the attack which followed, two of Philip's capital warships were captured and two (one of them the *San Felipe,* which had been the first to grapple with the *Revenge* at Flores five years before) were sunk with appalling loss of life among their crews, as recorded by the young John Donne:

So all were lost which in the ship were found:
They in the sea being burnt, they in the burnt ship
drowned.

After the holocaust in the outer harbour – 'if any man had a desire
to see hell itself, it was there most lively figured', commented Walter
Raleigh – no further resistance was offered and everyone stormed
ashore, the commanders anxiously jostling one another for the greatest share of any available glory in true Elizabethan style. All the
same, it was a pity that, in the general excitement, merchant shipping
valued at twelve million ducats trapped in the inner harbour at
Puerto Real should have been overlooked until too late, the Spaniards
themselves having set fire to it.

A pleasurable and profitable fortnight passed in ransacking the
city, 'the pearl of Andalusia', and then the question arose of what
next? Essex wanted to hold Cadiz and use it as a base for further
operations designed to cut King Philip off from 'his golden Indian
streams'. As he later pointed out, 'Lisbon and Seville are the cisterns
that first receive the wealth, and the Bay of Cales and the river of
Tagus the ports whereby the King of Spain's fleets for the Indies ever
go forth and to which they ever return: so as impeach him in these
places and we impeach him in all.' This was true enough, and certainly the present large and well-found expedition could have remained on the Spanish coast at least for long enough to inflict some
further and perhaps even decisive damage. But Essex was overruled
by a majority of his fellow commanders. The plain truth, of course,
was that the majority considered honour had been satisfied and were
now in a hurry to get home with their swag. Even if the Council of
War had voted to stay, it is more than doubtful whether they could
have controlled the rest of the army which, bulging with the spoil of
Cadiz, had frankly lost its enthusiasm for 'greater enterprises'. As
William Monson, captain of the *Rainbow,* was to put it, 'some men's
desires homeward were so great, that no reason could prevail with,
or persuade them'.

The fleet therefore sailed for home, pausing only to make a landing
at Faro on the Algarve coast of Portugal, 'a place of no resistance or
wealth' according to Monson. It did, however, yield an interesting
collection of books and manuscripts belonging to the local bishop,
which were subsequently presented by Essex to his friend Thomas
Bodley who was engaged in founding a new library at Oxford. Off
the Rock of Lisbon the Generals took Council again and Essex, supported by Lord Thomas Howard and the Dutch admiral, offered 'with

great earnestness' to stay behind with no more than a dozen ships for
as long as their victuals lasted, in the hope of intercepting either the
treasure fleet or the East Indian carracks. But again he was overruled
by a majority headed by Walter Raleigh, who had no intention of
letting their enterprising colleague out of their sight, and the expedition continued on its homeward way – incidentally missing the treasure fleet by no more than a couple of days.

When the first reports from Cadiz reached her, the Queen had been
generous in her praise. 'You have made me famous, dreadful and
renowned', she wrote, 'not more for your Victory than for your
Courage . . . Let the Army know I care not so much for being Queen,
as that I am sovereign of such subjects.' But this blaze of royal
sunshine soon began to cloud over and by the time the expedition
returned to its home ports in early August a distinctly chilly wind
was blowing from Whitehall.

Elizabeth had not been best pleased to hear that the shipping at
Puerto Real had been given time to destroy its valuable cargoes. Nor
was she pleased that a fleet which had cost her fifty thousand pounds
to equip and which could have kept the seas for several more weeks,
had come stampeding home without even attempting to seize the
Indian flotas. Annoyance turned to rage when the reason for this
indecent haste became apparent and it was realised just how much
of the booty from Cadiz had found its way into unauthorised hands.
When the Lord Admiral actually had the gall to ask for more money
to pay the wages of soldiers and mariners already weighted down
with plunder which should have gone into the exchequer, the Queen
exploded. She had always known how it would be, 'rather an action
of honour and virtue against the enemy, and particular profit by spoil
to the army, than any way profitable to ourself'. The government
fought a protracted and determined battle to separate the army from
its ill-gotten gains, but without any very noticeable success. Sir Anthony Ashley, the Secretary-at-War, who had sailed with the fleet
especially to watch over the Crown's interests had feathered his nest
with the others, and it was being whispered at Court 'that the Queen
should not hereafter be troubled with beggars, all were become so
rich at Cadiz'.

Both commanders-in-chief came in for a share of royal displeasure,
her Majesty not hesitating to remind them of their large promises of
'great profit and gain' which would more than repay all expenses and
without which, she declared, she would never have agreed to the
voyage in the first place. But her particular wrath seems to have been
reserved for the Earl of Essex. He had been prevented from publish-

ing his own version of the Action at Cadiz and the Queen was heard to say 'that she had hitherto, to her great damage, been contented to follow the earl's humours; and now he had had his desire; but from henceforth she would please herself, and serve her own'.

Essex, who had returned home with a beard and looking older – he would, after all, be twenty-nine that autumn – accepted his 'crabbed fortune' gloomily. 'I see', he wrote to faithful Anthony Bacon, 'the fruits of these kinds of employments, and I assure you I am as much distasted with the glorious greatness of a favourite, as I was before with the supposed happiness of a courtier, and call to mind the words of the wisest man that ever lived, who, speaking of man's works, cryeth out, Vanity of vanities, all is vanity.'

But if the Queen saw Cadiz as a hollow victory which had not even paid for itself, there is no doubt that it had scored an immense *succès d'estime*. The taking of the city had been another humiliating slap in the face for the King of Spain, another brilliant demonstration of English audacity, and the island's international prestige was back where it had stood in Armada year. 'Great is the Queen of England!' they were exclaiming in Venice, 'Oh, what a woman, if she were only a Christian!', which last unfortunate misapprehension Dr Hawkyns, the royal agent, did his best to correct by circulating copies of the prayer specially composed by the Queen of England for her army's success.

At home, the victory, hollow or not, came as a much needed fillip to a war-weary nation and no matter what was being said at Court, the Londoners had no hesitation in ascribing all the glory to the Earl of Essex. A sermon preached at St Paul's by Dr William Barlow sounding his lordship's 'worthy fame, his justice, wisdom, valour and noble carriage in the action' was received with sustained applause by the congregation, and even in Spain Essex was being acclaimed as a great captain and praised for his courtesy, clemency and magnanimity.

None of this made him any more popular with the Queen. Even when his judgement was vindicated by news of the safe return of the treasure fleet barely forty-eight hours after the English had left Cape Roca, her temper did not improve to any marked degree; although the Earl's 'backward friends', who had been busy putting it about that the real credit for Cadiz belonged to Walter Raleigh and the Lord Admiral, fell suddenly silent. Among other things, Elizabeth was angry about the excessive number of knighthoods conferred by Essex during the expedition. She expected this privilege to be used sparingly by her commanders in the field, for otherwise it cheapened honour – something she had always been careful to avoid. What was more, an Essex knight would become an Essex man and, in the Queen's opinion, his lordship's military clientele was already too numerous for comfort.

The chief bone of contention, however, remained the financial deficit, and as the weeks went by and it grew increasingly obvious that only a small proportion of the spoil of Cadiz was ever going to be recovered, the Queen swore that Essex should pay for his carelessness and his prodigality with her money. Had he not made the soldiers dance *and* paid the piper? In short, she intended to confiscate his share of the ransoms paid by the wealthy Spanish prisoners.

When Lord Burghley, feeling perhaps that matters had gone far enough, was rash enough to intervene, Elizabeth turned on him with 'words of indignity', calling him coward and miscreant and accusing him of regarding the Earl of Essex more than herself. This very unfair attack (which, incidentally, is revealing of her intense nervous irritation at this time) wounded the old man deeply, and he wrote to Essex complaining that he was between Scylla and Charybdis. 'Her Majesty chargeth and condemneth me for favouring of you against her. Your lordship contrariwise misliketh me for pleasing of her Majesty to offend you.' Essex, to do him justice, replied gracefully, but Anthony Bacon could not resist crowing that: 'Our Earl, God be thanked! hath with the bright beams of his valour and virtue scattered the clouds and cleared the mists that malicious envy had stirred up against his matchless merit; which hath made the Old Fox to crouch and whine, and to insinuate himself by a very submissive letter to my lord of Essex.'

Although the ill-tempered aftermath of Cadiz continued to rumble on in the background, there is no question that, in the autumn of 1596, my lord of Essex was riding high. Hailed as the English Scipio, he had become a popular hero such as even Francis Drake had never been – a cult figure surrounded by an adoring entourage, his every public appearance drawing an eager, jostling crowd. Internationally his reputation now stood almost, if not quite, as high as the Queen's. The King of France addressed him as 'Cousin' and foreign diplomats were careful to pay as much respect to Essex House as to Lord Burghley himself. Amidst all this adulation only the founder member of the Essex party stood aside, taking a long cool look at the phenomenon he had helped to create.

Francis Bacon was worried. The significance of Sir Robert Cecil's long-delayed appointment as Secretary while Essex was safely out of the way playing soldiers had not escaped his notice, and ever since the expedition's return he had been watching the political barometer with close attention. At last, in the first week of October, he wrote a long, minutely considered letter to his patron. He would yield to none in true congratulation, but felt bound by duty and friendship to speak his mind – to offer both counsel and warning. Above all, Essex must keep the Queen's trust and favour: 'if this be not the beginning, of any other course I see no end'. But was he going the right way about it? What, after all, was the Queen to think of 'a man of a nature not to be ruled; that hath the advantage of my affection and knoweth it; of an estate not grounded to his greatness; of a popular reputation; of a military dependence: I demand', asked Bacon forthrightly, 'whether there can be a more dangerous image than this represented to any monarch living, much more to a lady, and of her Majesty's apprehension?'

Bacon clearly feared for the future if this unfortunate 'image' was allowed to become fixed in the Queen's mind, and he went on to urge his lordship first and foremost to try and remove the impression that he was 'not rulable'. He must be more attentive, appear more amenable to her Majesty's wishes, take more trouble to please her in small ways, and make his pretty speeches as if he really meant them. As for his 'military dependence', let him keep the substance of it if he must, but for heaven's sake stop flaunting it before a nervous Queen, who was known to love peace, to hate the expense and uncertainty of war and who might easily grow suspicious of a subject with too great a military following. Bacon who, like the Queen, was a lover of peace would have much preferred to see Essex delegate martial matters to a subordinate and himself seek a civilian office like that of Lord Privy Seal which, as he wistfully pointed out, was a fine honour and a quiet place worth a thousand pounds a year with, moreover, 'a kind of superintendence over the Secretary'.

All this, of course, would have been excellent advice for a man seriously seeking to consolidate his power and influence in the state, but it was of little use to a maverick like Essex, whose restless self-destructive spirit would always reject the sensible, the politic course. In any case, it would by now have been difficult, if not impossible, for him to have relinquished his military role. After Cadiz he was irrevocably type-cast as England's leading man of war, and there was to be more work for him that autumn.

Even while Bacon was composing his carefully rounded periods, the King of Spain, roused from the lethargy of old age and mortal sickness by the disgrace of seeing one of his principal ports fall so effortlessly into enemy hands – he was said to wish to live only till he might satisfy his vengeance – was hustling his reluctant admirals into an immediate counter-attack, despite the lateness of the season. On 10 October the Venetian ambassador in Madrid reported that great preparations were going on in Lisbon under the command of Don Martin de Padilla, Adelantado or Governor of Castile. A fleet of ninety-odd miscellaneous craft had been assembled of which, according to the Venetian ambassador, a third would be fit to fight. 'There are 12,000 men on board', he went on, 'including seamen. Ships and munitions are very poor; there is a great lack of biscuit.' However, the extent of the preparations, the variety of the provisions and the anxiety of the Adelantado were leading people to believe that he meant to sail as soon as possible. His destination remained a closely guarded secret, 'but common conjecture points to Ireland or England'.

Intelligence reports reaching Anthony Bacon from his agent at Fuenterrabía and letters from a spy entrenched in the Escorial itself had already given warning that Spain was on the move, and towards the end of October the crews of some captured Portuguese caravels confirmed that the Armada had already sailed. The Queen at once turned to the Earl of Essex to organise a Council of War and the whole of the south of England was put on general alert. The militia was mobilised, warning beacons prepared, strategic points along the coast reinforced, and contingency plans for a scorched earth policy in case of an enemy landing were drawn up. After its summer service the navy was laid up in harbour for refitting, but five vessels were already in commission in the Channel and at the beginning of November orders were issued for the hasty provisioning of another sixteen. The alarm lasted about a month but no more was heard of the Spanish fleet. Not until Christmas did reliable news come in that it had been scattered by a storm off Cape Finisterre and driven back onto its own coasts with heavy losses.

For the Queen 1596 had been an eventful and an upsetting year, and one which had seen the disappearance of still more familiar faces. In April John Puckering, Lord Keeper of the Great Seal, died of an apoplexy and Elizabeth had at once replaced him by Sir Thomas Egerton, a friend of Essex but an able and experienced lawyer whose talents she valued. The office of Lord Keeper was, in fact, the same as Lord Chancellor, but the latter title was only bestowed on those of noble or gentle blood and Egerton had risen from the ranks. After she had handed him his seals in a ceremony in the Privy Chamber, the Queen, wearing a gown of straw-coloured satin heavily trimmed with silver and standing on a Turkey carpet under the cloth of estate,

remarked that she had begun with a Lord Keeper, Nicholas Bacon –
'and he was a wise man, I tell you' – and would end with a Lord
Keeper. Lord Burghley, who was also present, exclaimed: 'God forbid, madam. I hope you shall bury four or five more.' 'No', said
Elizabeth, 'this is the last' and burst into tears. Egerton murmured
awkwardly that the first Lord Keeper had indeed been a wise man,
but the Queen still wept, 'clapping her hand on her heart', and turned
away, saying: 'None of the Lord Treasurer's men will come to fetch
him so long as I am here. (Burghley now had to be carried in a chair.)
Therefore I will be gone.' At the door, perhaps to cover her embarrassment at this uncharacteristic breakdown, she suddenly shouted:
'He will never be an honest man until he be sworn. Swear him! Swear
him!'

Her first cousin, Henry Carey Lord Hunsdon, son of her maternal
aunt Mary Boleyn, also died that spring and was followed in July by
Essex's grandfather, that stout old Puritan Francis Knollys. But in
spite of these unwelcome intimations of mortality, it was very rare
for the Queen to give way to melancholy and foreign visitors were
greatly struck by her elegance and vitality. The Duke of Württem-
berg, who saw her in 1592, had declared, with possibly rather more
enthusiasm than accuracy, that to judge from her person and appearance she need not yield much to a girl of sixteen; while in 1595
another German had been deeply impressed by the splendour and
richness of her Court and by the fact that her Majesty, dressed in a
red robe interwoven with gold thread and sparkling with diamonds,
had stood talking to him for more than a full hour by the clock –
something which he considered astonishing for a Queen of such great
age and eminence.

Of course no one could any longer pretend that the Queen was still
in the prime of life, but her stamina and her resilience were surely
astonishing as, at sixty-three, she continued to cope with a daily diet
of problems which might have daunted any working monarch. Apart
from the perennial anxieties about money and the fluctuating international situation, Elizabeth was now seriously worried by economic
depression and 'dearth' at home. 1596 had been the third consecutive
drenching summer when crops rotted in the ground and food prices
rose to unprecedented heights. In the north wheat was up to eighteen
shillings a bushel, rye to fifteen shillings and even at these famine
prices hard to come by. Local authorities did their best to provide
relief; some grain was imported from Germany and Denmark, and
the Privy Council issued a stream of regulations intended to prevent
hoarding and profiteering. But still the poor died of want and hungry

children cried in the streets, 'not knowing where to have bread'. There were bread riots in Oxfordshire and some other places that autumn and a good deal of hot-headed talk by men with empty bellies, while the justices of the peace lived in dread of more widespread disturbances. After the boom years of the seventies and early eighties trade was in recession, and the law and order situation was not improved by the numbers of discharged soldiers now being thrown onto the labour market. Many of these unfortunates, unable or unwilling to return to a life of honest toil, took to roaming the countryside in gangs, terrorising isolated villages and farmsteads, or else gathered in the cities – a social nuisance and ready-made fodder for agitators and trouble-makers.

Then there was always the Earl of Essex. His lordship had come back from Cadiz in one of his hair-shirt moods, attending prayers regularly and prepared to devote himself entirely to business with, so he said, 'no ambition but her Majesty's gracious favour and the reputation of well serving her'. Unfortunately it was not a lasting mood. At the beginning of 1597 plans were already under discussion for yet another 'design against Spain' to be undertaken in the summer, and the Earls of Cumberland and Essex both put forward schemes for an attack on Ferrol, where yet another Armada was being laboriously collected. Essex's plan was, typically, the more grandiose. He wanted a large amphibious force of the kind which had gone to Cadiz – a fleet of ten or twelve Queen's ships, supported by twelve Londoners and twenty Dutchmen, with an army of five thousand and a free hand for himself. Elizabeth was lukewarm; there were rumours that Walter Raleigh and Lord Thomas Howard might be promoted to command and the upshot was a furious row between Queen and favourite. Essex took to his bed – a ploy he was to make use of more and more as time went on. Meanwhile Sir Robert Cecil was noted to be in great credit, the Queen spending most of the day in 'private and secret conference' with her new Secretary.

The changing state of the parties was naturally a matter of intense interest at Court, and that assiduous correspondent Rowland Whyte informed Sir Robert Sidney in a letter dated 19 February that the Earl of Essex had 'kept in' for a full fortnight, although the Queen often sent to see him and he, too, was going privately to see her almost every day. On 25 February Whyte had met my lord of Essex coming out of his chamber in his gown and nightcap and was able to report that there had been a reconciliation. 'Her Majesty', he wrote, 'as I heard, resolved to break him of his will, and to pull down his great heart, who found it a thing impossible, and says he holds it from the mother's side; but all is well again, and no doubt he will grow a mighty man in our State.'

Two days later there was more trouble, with Essex in the sulks again and announcing that he meant to visit his estates in Wales for his health's sake. 'Truly', commented Rowland Whyte, 'he leads here a very unquiet life.' Robert Cecil had apparently been to see him on a conciliatory mission which 'took not that success which was looked for' and now, again according to Whyte, Walter Raleigh was often very private with the Earl, having become 'a mediator for peace' between his lordship and the Secretary.

In the middle of these delicate negotiations came the death of Lord Cobham, Warden of the Cinque Ports. Essex was pushing Robert Sidney, younger brother of the dead hero Philip Sidney and currently Governor of Flushing, as his candidate for the vacant office, but the Queen rejected him out of hand. Sidney was too young and, in any case, was already fully occupied with his present job. Besides, she added, it would be an insult to the Brooke family to bestow the Wardenship on a man of lesser rank and indicated that she had more or less decided to give it to the new Lord Cobham.

Essex, who as usual was making the affair an issue of confidence, retorted that if Robert Sidney's rank was not high enough, he would stand himself. At a Council meeting on 7 March he declared that he had cause to hate Lord Cobham for his villainous dealing (Henry Brooke had been one of the more outspoken critics of the Cadiz operation), and if the Queen were to grace so unworthy a man, then he, Essex, would have every reason to think himself little regarded by her.

Nevertheless, two days later, the Queen told him that she had definitely decided that Lord Cobham should have the Cinque Ports. In a furious temper the Earl at once got ready to set out on his Welsh journey, but was recalled before he had left London and in a private interview Elizabeth offered to make him Master of the Ordnance. This was an important military post and just the kind of office which Francis Bacon had tried to warn him against, but Essex accepted without a second thought and, for the time being at least, was happy again.

Although the fleet was now being put into commission, a good deal of doubt remained as to what, if any, aggressive action would be attempted in 1597. Reports coming in from Spain of famine, desertion and sickness at Ferrol seemed to discount any immediate danger from that quarter, and one school of thought still held that the recovery of Calais ought to have first priority. This had been suggested to the King of France – a relieving force on the same conditions as before with the Earl of Essex in command – but the King is said to have replied, 'with a disdainful smile', that he was sure her Majesty would never allow his cousin of Essex to leave her skirts. To bait the lioness was to invite a punishing swipe of her claws and this insult, being faithfully repeated back, provoked four lines written in her Majesty's own hand which caused the King to change colour and almost to strike the messenger. Anthony Bacon was afraid that, if the story were true, 'some effects' would follow, and certainly Anglo-French relations took a distinctly chilly turn that summer.

Nothing had been decided when, on 18 April, at a dinner party at Essex House, Robert Cecil, Essex and Walter Raleigh agreed to settle their differences. The alliance was based on mutual self-interest. Cecil was angling in his quiet way for the Chancellorship of the Duchy of Lancaster. Raleigh wanted to get back his old job of Captain of the Guard, and in return offered to find victuals at ninepence a day for six thousand men for any forthcoming venture; while Essex, who was determined to have sole command this time, wanted all the support he could get. The new triumvirate made a formidable combination and by the end of the month Rowland Whyte was able to tell Robert Sidney that 'our preparation for sea for her Majesty's fleet goes well forward, so doth the victualling of six thousand foot, on expectation of some secret enterprise against the common enemy'.

Three weeks later came the usual hitch. 'Here', wrote Whyte, 'hath been much ado between the Queen and the Lords about the preparation for sea; some of them urging the necessity of setting it forward for her safety; but she opposing it, by no danger appearing towards her anywhere, and that she will not make wars, but arm for defence; understanding how much of her treasure was spent already in victual, both for ships and soldiers at land. She was extremely angry with them that made such haste in it, and at Lord Burghley for suffering it, seeing no greater occasion.' It seemed that no reason or persuasion could prevail and the Queen had given orders 'to stay all proceeding'. 'How her Majesty may be wrought to fulfil the most earnest desire of some to have it go forward', added Whyte, 'time must make it known.'

Time made it known within a few days, Elizabeth's struggles having been overcome, probably by sheer weight of numbers. The expedition was on again and Essex was 'to be chief of all'. With the Cecils behind him he had become well nigh irresistible; everything was still love and kindness between them and 'all furtherance given to his desires, especially in the matter now in hand'.

Walter Raleigh, too, was getting his reward. At the beginning of June Robert Cecil had brought him in to see the Queen, who received him graciously and reinstated him as Captain of the Guard. Elizabeth was pleased to have her old friend back. She took him out riding with her that evening and he was soon back on the old footing, coming and going boldly in the Privy Chamber 'as he was used to do'. All this took place in Essex's absence, but the Court knew it had his approval.

Having got his own way, the Earl, as always, was ready to call the whole world brother and, in any case, he was often away from Court these days. His steward, Gilly Meyrick, told Rowland Whyte complacently that his lordship was so full of the business now in hand that everyone must have patience till his return, when he would be able to do something for his friends.

Essex, in fact, looked all set for further glory and on 15 June his commission as 'lieutenant-general and admiral of our army and navy' was signed by the Queen. His instructions were to go first to Ferrol and destroy the Spanish fleet. 'For the doing whereof, you . . . will discreetly in God's name and with the least danger and loss of our people, expedite this special service for the ruin of the enemy, especially by the destruction of his ships; which being well executed, there is no cause for us to doubt of any peril to come for a long time, though his mind be never so malicious.' It was 1589 all over again, for only after accomplishing this 'special service' was the Lord General authorised to stand over to the Azores in pursuit of that eternal chimera, the treasure fleet, and also to explore the possibility of establishing a permanent base on the island of Terceira – that other long-cherished but by now impractical dream.

The expedition was a large one, much on the lines of the previous year's – seventeen of the Queen's ships and twenty-four troop carriers. Thomas Howard and Walter Raleigh were sailing as vice and rear admirals as before, and the fleet would again be reinforced by a strong Dutch squadron. Everyone was hoping for another Cadiz and Essex, setting out on his first independent naval command, wrote to the Queen that he would strive to be worthy of so high a grace and so blessed a happiness.

Unfortunately, the Islands Voyage, as it came to be known, got off to a disastrous start. Contrary winds in the Channel delayed the rendezvous at Plymouth for the best part of a month, while morale sagged and provisions were eaten up at an alarming rate. At last, on Sunday 10 July, they were able to get away, but almost immediately a great storm blew up from the south-west and raged for four horrible days. The fleet soon lost contact and ships and men suffered severely from the tremendous buffeting of wind and sea. It was too much for Walter Raleigh and too much for Essex, although he hung on as long as he dared, and by the nineteenth everyone except Lord Thomas Howard, who had triumphantly ridden out the gale and was now cruising off Corunna, had crawled exhaustedly back to port.

It was a bitter disappointment. There had been no actual losses but most of the ships were in need of repair – Essex's own flagship, the *Merhonour,* was leaking so badly that he had had to abandon her – and this would mean more delay with the campaigning season already well advanced. They would also need more provisions, which would mean more expense. The Earl wrote off anxiously to London – this was just the kind of setback calculated to annoy the Queen and perhaps make her decide to cancel the whole operation – but he was lucky enough to catch her in a relaxed mood. She was thankful that the fleet and its commander were safe. She was willing for the voyage to continue, and would send the *Lion* to replace the crippled *Merhonour* with another three months' provisions, though, wrote Robert Cecil, 'she stuck at that at first'. Clearly the Cecil influence was still favour- able and in another letter Sir Robert assured the absent Essex that 'the Queen is so disposed now to have us all love you, that she and I do every night talk like angels of you'.

It was while the two admirals were working like demons to refit and get to sea again that the famous episode of the Polish ambassador took place. This had begun as a routine piece of diplomatic business, but as the Queen preserved pleasant memories of the King of Po- land's father, who had visited her once long ago in her giddy courting days, and as his envoy was said to be a handsome, well-spoken fellow, she decided to honour him with a public reception in the Presence Chamber, with the lords and officers of the Court gathered round making an occasion of it.

The ambassador was duly brought in, attired in a long robe of black velvet 'well jewelled and buttoned', and kissed hands before retiring a few paces to make his oration; while the Queen, standing under the canopy of estate, waited to listen kindly to the usual complimentary Latin address. But it was not a complimentary address. On the con- trary, the Polish ambassador was uttering threats. His master, he said, complained that, despite repeated protests, the Queen was allowing his ships and merchants to be spoiled in the pursuance of her quarrel with Spain, thus violating the laws of nature and of nations. By attempting to prohibit their freedom of trade, the Queen was assum- ing a superiority over other princes which he found intolerable and would no longer endure. He regarded Spain as his friend, and if her Majesty would not speedily reform these abuses, then he would do it for her.

For an ambassador supposedly come in peace to launch such an unheralded attack was, of course, a shocking breach of protocol and his audience heard him out in frozen silence. But if the King of Poland had expected to flummox the Queen of England, he was about to be disappointed. Her Majesty took up the challenge without hesitation, and there and then in fluent and flawless off-the-cuff Latin, proceeded to wipe the floor with his unhappy spokesman. 'Expectavi legationem, mihi vero querelam adduxisti . . .' If the King were really responsible for such language, then it must be attributed to youth and inexperience and also, no doubt, to the fact that he was a king not by right of blood but only by election. As for the ambassador, he might consider himself an educated man who had read many books, but clearly he had never come across the chapter which prescribed the proper forms to be used between kings and princes. If it were not for his privileged status, she added, she would have dealt with his impertinence 'in another style'. She then dismissed him contemptuously, promising to appoint some of her Council 'to see upon what ground this clamour of yours hath its foundation'.

Justly pleased with her performance, Elizabeth is said to have turned to the awed and admiring bystanders, exclaiming 'God's death, my lords! I have been enforced this day to scour up my old Latin that hath lain long rusting'. A little later she remarked wistfully that she wished the Earl of Essex might have been present to hear her and Robert Cecil, taking the hint, had a full account of the incident sent down to Plymouth. Essex – harassed by problems of sickness, desertion and shortage of victual, while persistent south-westerly gales continued to keep the fleet bottled up in harbour – nevertheless made haste to send congratulations on her Majesty's princely triumph over 'the braving Polack'. Surely she was made of the same stuff of which the ancients believed the heroes to be formed – 'that is, her mind of gold, her body of brass'.

The Earl may well have wished similar heroic attributes for himself during those frustrating weeks of struggle to salvage something from the wreckage of his great command. 'Such contrariety of winds and such extreme weather at this time of year, hath not been seen', he wrote dispiritedly to his secretary, Edward Reynolds. All the same, he intended, by God's grace, to live at sea until winter came in. 'We will fare hardly, but we will offer to dispute the cause with the Adelantado if he mean to look abroad this year.'

It was more than half way through August before a much depleted expedition finally set sail, Essex having at the last moment decided to discharge nearly all his infantry, keeping only the hard core of veterans who had come with Francis Vere from the Netherlands. This, of course, meant that there would now be no chance of landing at Ferrol and, although the Queen was still insisting on a naval assault, Robert Cecil no longer expected to see any results beyond 'the keeping up of the journey's reputation, by keeping the sea as long as the time of year doth serve for the Spaniards to come out, and to lie off at the Islands to interrupt the Indian fleet'.

In the event, Essex and Raleigh never went to Ferrol at all. Relying on reports that the Adelantado was too weak to come out anyway and using the weather as a convenient excuse (the fleet had again been separated by gales), they disobeyed instructions just as Drake had done before them and rendezvoused at the Azores on 14 September. Here they found that the treasure ships had not yet arrived, nor had the usual escort sailed to meet them. Hopes of making a killing rose sharply but Essex, either from over-excitement or over-anxiety or both, proceeded to behave like a neurotic sheepdog, constantly chasing after shadows and regrettably failing to inform his rear admiral of his movements.

It was during one of the Lord General's sudden darts over the horizon that Walter Raleigh performed the only noteworthy exploit of the entire campaign, landing at Fayal, one of the islands in the central group, and taking the town. When Essex returned he was furious at having been cheated of the 'honour' and a full-scale row developed with Essex, egged on by the more hysterical members of his entourage, threatening to court martial Raleigh for going ashore without orders, and Raleigh, who was not a man to stand for nonsense of this kind, threatening to take himself and his squadron home. In the end good old Thomas Howard managed to patch things up, persuading Essex to accept an apology and Raleigh to make one, but it was a fragile truce and feelings continued to run high between the Earl's followers and Raleigh's Westcountrymen.

Leaving the Dutch to guard the southern approaches, the English fleet now moved in a body to La Gratiosa in the north. The flota, which was expected at any moment, would arrive from the west and would have to be intercepted before it reached sanctuary in the heavily fortified roadstead at Terceira, but on 27 September the Earl of Essex, for reasons which remain mysterious, decided to make for St Michael's, the eastern-most island, arriving at dawn on the twenty-ninth. Meanwhile, the flota, accompanied by eight galleons of the Indian Guard, had duly appeared on the western horizon and, before the English could retrieve their general's horrifying blunder, had sailed placidly into the Angra Road at Terceira and anchored under the protection of the most formidable shore batteries then known.

In 1585 Drake had missed the treasure fleet by a margin of twelve hours for reasons 'best known to God'. Essex had missed it by a margin of three hours, in circumstances which could only be explained by his own shortcomings as a commander. William Monson in the *Rainbow,* who had the mortifying experience of actually encountering the flota but being unable to impede its progress, considered that none of the captains could be blamed. 'All', he wrote later, 'is to be attributed to the want of experience in my lord and his flexible nature to be over-ruled.'

Since it would have been suicidal to attempt a direct assault on Terceira with the forces at its disposal, the expedition's only remaining hope – and that was a forlorn one – was to try and take one of the other islands, replenish their supplies and then hang on until the Spaniards were forced to put to sea. Accordingly the fleet sailed despondently back to St Michael's. Here it was agreed that while Raleigh created a diversion off Punta Delgada, Essex should take his soldiers round the headland and make a landing at Villa Franca where the coast was more sheltered. He would then march across country to take the town and fort of St Michael's from the rear. The first part of this plan was carried out but, having discovered Villa Franca to be a pleasant spot, well provided with the comforts of life, the army showed a marked reluctance to leave it. Essex listened to his officers' gloomy assessments of the probable hazards of the overland journey and the difficulties likely to be experienced in taking St Michael's from any angle and, with his usual weakness for cheap popularity, allowed himself to be persuaded. They would stay where they were and send for the fleet to join them, but not just yet – all those thirsty seamen would soon dispose of the wine and other goodies so thoughtfully left behind by the inhabitants of the town. It was an inexcusable decision whichever way you looked at it, made still worse by the deliberate failure to inform Walter Raleigh, left in suspense on the other side of the island with many of his ships beginning to run short of fresh water.

But while the fleet waited, at first puzzled and then angry, a prize offered itself which might very satisfactorily have wiped the army's eye. A huge East India carrack, homeward bound and fully laden, was sighted making trustfully for the road at St Michael's and, hardly daring to breathe, Raleigh ordered all flags to be struck, not a move to be made, until she had rounded the point. It could so easily have been the *Madre de Dios* all over again, if one of the Dutch captains had not lost his head and opened fire at almost the last moment. The carrack took fright and helped by a sudden shift of wind was able to run herself aground under the guns of the fort. The townspeople swarmed out to help unload her and by the time the English flyboats had managed to cover the three intervening miles of choppy water, her captain had set her alight.

This was the last straw as far as the sailors were concerned, for if Essex had kept his part of the bargain, the shore would have been in the hands of the army and some fortunes at least would have been made. The fleet had had enough and this final fiasco marked the end of a useless and inglorious voyage, remarkable for nothing but bad luck, bad judgement and bad feeling. In any case, it was now October, the weather was breaking up and everyone wanted to go home. The army was re-embarked and, after watering at Villa Franca, the expedition prepared to sail. Little attempt was made to keep formation and when a brief storm blew up, scattering the squadrons, they simply steered their own course for Plymouth, the more weatherly ships drawing ahead and leaving stragglers to fend for themselves. This rush for home was due primarily to the desire of individual captains to get their stories in first, since none of the disgruntled and disappointed crews was yet aware that they had company; that on 9 October, the very day they had left the Islands, the fleet in Ferrol so casually ignored by Essex and Raleigh had put to sea and was making for the Channel ahead of them.

The moment he realised that the English fleet was heading for the Azores, Philip of Spain had become possessed by the resolve to seize this apparently heaven-sent opportunity to sink his teeth into his arch-enemy while she lay virtually undefended. The King knew that he was dying. He knew that this would be his last opportunity to do God's work and, sweeping aside all objections, ignoring 'the unwillingness to sail which filled the minds of everyone . . . and of the absolute lack of all that was essential to the success of the enterprise', he literally drove the unhappy Adelantado of Castile to sea.

Don Martin's orders were to sail for Brittany and pick up the squadron of galleys which was still based on the little port of Blavet. He was then to cross to Cornwall, capture Falmouth and establish a base there, before returning to the Scillies to lie in wait for the English fleet. 'On winning a victory, as was expected, he was again to enter Falmouth and land the rest of his troops. From Falmouth he was to press forward and capture all he could.'

Whether Philip, carried away as most people seemed to believe by a passion for revenge, really expected this ingenious plan to result in the subjugation of England, or whether he was simply hoping to frighten Elizabeth into deserting her Dutch allies and agreeing to make peace on his terms, it is impossible to say. But, as the Venetian ambassador later remarked, no impartial observer had ever thought for a moment that, in a bad season, with a weak Armada, the King's 'violent resolution' could possibly result in anything except another humiliating failure. Nevertheless, late, creaky, ill-prepared, ill-equipped and reluctant though it was, the Armada got as far as Brittany and some of the ships were actually sighted off the Lizard.

An attack in such circumstances, with her own fleet straggling home in disorder after an unsuccessful voyage, was the sort of nightmare which had always haunted the Queen, and when Essex arrived in Plymouth on 26 October, he found that 'the Spaniards were upon the coast' and everyone in an acute state of alarm. The Earl, who was probably not sorry to have attention diverted from his own recent performance, prepared to rise magnificently to the occasion and assist at the destruction of a fleet which he should have finished off three months ago. 'If we do not bestir ourselves as never men did', he wrote excitedly, 'let us be counted not worthy to serve such a Queen.' As soon as he had set his sick men ashore and taken on fresh water, he would be out with as many ships as he could, even if they had to eat ropes' ends and drink rain water.

The Queen was not pleased with Essex, who had 'given the enemy leisure and courage to attempt us', but in this emergency she authorised him to assume command and take whatever action seemed necessary, with the proviso that he must not leave England unprotected upon any 'light advertisement'. However, if the Spaniards appeared to be making for Ireland, then he should follow them. It would not be necessary to eat ropes. 'For treasure, for victual, and what may be fit for us to send, you shall find that you serve a Prince neither void of care nor judgement what to do that is fit in cases of this consequence.'

As it turned out, no action was necessary. A brisk north-easterly was already scattering Don Martin's unenthusiastic fleet, and by the end of the month they were scuttling thankfully for home. It was the last Armada – just as the Islands Voyage was to be last big combined operation in Spanish waters. Although no one yet realised it, the stormy, unfruitful autumn of 1597 marked the end of an era.

VI
A Very Great Princess

Love wing'd my Hopes and taught me how to fly
Far from base earth, but not to mount too high:
  For true pleasure
  Lives in measure,
  Which if men forsake,
Blinded they into folly run and grief for pleasure take.

'We may say, and that truly, that God fought for us . . . for certainly the enemy's designs were dangerous, and not to be diverted by our force; but by His will who would not suffer the Spaniards in any of their attempts to set footing in England.' This, at least, was the considered verdict of William Monson on the Armada of 1597 and one which was most probably shared by Queen Elizabeth. Having once more been obliged to watch her men of war deliberately disobeying their instructions with what might have been very serious consequences, it would hardly be surprising if she had come to regard the Almighty as her only reliable supporter.

Nor was it surprising that the Earl of Essex should have received a chilly welcome when he returned to Court at the end of October. The Queen had been listening to Walter Raleigh's friends and made no secret of her anger and disappointment with her commander-in-chief. It was the return from Cadiz all over again, but this time there was no compensating triumph. This time, too, Essex, himself deeply disappointed, overtired, irritable and on the defensive, was in no mood of resignation and quickly found a grievance of his own to exploit.

After church on Sunday, 23 October, in a grand ceremony in the Presence Chamber, the Queen had conferred the earldom of Nottingham on Charles Howard – an event made the more noticeable by the extreme rarity of Elizabethan peerages. Some people might have seen this one as a well-deserved, if belated, recognition of a distinguished servant of the Crown. Essex chose to see it as a deliberate insult, taking special umbrage over the wording of Howard's patent, which not only mentioned his great services against the Armada of 1588, but also in the action at Cadiz, the credit for which, in Essex's opinion, belonged to him alone. To make matters worse, the new earl, as Lord High Admiral and Lord Steward of the present Parliament, would now take precedence over him on public and state occasions – a humiliation Essex was not prepared to endure. He took himself off to his house at Wanstead on the pretext of having to attend to his own long-neglected affairs and proceeded to indulge in an attack of galloping self-pity. Being Essex, of course, he was over-reacting, but the timing of Charles Howard's elevation does lead to the suspicion that it had been intended, if not as a direct snub, at least as a strong hint that the Queen's favour was not to be considered as anyone's exclusive property.

The absence of my lord of Essex naturally became the chief topic of conversation at Court, Rowland Whyte speculating that the peace concluded between him and Robert Cecil would once more 'burst out to terms of unkindness'. The Queen, faced with this fresh evidence of irresponsibility in one who, like it or not, was still a popular hero and a leading public figure, grumbled that a prince was not to be contested withal by a subject; but she would not take up the challenge. She would not order Essex to return, his place and duty ought to be enough to command him, she said, and Lord Hunsdon was able to tell the sulking Achilles that he could find 'nothing but comfort and kindness towards your lordship, if you will but turn about and take it'.

In spite of strenuous efforts by his well-wishers to make him see the futility of his behaviour, Essex stayed obstinately at Wanstead for a full fortnight and, for the sake of appearances, Elizabeth was obliged to accept the excuse of his 'want of health'. When at last he condescended to come back to town, he persisted in his refusal to take his seat in Parliament or attend Council meetings, in case he should meet the Lord Admiral and be unable to control himself. He insisted that the Queen should be pleased to see the wrong done unto him and that the wording of the Earl of Nottingham's patent should be altered – a demand which the Earl of Nottingham understandably refused even to consider. An element of fantasy was introduced into the situation when Essex offered to settle the matter by personal combat, either with the Lord Admiral himself (a man twice his age, who had cried off the Islands Voyage because of 'indisposition of body'), or with one of his sons or kinsmen. Christmas approached and still the quarrel and its various ramifications were keeping the Court in a state of uproar. 'Here is such ado about it', reported Rowland Whyte, 'as it troubles this Place and all other proceedings.' 'All other proceedings' was the key phrase, for by December Essex's tantrums had begun to interfere with the progress of an important item of international business.

The Kings of France and Spain were now moving towards a settlement of their differences, and the King of France – mindful of his treaty obligations not to conclude a separate peace – had despatched a special envoy to London charged with the delicate task of discovering how Queen Elizabeth would react to the idea of taking part in joint negotiations with Spain. Elizabeth was naturally anxious that her Council should present a united front on such a vital issue and it would, of course, be acutely embarrassing if Essex, as a particular friend of Henry IV's, refused to meet his ambassador. André Hurault, Sieur de Maisse, was therefore kept waiting for his first audience while renewed behind-the-scenes moves were made to pacify the intransigent Earl.

De Maisse, an experienced and skilful diplomat, soon became maliciously aware of the English government's predicament, nor did it take him long to evaluate the probable response to his mission. The Queen, he thought, was inclined to peace and would welcome it, if some way could be found of including the Netherlands. Old Lord Burghley, too, was likely to be in favour, and where he led, his son and the rest of the Cecil faction would follow. Opposition could, however, be expected from the Essex party, for while de Maisse did not believe that the Earl would be so rash as to speak openly in favour of war, he undoubtedly had no desire for peace. Why should he, after all? 'He is courageous and ambitious', commented the ambassador, 'and a man of great designs, hoping to attain glory by arms, and to win renown more and more.' With the coming of peace, his shining public image would quickly fade and he would become no more than just another Council lord, forever playing second fiddle to Mr. Secretary and falling ever deeper into debt.

André de Maisse was a conscientious man, keeping a faithful daily record of his observations of the English Court. The Queen, in particular, fascinated him and from the pages of his Journal there emerges an unforgettable picture of Elizabeth as she was in the fortieth year of her reign.

The ambassador was finally summoned to the presence on 8 December and found the Queen *en déshabillé*. She told him that she had had a boil on her face which had made her feel wretched, and although she apologised profusely for receiving him in her nightgown, his first impression was of a somewhat outlandish old lady, wearing a great reddish coloured wig covered with gold and silver spangles, and perpetually fidgeting – twisting and untwisting her long hanging sleeves, or jerking open the front of her robe 'as if she was too hot'. Her face was long and thin and appeared very aged, and her teeth were discoloured and uneven. Many of them were missing, so that it was difficult to understand her when she spoke quickly. The whole effect was definitely weird, and yet the charismatic grace and dignity were still unmistakable.

Elizabeth was at her most affable, ordering a stool to be brought for de Maisse and telling him to remain covered. But, he wrote, 'all the time she spoke she would often rise from her chair and appear to be very impatient with what I was saying. She would complain that the fire was hurting her eyes, though there was a great screen before it and she six or seven feet away; yet did she give orders to have it extinguished, making them bring water to pour upon it. She told me that she was well pleased to stand up, and that she used to speak thus with the ambassadors who came to seek her and used sometimes to tire them, of which they would on occasion complain. I begged her not to overtire herself in any way, and I rose when she did; and then she sat down again, and so did I. At my departure she rose . . . and again began to say that she was grieved that all the gentlemen I had brought should see her in that condition, and she called to see them. They made their reverence before her, one after the other, and she embraced them all with great charm and smiling countenance.'

When de Maisse saw the Queen again a week later, she was looking better and was rather more conventionally dressed, in black taffeta bound with gold lace and lined with crimson over a petticoat of white damask. All the same, he noticed that 'when she raises her head she has a trick of putting both hands on her gown and opening it insomuch that all her belly can be seen'. During the course of conversation Elizabeth often referred to herself as 'foolish and old', saying she was sorry that de Maisse, who had known so many wise men and great princes, should come at length to see a poor woman and a foolish. The ambassador, who knew better than to be taken in by this kind of talk, remarked that the Queen liked to speak slightingly of her intelligence 'so that she may give occasion to commend her'. She was obviously pleased when he praised her judgement and prudence, but said modestly 'that it was but natural that she should have some knowledge of the affairs of the world, being called thereto so young'. 'When anyone speaks of her beauty', wrote de Maisse, 'she says that she was never beautiful, although she had that reputation thirty years ago. Nevertheless, she speaks of her beauty as often as she can.'

The Earl of Essex was still conspicuously absent from the gathering in the Privy Chamber and de Maisse was afraid that until he returned to Court 'they (the English) will do nothing in good earnest in the business which I have discussed'. But now, at last, there were signs of a breakthrough. Rowland Whyte, writing a few days before Christmas, was able to tell Robert Sidney that 'the gallant Earl doth now show himself in more public sort than he did', and shortly afterwards the word went round that Essex was to be given the office of Earl Marshal which would restore his precedence over the Lord Admiral. The Admiral was not pleased and went off in a huff to his house at Chelsea, but the deadlock seemed to have been broken and when de Maisse had his third audience with the Queen on Christmas Eve he found her in excellent spirits, wearing a very low cut gown of cloth of silver and listening to a pavane being played to her on the spinet.

Elizabeth had obviously warmed to the urbane and civilised Frenchman and was taking a good deal of trouble over him, chatting freely on a wide range of subjects from music to religion, reminiscing and entertaining him with a selection of anecdotes from her extensive repertoire. 'Whilst I was treating with her in the matter of my charge', de Maisse recorded, 'she would often make such digressions, either expressly to gain time . . . or because it is her natural way. Then would she excuse herself, saying, "Master Ambassador, you will say of the tales I am telling you that they are mere gullery. See what it is to have to do with old women such as I am"'. But the ambassador thought that apart from her face, which looked old, and her bad teeth, it would not be possible to see a woman of so fine and vigorous disposition, both in mind and body. She knew all the ancient histories, he wrote, and 'one can say nothing to her on which she will not make some apt comment'. In fact, despite her various little oddities, he had come to feel an enormous respect for the Queen. 'She is a very great princess who knows everything' was his considered judgement.

Elizabeth had promised that de Maisse should confer with her Council on the matter in hand, but it seemed that the Earl of Essex was still making difficulties and was now threatening to go back to the country again. De Maisse thought this was very foolish, for the Earl would only be giving his enemies a further opportunity to make mischief behind his back, and if he persisted in 'withdrawing' himself in this fashion the Queen might well begin to suspect that he was up to no good. The ambassador did not pretend to understand all the mysterious ins and outs of the quarrel, but he was becoming more than a little irritated by it and grumbled in his Journal that 'the King's affairs remain at a standstill by reason of these trifles'.

A few days later he heard that there had been a reconciliation and all the Court was rejoicing, but another week went by before Essex was finally satisfied with the wording of his patent and had been ceremoniously installed as Earl Marshal. The way was now clear at last for a meeting of the full Council and, as de Maisse had anticipated, everyone appeared to be cautiously in favour of peace except Essex, who sat sulkily silent through most of the proceedings. The ambassador was told that the Queen had decided to send her own commissioners to France to take counsel with his Majesty as to what should be done and, since this was a game for three players, she understood that the Dutch would also be sending representatives. De Maisse pointed out that he had been kept waiting six weeks for this not very startling resolution and put in an urgent plea that the commissioners should be despatched as soon as possible with full powers to treat 'as much for war as for peace'.

When the meeting broke up, he went to take his leave of the Queen who apologised for having detained him so long and then drew him aside for a private word. There was no creature on earth who bore the King of France so much affection, or so greatly desired his welfare and prosperity as she did, but at the same time she must beg him to consider her position. She was only a woman, old and capable of nothing by herself. She had to deal with nobles of divers humours and a people who, although they made great demonstrations of love towards her, were notoriously fickle and inconstant, and as a result she was beset by fears and troubles on every side.

From even a short acquaintance with her Majesty, this affecting picture of a poor, helpless old lady must have struck de Maisse as a trifle unconvincing; and no doubt the Queen was equally sceptical of his earnest assurances concerning the King's undiminished goodwill and gratitude for past favours, and his intention, once his own affairs were straightened out, of repaying the like to his friends – an oblique reference to the matter of King Henry's formidable debt to the English treasury, which had come up more than once during the past six weeks. However, the two parted on the best of terms, Elizabeth saying that she was glad to have known de Maisse and would always think most highly of his merits. She turned to the Admiral, who happened to be standing near, and ordered him to make sure the ambassador was given a good ship for his passage home, adding with a laugh that he might be taken prisoner by the Spaniards, to which de Maisse replied gallantly that marching under the Queen's banner he had no need to fear them.

Before de Maisse left the country he paid the usual round of farewell courtesy visits and saw the Earl of Essex alone for the first time. Essex still seemed rather gloomy and out of sorts, referring to the 'great cloud' which had hung over him ever since his return from the Azores but which was now, he hoped, beginning to dissipate. He told the ambassador that he had been suggested as one of the commissioners to go to France but had excused himself, because he knew the peace party would blame him if the talks failed. He went on to remark that in England, as in France, there were contrary parties each with their own designs, adding that in England they suffered from delay and inconstancy 'which proceeded chiefly from the sex of the Queen'.

Essex was evidently of the opinion that he had received no more than bare justice in his recent contest with Elizabeth, but as usual failed to appreciate that the battle should never have been fought at all. The Queen had no taste for farce under duress and it seems reasonable to assume that this latest exhibition had destroyed any lingering remnants of her personal fondness for Robert Devereux. Once more, though, all appeared to be well on the surface. Essex was back in his accustomed place at Court and Robert Cecil had persuaded the Queen to show unusual generosity over the disposal of some cargoes of cochineal brought back from the Islands Voyage, as well as making his lordship an unconditional gift of seven thousand pounds. The arguments the Secretary had used with her Majesty were not revealed but there was no secret about his motives, for it was about to be Cecil's turn to go abroad. He had been nominated to lead the forthcoming delegation to France, leaving Essex to take his place at the Queen's right hand, and in typically Cecilian fashion was taking every precaution to secure his rear. Rowland Whyte heard that 'he was resolved not to stir one foot till the Earl of Essex did assure him that nothing should pass here that might be a prejudice or offensive unto him'.

As it turned out, Cecil needn't have worried. Francis Bacon, making one final attempt to offer sensible political advice, had urged Essex to start taking an interest in Irish affairs which, 'being mixed with matter of war', should be congenial to him – quite apart from the fact that anyone who could make a constructive contribution towards solving the Irish problem would certainly gain in credit and reputation. But although my lord of Essex was reported to be in very diligent attendance upon the Queen and 'in some sort takes upon him the despatching of all business in the absence of Mr. Secretary', he squandered what was to be his last opportunity to re-establish himself with her Majesty by nagging her to agree to receive his mother at Court.

The former Countess of Leicester, now married for the third time to Christopher Blount, one of her son's cronies, was a woman of considerable physical attractions, forceful personality and slightly doubtful reputation. The Queen had loathed her ever since the mid-sixties when she and the Earl of Leicester had first embarked on an ostentatious flirtation, and after her marriage with Leicester she became a non-person as far as Elizabeth was concerned. The prospect of being obliged to see her again was distasteful to say the least but Lady Leicester, as she was still known, would not let the matter drop and eventually, probably for the sake of peace, the Queen gave in. The two women met briefly in the Privy Chamber and embraced, but this was as far as Elizabeth was prepared to go. When she heard that Lettice wanted a repeat performance with more publicity, she refused with 'some wonted unkind words'. Mother and son had gained a technical victory, but neither achieved anything in the long run by 'importuning the Queen in these unpleasing matters'.

The spring of 1598 marked the lull which preceded the last great crisis of the reign. The Queen was reported to be very well and celebrated the Garter Feast of St George's Day in splendid style. Elizabeth had now become one of the great tourist attractions of the western world and whenever she was in London foreign visitors flocked to Greenwich or Whitehall or Hampton Court to see the Sunday church parade. Paul Hentzner, a German lawyer bear-leading a young nobleman on the Grand Tour, was at Greenwich that summer and, together with other selected outsiders, was admitted to the Presence Chamber to watch the Queen and her ladies pass by on their way to the chapel, escorted by the great officers of state and guarded by a contingent of gentlemen pensioners with their gilt battle axes.

Hentzner must have had a good view, for he described the Queen as looking 'very majestic, her face oblong, fair but wrinkled, her eyes small, yet black and pleasant, her nose a little hooked, her lips narrow and her teeth black'. (All the English were inclined to have bad teeth, a defect which, in Hentzner's opinion, was due to their inordinate fondness for sweetmeats.) Elizabeth was wearing a pair of very fine pearl earrings and a small crown on top of an obvious red wig. 'Her bosom was uncovered, as all the English ladies have it till they marry; and she had on a necklace of exceeding fine jewels. Her hands were small, her fingers long, and her stature neither tall nor low; her air was stately, her manner of speaking mild and obliging.' That particular Sunday she was dressed in white silk bordered with pearls the size of beans, and over it a mantle of black silk shot with silver threads, her train being carried by a marchioness. Hentzner was much impressed by all this magnificence and as the Queen passed, he says, 'she spoke very graciously, first to one, then to another, whether foreign ministers, or those who attended for different reasons, in English, French and Italian; for besides being well skilled in Greek, Latin and the languages I have mentioned, she is mistress of Spanish, Scotch and Dutch'. He remarked on the great respect with which she was treated. 'Whoever speaks to her, it is kneeling; now and then she raises some with her hand. While we were there . . . a Bohemian baron had letters to present to her; and she, after pulling off her glove, gave him her right hand to kiss, sparkling with rings and jewels, a mark of particular favour. Wherever she turned her face, as she was going along, everybody fell down on their knees.'

While the Queen was at prayer, the visitors were able to watch the ceremonial laying of the royal dinner table – the various officials responsible for spreading the cloth and carrying the bread and salt prostrating themselves and behaving with as much awe and reverence as if the Queen had been present. The meal itself, served on gilt plate, was brought in by the yeomen of the guard in their scarlet coats while the hall rang with the braying of trumpets and rattle of kettle drums. After each dish had been assayed, or tasted, for poison, the maids of honour appeared and, 'with particular solemnity', lifted the meat off the table and bore it away to the private apartments. 'The Queen dines and sups alone', wrote Hentzner, 'with very few attendants; and it is very seldom that anybody, foreigner or native, is admitted at that time, and then only at the intercession of somebody in power.' Paul Hentzner did not command that sort of influence and had to be content with the public part of the show; but just to have seen the great Queen of England go by on her way to church was something well worth storing up to tell one's grandchildren about.

The tourists who came to gaze and to admire the splendour of the English Court, who strained to catch a glimpse of the incredible woman around whom all this well-ordered, pompous ritual revolved, naturally knew nothing of the tensions building up behind the glittering and bejewelled facade as the Queen grew older and the power struggle rending the younger generation intensified. To the outward eye Gloriana at sixty-four still appeared to be fully in command, universally loved, feared and respected. It was an appearance which had at all cost to be maintained. Only the Queen herself knew the cost in terms of mental and physical strain, or how fragile the facade of power really was. She knew that the greedy, ruthless condottiere surrounding the Earl of Essex were becoming increasingly impatient of an old woman's rule and that the old order, the old system of checks and balances, the old game of playing one faction against the other which, in the last resort, had depended on the willingness of the factions to abide by its unwritten rules, was slowly but inexorably sliding out of control. The new men, who knew little and cared less of the past and its painfully accumulated conventions, were thinking of the future, of a time when they would no longer be encumbered by a living monument, her hands clamped firmly on the purse strings, her iron will damming the golden stream of patronage and preferment which might flow so freely from a more easy-going monarch.

The danger that such men would not be prepared to wait for nature to take its course – although in large part neutralised by their general incompetence and lack of cohesion – was by no means imaginary. In Scotland James Stuart, his naturally suspicious mind poisoned against the Cecils by his friend Essex, was also becoming increasingly dissatisfied with his admittedly anomalous position, and was busy intriguing abroad for support for his claim to be publicly recognised as the Queen's heir; while in the shadow world inhabited by spies, informers, political refugees and Catholic exiles, rumours proliferated that the King of Scots 'would attempt to gather the fruit before it is ripe'.

But troublesome though he might be, Elizabeth never doubted her ability to deal with young James. Of far more pressing concern in the summer of 1598 was the question of peace with Spain. Robert Cecil and his colleagues had returned home in April to report the failure of their mission to the King of France. Henry, with an empty treasury and a shattered country to rebuild, was set on peace without delay and, after safeguarding the rights of his Huguenot subjects by the Edict of Nantes, he signed a separate treaty with Spain at Vervins that May, but he stipulated that the English were to be granted a period of six months to decide whether or not they wanted to join in.

That both the Queen and Lord Burghley wanted peace is not in doubt. Its advantages were too obvious. The frightening drain on the exchequer would be checked, European trade would revive and the Irish rebels, cut off from any hope of Spanish aid, could be dealt with more or less at leisure. But it was not, of course, as simple as that. As the Earl of Essex passionately pointed out, the Queen and her advisers were proposing to negotiate with a nation which, for as long as most people could remember, had been dedicated to the destruction of Protestant England and all she stood for. It was impossible, he argued, to deal in good faith with a popish Prince who never treated with heretics but to deceive them, and who would simply seize the chance of a breathing space to re-group and re-arm while England allowed her military forces to decay. Philip and his successors would think it no crime to break a treaty any time it suited them. Even if they did, they could easily obtain the Pope's absolution. After all, were they not still bound to obey *Regnans in Excelsis,* the bull of excommunication which enjoined the Catholic powers to depose the bastard, heretical and usurping Queen of England by fair means or foul?

This was a familiar argument and had been used in pre-Armada days by councillors terrified that the Queen, in her reluctance to commit herself to all-out war, might be lured into dropping her guard by false hopes of peace. But the situation was very different now. Ten years after the Armada no one could seriously maintain that England was any longer in danger of invasion. She could not afford to go on fighting a holy war just for the sake of it and thus run the risk of incurring the disapproval of world opinion as an obstinate disturber of the peace. At one of the last Council meetings he attended Lord Burghley told Essex that he breathed nothing but war, slaughter and blood and, drawing out his prayer-book, the old man pointed solemnly to the words of the psalm: 'the bloodthirsty and deceitful men shall not live out half their days'.

This well-known incident proved prophetic enough, but Essex was not to be silenced by psalms and he proceeded to bring the debate out into the open by publishing – or allowing Anthony Bacon to publish – a letter in which he defended himself vigorously against those critics who accused him of war-mongering and of using his influence to prolong the conflict at a time when peace might be had, in order to further his own career and serve the selfish interest of his military followers. This letter, or Apology as it became known, was a naked appeal to the passions and prejudices of the mob over the government's head and it naturally infuriated both the Queen and the Cecils. But in the final analysis it was not the Earl of Essex who blocked the road to peace.

The Dutch people had suffered bitterly in their twenty year long struggle for freedom from the overlordship of Spain. By the mid-nineties, though, the United Provinces or States of Holland were at last beginning to emerge as an independent nation (Philip's ill-advised intervention in French affairs had helped to take the pressure off them at a crucial moment), and nothing and nobody was going to persuade them to accept even the most carefully hedged form of compromise, even the most nominal form of Spanish sovereignty – always supposing Spain was disposed to be so generous. Elizabeth had never cared for the Hollanders, regarding them as greedy, stubborn, ungrateful and Calvinist, but she could scarcely in honour abandon them now. Nor, for that matter, could she risk exposing them to a renewed onslaught from the south, perhaps wasting all the precious lives and treasure which had been poured in aid across the North Sea and saying goodbye to any hope of repayment of her numerous loans. So Francis Vere went back to strengthen the bonds uniting the two remaining members of the Triple Alliance, and the war in the Netherlands went on. But it had at least become a limited war and was, in its way, quite useful as a military training ground.

The other major problem which continued to preoccupy the Queen and her Council was, of course, Ireland, where the situation had been steadily deteriorating over the past two years and where the English presence was now effectively confined to the area of the Pale round Dublin. The appointment of a new Lord Deputy had become a matter of urgency but, not surprisingly, no one was eager to be banished to a country which had earned the reputation of a white man's grave, or to accept an office which in recent years had generally led to the financial ruin as well as the death of its incumbent.

The subject came up for discussion again early in July at a meeting which consisted of the Queen, the Earl of Essex, the Lord Admiral, Sir Robert Cecil and Thomas Windebank, Clerk of the Signet. The Queen's favoured candidate was William Knollys, Essex's uncle and one of his principal supporters on the Council. Essex proposed Sir George Carew, an able man but, more to the point, a prominent member of the Cecil faction and one who might with advantage to the Earl be taken out of circulation. The Queen rejected the suggestion out of hand. Essex persisted. The argument grew heated and then suddenly exploded into a violent scene. According to the brief, dispassionate account left by the historian William Camden, who probably had it from Robert Cecil, Essex turned his back on the

Queen in a deliberate gesture of contempt. Elizabeth, thus provoked, lost her temper and boxed his ears, telling him to go and be hanged! The Earl made as if to draw his sword and, as the Lord Admiral hastily made to intervene, swore that he neither could nor would take such an insult from anyone. He would not have endured it even from King Henry VIII himself! There was, one may imagine, a second's horrified silence before Essex flung away and slammed himself out of the room.

It had been an ugly and revealing episode which reflected no particular credit on either of the contestants, both of whom were now standing stiffly on their dignity. Essex, who had retreated to Wanstead, characteristically considered himself the injured party, as he made abundantly clear in a letter to the Queen reproaching her for 'the intolerable wrong you have done both me and yourself'. 'I am sorry to write thus much', he went on, 'for I cannot think your mind so dishonourable but that you punish yourself for it, how little soever you care for me. But I desire whatsoever falls out, that your Majesty should be without excuse, you knowing yourself to be the cause, and all the world wondering at the effect. I was never proud, till your Majesty sought to make me too base. And now since my destiny is no better, my despair shall be as my love was, without repentance . . . I must commend my faith to be judged by Him who judgeth all hearts, since on earth I find no right. Wishing your Majesty all comforts and joys in the world, and no greater punishment for your wrongs to me, than to know the faith of him you have lost, and the baseness of those you shall keep.'

This was a pretty amazing letter for any sixteenth century subject to address to the monarch and William Knollys, writing to his nephew about the middle of July, could only say that 'between her Majesty running into her princely power and your lordship's persisting in your settled resolution, I am so confounded as I know not how nor what to persuade. I will therefore leave it to God's work, to whom I heartily pray to settle your heart in a right course; your Sovereign, your country, and God's cause never having more need of you than now'. Sir William more than hinted that her Majesty would be prepared to accept an apology and ended with a plea that 'if in substance you may have a good peace, I beseech your lordship not to stand upon the form of treaty'.

But Essex refused to budge and a few days later his friend Lord Keeper Egerton took a hand. 'I will not presume to advise you', he wrote, 'but shoot my bolt as near the mark as I can and tell you what I think . . . You are not so far gone but you may well return. The return is safe, but the progress dangerous and desperate in this course you hold. If you have enemies, you do that for them which they could never do for themselves; whilst you leave your friends to open shame and contempt, forsake yourself, overthrow your fortunes, and ruinate your honour and reputation, giving that comfort to our foreign foes, as greater they cannot have . . . You forsake your country when it hath most need of your help and counsel: and lastly, you fail in your indissoluble duty, which you owe to your most gracious Sovereign.'

The best, indeed the only, way out of the present impasse Egerton concluded was 'not to contend and strive, but humbly to submit'. 'When it is evident that great good may ensue of it to your friends, your country and Sovereign, and extreme harm by the contrary, there can be no dishonour or hurt to yield; but in not doing it, is dishonour and impiety. The difficulty, my good Lord, is to conquer yourself, which is the height of all true valour and fortitude.'

This was plain speaking and Essex responded with some even plainer. He repudiated the charge that he was forsaking his country at a time of need. 'If my country had at this time any need of my public service, her Majesty, that governs the same, would not have driven me into a private kind of life.' The only indissoluble duty which he owed the Queen was that of allegiance 'which I never will, nor never can, fail in'. He had been content in the past to do her Majesty the service of a clerk, but could never serve her as a villein or slave.

As for Egerton's advice to yield and submit – 'I can neither yield myself to be guilty, or this imputation laid upon me to be just. I owe so much to the Author of all Truth, as I can never yield falsehood to be truth, nor truth falsehood . . . When the vilest of all indignities are done unto me, doth religion enforce me to sue? Doth God require it? Is it impiety not to do it? What, cannot Princes err? Cannot subjects receive wrong? Is an earthly power or authority infinite? Pardon me, pardon me, my good Lord, I can never subscribe to these principles . . . Let those who mean to make their profit of Princes show to have no sense of Princes' injuries; let them acknowledge an infinite absoluteness on earth, that do not believe in an absolute infiniteness in heaven.'

It would be easy to assume from the tone of this letter that, instead of being asked to say he was sorry for having been rude to the Queen, at the very least Essex's paternity was in question or that he'd been accused of some heinous form of treason. In fact, in the sixteenth century context, the sentiments expressed in it were not far short of treason. If any less favoured individual had stood up in public and said anything of the kind, he would quickly have found himself in serious trouble. But my lord of Essex, it appeared, remained a law unto himself and the Queen continued to ignore him.

As it happened, the Queen had other things on her mind just then, for Lord Burghley was failing at last and Elizabeth was sitting at her old friend's bedside feeding him his gruel. In his last letter to his son, the dying man wrote: 'I pray you diligently and effectually let her Majesty understand how her singular kindness doth overcome my power to acquit it, who though she will not be a mother (remembering all those years when he had tried so hard to get her married), yet she showeth herself by feeding me with her own princely hand, as a careful nurse, and if I may be weaned to feed myself, I shall be more ready to serve her on earth, if not, I hope to be in heaven a servitor for her and God's church.' And he added a postscript. 'Serve God by serving of the Queen, for all other service is indeed bondage to the devil.'

Burghley died on 4 August, having served the Queen for very nearly forty years, and for Elizabeth it was a break with the past more complete than any she had yet known. Her association with William Cecil went back to childhood days when, as a rising young government servant, he had been friendly with her much-loved governess Katherine Ashley. When she was sixteen the princess, who knew an honest man when she saw one, took the opportunity of attaching him to her interests by asking him to act as Surveyor of her landed property at a salary of twenty pounds a year. They kept in discreet touch during the dangerous years which followed and almost her first act as Queen had been to appoint him Principal Secretary of State. 'This judgement I have of you', she said on that occasion, 'that you will not be corrupted by any manner of gift and that you will be faithful to the state; and that without respect of my private will you will give me that counsel which you think best.' She had never had occasion to alter that judgement and their partnership remains something unique in history. Lord Burghley, wrote his friend William Camden, was 'a singular man for honesty, gravity, temperance, industry and justice. Hereunto was added a fluent and elegant speech ... wisdom strengthened by experience and seasoned with exceeding moderation and most approved fidelity ... In a word, the Queen was most happy in so great a Councillor and to his wholesome counsels the state of England for ever shall be beholden'.

When they brought her the news of his death, Elizabeth went away to mourn in private. But she made no attempt on this occasion to hide her grief. It was noticed that for months afterwards she could not speak Burghley's name without tears and would turn aside when other people brought it up. Her godson, John Harington, found this very understandable. When, after all, would the realm see such a man again, or such a mistress have such a servant. 'Well might one weep when the other died', he commented.

Meanwhile, the Earl of Essex, that so much less admirable servant of the state, was still absent from his appointed place and his friends, many of whom had built their own careers on his influence and patronage, were growing increasingly worried. As William Knollys pointed out, this was no time to be away from Court if the Earl wanted any say in the disposal of Lord Burghley's offices. 'Remember, I beseech you', he went on, 'that there is no contesting between sovereignty and obedience; and I fear the longer your lordship doth persist in this careless humour of her Majesty, the more her heart will be hardened; and I pray God your contending with her in this manner do not breed such a hatred in her, as will never be reclaimed.'

Shortly after this, Essex was summoned to attend a Council meeting at the Lord Keeper's house. He came, but declined to take any part in the proceedings unless the Queen agreed to see and listen to him first. She would not and he went away again. How long the stalemate might have continued is impossible to say, but before the end of August outside events supervened and made the domestic quarrels of the English Court seem more than usually irrelevant. On the fourteenth of the month the army in Ireland, some four thousand men under the command of Sir Henry Bagenal, had marched out of Armagh in a show of strength to relieve the garrison of a key fort on the Blackwater river, only to be outflanked and overwhelmed by the rebel forces under the Earl of Tyrone. Bagenal himself and half his army, including some of the best officers, were killed and the survivors driven back in disorder to Armagh.

The disaster at the Yellow Ford brought the running sore of Ireland to a festering head. The news also brought the Earl of Essex back to town. He was present at a Council meeting on the 22nd, but still the Queen would not see him, nor would she accept a written memorandum of advice on the Irish crisis, and it began at last to dawn on Essex that this time she was not playing games. Her Majesty had been heard to remark that the Earl had played long enough upon her and that now she meant to play awhile upon him, 'and so stand as much upon her greatness as he hath done upon stomach'. In other words, as she had already made clear in messages to Essex, he must apologise and 'submit' before he could hope to return even to limited favour.

Essex appeared prominently among the five hundred black-hooded mourners at Lord Burghley's funeral and was noticed to carry 'the heaviest countenance of the company', although at least one cynical observer was moved to speculate on how much of this gloom was due to grief for the departed and how much to 'his own disfavours'.

The Earl vanished to Wanstead again as soon as the funeral was over and conveniently went down with an ague. His fever may or may not have been genuine, but it did offer both sides an opportunity to retreat from their heavily entrenched positions without too much loss of face. Elizabeth, always concerned in cases of sickness, sent the invalid a kind message, followed by one of her own doctors, and let it be known that the gentlemen of the household might visit him without causing offence. By the second week of September he had recovered and was back at Court and apparently back in favour. By the beginning of October, Robert Cecil, writing to Thomas Edmondes in Paris, mentioned casually that any misunderstanding between her Majesty and his lordship 'was now clearly removed, and all very well settled again'.

This time, though, few people believed the reconciliation to be genuine. Francis Bacon, in a letter of congratulation to the Earl on his reinstatement, hoped that this would be the last of his 'eclipses' and that 'upon this experience may grow more perfect knowledge, and upon knowledge more true consent' between him and the Queen. But from his own knowledge of his patron, Bacon was probably more optimistic than convinced. What passed between Elizabeth and Essex in private is a matter of conjecture – all the same, it seems logical to suppose that this was the occasion of the Queen's warning to content himself with displeasing her and insolently despising her person, but to be very careful indeed of touching her sceptre. Of the numerous warnings Essex received during the course of his career it was this one, above all others, which he would have been wise to heed, but there is little indication that he did so. Within a matter of weeks he was back at his old tricks of trying to bully the Queen into giving him Lord Burghley's influential and potentially very profitable Mastership of the Court of Wards. The Queen took no notice. Burghley's Lord Treasurership went to Lord Buckhurst and, in the fullness of time, the Court of Wards was bestowed on the dead man's son.

There had been another notable death that summer when, on 10 September, Philip of Spain finally succumbed to the disease which was consuming him. It's hardly likely that Elizabeth shed tears for her old antagonist, but his going snapped another link and it is tempting to wonder if, when the news reached her, her thoughts went back to that long-ago summer when she had flirted discreetly with her sister's husband in the gardens of Hampton Court, while Queen Mary waited in desperate, deluded optimism to bear the half-Hapsburg son who would have altered the course of European history. Nearly half a century had gone by since Philip's brief sojourn in England as Mary Tudor's consort, but Elizabeth would certainly not have forgotten her first and only personal contact with the man to whom she was destined to be bound by ties of enmity as compelling in their way as those of love.

But the Queen had small leisure for dwelling on the past. Now, in what were to be the closing years of her life, she must turn to face new challenges to her authority and to the security of her realm – challenges as urgent and dangerous in their way as any she had met before and which were to drain the last of her strength.

VII
The General
of Our Gracious Empress

Now Scipio sails to Affrick far from home,
The Lord of Hosts and battles be his guide;
Now when green trees begin to bud and bloom,
On Irish seas Eliza's ships shall ride:
A warlike band of worthy knights, I hope,
Are arm'd for fight, a bloody brunt to bide,
With rebels shall both might and manhood cope,
Our country's right and quarrel to be tried:
Right makes Wrong blush, and Truth bids Falsehood fly,
The sword is drawn, Tyrone's dispatch draws nigh.

The Irish problem, now occupying the attention of Queen and Council to the exclusion of almost everything else, was not, of course, a new one. It had been a matter of intermittent concern throughout the Tudor century and its origins, which were geographical and ethnic quite as much if not more than political, went back even further.

The Plantagenet kings, with their numerous other outside interests, had been content to exercise their feudal overlordship of Ireland at second-hand and, apart from a few brief personal incursions, had left control of the island's affairs in the hands of the Anglo-Norman feudal barons, 'planted' there after the Conquest. These families, notably the Burkes, the Butlers of Ormonde and the Fitzgeralds of Desmond and Kildare, had intermarried extensively with the Irish tribal aristocracy and over the years had become almost totally absorbed into Irish tribal society. But so long as they were left undisturbed to pursue their private struggles for ascendancy among themselves and over the native clans or septs, they were willing enough to stay loyal to the Crown.

This mutually convenient state of affairs began to come to an end with the arrival of the new dynasty. The mighty Geraldines of Kildare had taken the Yorkist side in the English civil wars and Ireland therefore became a natural breeding-ground for Yorkist resistance, forcing the first Tudor monarch to intervene. Henry VII's attempt to impose a form of direct rule met with only partial success, and when the Yorkist challenge fizzled out, he let the experiment lapse, recalling his Lord Deputy and allowing the great Earl of Kildare to resume his position of uncrowned king.

The next encounter came in the 1530s when Henry VIII and Thomas Cromwell, conscious of the danger of papal interference in their revolutionary doings via the Irish back door, began to place new English officials in key offices and to establish a permanent presence in Dublin, to the acute irritation of the 'old' English. The Fitzgeralds revolted, but on their own they were no match for Tudor imperialism and their reign was finally brought to an end by a judicious mixture of treachery and gunpowder. In 1541 Henry adopted the title of King of Ireland and embarked on a determined campaign to anglicise and civilise the wild Irish, persuading some of the chieftains – notably the O'Neills of Ulster – to surrender their tribal independence in exchange for English-style peerages and an oath of allegiance. Again, this policy enjoyed a superficial short-term success, but the task of grafting an alien system of law, language and land tenure onto a primitive and uncomprehending pastoral society by 'circumspect and politic ways' was beyond the capabilities of the Tudor machine. The Earl of Surrey, who held the office of Lord Lieutenant in 1520, had given it as his poor opinion that Ireland would never be brought to good order and due subjection but only by conquest, and time was to prove him right. Nevertheless, conquest continued to be regarded as a last resort by successive Tudor governments.

Under Mary, and later under Elizabeth, efforts were made to speed up the civilising process by bringing in more English settlers who would, it was hoped, insert a solid and industrious wedge whose loyalty could be relied on in time of trouble. Richard Grenville and Walter Raleigh both invested heavily in these new 'plantations' and so, to a lesser extent, did Edmund Spenser the poet. But the immigrants led a precarious existence, constantly harassed by the wild Irish, much as the early American colonists were harassed by wild Indians, and few stood the course. Many of them, indeed, rented their holdings back to the dispossessed tribes, thus defeating the

whole object of the exercise and laying the foundations of the notorious absentee landlord syndrome. By the end of the 1580s, despite the
endeavours of successive Elizabethan Lord Deputies to bring the
Queen's ungrateful Irish subjects the benefits of the rule of her law,
the fact had to be faced that Ireland was as far, if not further, from
becoming peacefully integrated into the English social system as it
had been in the previous generation, and by this time, of course, the
religious aspect was providing additional complications.

Henry VIII's Reformation had made no martyrs in Ireland for the
sufficient reason that, St Patrick regardless, the indigenous population of the Island of Saints continued to set very much greater store
by their own charms and spells and esoteric deities than on the
Roman form of worship – in its way just as foreign to the Gaelic
culture as the doctrines evolved by Martin Luther, John Calvin or the
second Henry Tudor. But Ireland's long isolation from the main-
stream of European life was coming to an end and, as the shock waves
of the ideological revolution convulsing Western Christendom
spread inexorably outwards, certain Irishmen began to grasp the fact
that here was a weapon capable of being turned against the Anglo-
Saxon intruder. The tide of religious fanaticism which was to cause
such untold suffering in the unhappy island did not reach its flood
until the next century, but already it offered a focal point of resistance, a force potentially powerful enough to unite the perpetually
squabbling tribes and transform their localised resentments into a
holy war to drive out the heretics.

The first manifestation of this new initiative showed itself in the
Earl of Desmond's rebellion of 1579–80. The rising was savagely
suppressed but thereafter there was a fairly constant traffic between
Ireland, Spain and Rome, as the missionary priests of the Counter-
Reformation worked to consolidate the Catholic revival, especially in
the south and west. After the failure of the 1588 Armada Philip
began seriously to reflect on the strategic advantages of establishing
a bridgehead on Irish soil – the ill-fated expedition of 1596 had, in
fact, been intended for an Irish destination – and Irish leaders,
through their priestly emissaries, continued to press urgently for
Spanish aid.

In the circumstances, therefore, it was ironical that the crisis situation facing Queen Elizabeth's government in 1598 should have originated in the north, in Ulster, the most backward and least Christian-
ised of all the Irish provinces. It was ironical, too, that Ulster's
paramount chief should have been by far the most sophisticated and
able figure Ireland had yet produced, an astute and plausible politi-

cian as well as an efficient military commander. But Hugh O'Neill, Earl of Tyrone, had been brought up in England at the Sidneys' great house at Penshurst, and had learned his soldiering serving with the English army in Ireland, absorbing all the enemy could teach him and storing it away for future use. A devious and patient man, he was content to bide his time and his defection, when it came, was well-thought-out and well-organised.

Although careful to present his cause as a crusade for the extirpa-tion of heresy – the only banner under which he could hope for Spanish support and the equally essential support of his fellow chief-tains – Tyrone's real motives were political. He was determined to preserve the old Celtic order in his own territories and with it, of course, his own local supremacy; but there is little doubt that he also dreamed of seeing the English driven out altogether and of setting himself up as High King of an independent and re-celticized Ireland. In 1598 that dream looked tantalisingly close to becoming a reality, for his brilliant victory at the Yellow Ford had lit a spark of revolt which ran like wildfire through the whole country. Everywhere the tribes were out, emerging from their impenetrable bogs and moun-tains to indulge themselves in an orgy of killing, burning and looting. The English settlers, among them Edmund Spenser, had to run for their lives to the doubtful sanctuary of the towns and even the Pale itself could no longer be regarded as safe. This was Tyrone's moment and an opportunity for mischief-making which Spain could hardly fail to exploit. Unless decisive action were taken quickly Ireland would be lost – a disaster in terms of England's national security and prestige which was not to be contemplated.

An army big enough and strong enough to reconquer the island and re-establish the authority of the Crown would somehow have to be raised and dispatched before the new King of Spain could provide the artillery which Tyrone lacked. This was not in dispute. The tricky problem now exercising Queen and Council was the identity of the new Lord Deputy and commander-in-chief. Elizabeth suggested Lord Mountjoy who, as Charles Blount, had first attracted her atten-tion ten years earlier and as a result had been challenged to a duel by the brash young Earl of Essex. Mountjoy had subsequently be-come a prominent member of the Essex set – his brother had married Lady Leicester and he himself was well known to be the lover of the Earl's fascinating sister, Penelope Rich. All the same, Essex opposed his friend's appointment. He was inexperienced, too bookish and 'not considerable enough by his fortunes and alliances' to attract a follow-ing. Such an important job required 'some prime man of the nobility, strong in power, honour and wealth, in favour with military men, who had been before general of an army'. A description by which, as few people failed to notice, the Earl 'seemed to point the finger at himself'.

Did Essex really want the Irish command, or was he by some sinister but unspecified means manoeuvred into it by his enemies, as some of his biographers have hinted? In fact, he was, as he himself admitted, tied by the reputation he had worked so hard to build. If, as he claimed, he was indeed the greatest man in the kingdom, then he could hardly shirk the greatest task when it presented itself – 'his honour could not stand without undertaking it'. In any case, Elizabeth had made up her mind. 'Into Ireland I go', wrote the Earl at the beginning of January 1599, 'the Queen hath irrevocably decreed it.'

It seemed a strange decision, both then and later. Mountjoy's secretary, Fynes Moryson, remarked that his lordship's embracing of military courses and his popular estimation had made him so much suspected of his sovereign, 'as his greatness was now judged to depend as much on her majesty's fear of him, as her love of him. And in this respect he might seem to the queen most unfit for that service ... The vulgar gave ominous acclamations to his enterprise; but wiser men rather wished than hoped happy effects either to his private or the public good.' Another contemporary observer was frankly puzzled. Robert Markham, writing from the Court to John Harington, who was to go with the army in Ireland, reported that 'in all outward semblance' the Queen had forgiven Essex for his shocking behaviour of the previous summer and was now apparently content to place every confidence in the man 'who so lately sought other treatment at her hands'; but her real feelings were anyone's guess and 'what betydeth the Lord Deputy is known to Him only who knoweth all'. For his part, Markham expected trouble and went on to warn the Queen's merry godson (who had recently been in disgrace with his formidable godmother for writing naughty verses to amuse the maids of honour) to be very careful not to meddle in politics while he was away, 'nor give your jesting too freely among those you know not'. There would be spies in the camp and it was a time when sensible men kept their opinions to themselves.

The general atmosphere of foreboding was intensified that February when Dr John Hayward brought out his history of *The First Part of the Life and Reign of King Henry IV* and dedicated it to the Earl of Essex. Eighteen months earlier, when the Lord Chamberlain's Men were performing William Shakespeare's *Richard II* in which that monarch is deposed by his cousin Henry Bolingbroke, it had seemed to the

more politically aware members of the audience that the playwright
had been drawing from life in his description of the usurper's methods of courting popularity.

> *Off goes his bonnet to an oyster-wench;*
> *A brace of draymen bid God speed him well,*
> *And had the tribute of his supple knee,*
> *With 'Thanks, my countrymen, my loving friends';*
> *As were our England in reversion his,*
> *And he our subjects' next degree in hope.*

The historical parallel was far from exact and certainly it would be
difficult to trace any noticeable resemblance between Elizabeth
Tudor and the unfortunate Richard Plantagenet, but the fact that the
romantic image of Essex as a second Bolingbroke should have gained
even a passing currency demonstrates the strength of his hold on the
public imagination. The Queen was well aware of the existence of the
comparison and took furious exception to John Hayward's little
book. Yet, at the same time, she was entrusting Essex with a large and
well-equipped army which would be operating within the bounda-
ries of her own realm. She was allowing him virtually untrammelled
power in the exercise of his command and had also, though reluctantly, agreed to sign a licence enabling him to return to England at
his own discretion.

So why did she do it? The suggestion that it was all part of a
deep-laid plot, master-minded by Robert Cecil and intended to give
Essex enough rope to hang himself, is surely about as paranoiac as
the Earl himself. The Irish crisis posed a real and urgent threat, not
something to play politics with, and raising the army had just about
scraped the treasury bare. If Cecil was planning the destruction of his
rival, he could hardly have picked a more expensive and chancy way
of doing it. A more likely, if less dramatic, explanation is that the
Queen, as much as the Earl, had found herself a prisoner of his
reputation. In spite of all that had happened since, the glory of Cadiz
still clung to Essex, giving him, both in the eyes of the general public
and of the military caste, an inalienable right to lead any major
expedition. Besides this, of course, his position as Earl Marshal did
give him a proscriptive right to command the Queen's armies, a fact
Elizabeth could scarcely ignore without courting further domestic
uproar. Then, again, the choice of suitable alternatives was severely
limited, Walter Raleigh having wisely refused to become involved.
Service in Ireland was notoriously unpopular at all levels, but the
soldiers would follow the magic name of Essex where they might not

follow anybody else and one is driven to the conclusion that, at a time when speed was of the essence, Elizabeth simply took the line of least resistance and hoped for the best – though her misgivings must certainly have been as strong as Robert Markham's.

Essex's own mood see-sawed between over-confidence and gloom. 'I have beaten Knollys and Mountjoy in the Council', he wrote to John Harington, 'and by God I will beat Tyrone in the field; for nothing worthy her Majesty's honour hath yet been achieved.' But in a letter to Lord Willoughby he spoke of his 'private problems and nightly disputations', dwelling with customary obsessiveness on all the 'practising enemies' who would take advantage of his absence to drop their poison in the Queen's ear. The war itself would be hard and while failure was dangerous, too much success would only lead to further envy and suspicion.

By the time the new Lord Lieutenant left to take up his duties towards the end of March, his gloom had deepened. Elizabeth had vetoed his appointment of the young Earl of Southampton as General of the Horse, nor would she allow his stepfather, Sir Christopher Blount, to be made a member of the Council of Ireland and Essex was already convinced that everyone at home was against him. He complained constantly and fluently of lack of support and understanding, and whined that he was being sent to perform an exceptionally difficult task without the inward comfort or outward demonstration of her Majesty's favour. The Earl was not helping himself by this characteristic orgy of self-pity, but no one minimised the formidable nature of his task.

To the average Elizabethan, Ireland was a soggy, savage wilderness where no sensible person would willingly set foot. The Spaniards soon came to regard it as a land fit only for the Prince of Hell and the average civilised Englishman agreed with them. The English could see nothing romantic or even faintly admirable in the ancient Celtic tribal system. To them the habits and customs of the wild Irish were barbarous, unhygienic and generally just plain nasty. They were horrified by the backwardness, the filth, the inefficiency and laziness of a people whose favourite sports appeared to be cattle-raiding and killing one another, and were shocked by the tyranny of their chiefs. To the soldier, Ireland offered no possibility of profit or glory, but only an excellent chance of dying miserably of dysentery or marsh fever – if, that is, he escaped being knocked on the head by some axe- or club-wielding tribesman. Elizabethan soldiers were no strangers to hardship but Irish hardships held special terrors, perhaps because of the untamed and uncharted nature of their surroundings.

On the continent, in France or the Netherlands, the landscape was at least tolerably familiar, with towns and highways and cultivated fields, the enemy recognisable as a fellow human being and not a howling hairy savage in a wolf pelt. Usually soaked to the skin, cold, disorientated and fed up, the troops grumbled that they would rather go to the gallows than the Irish wars and deserted in droves at every opportunity.

To the army commander, campaigning in Ireland presented tactical and logistical problems of an acute kind. It was, of course, classic guerilla war territory, with all the initial advantages on the side of an enemy fighting on his own ground, especially an enemy apparently able to subsist on grass and to be virtually independent of clothing, shelter and other such basic amenities of life. Communications and supply became a nightmare in a country where such roads as existed were often impassable to wheeled traffic and rain fell with deadly persistence. Corruption, that universal bugbear of sixteenth century warfare, was rampant – with their pay, as always, in arrears, the soldiers sold their arms and even their clothes to Irish middlemen who sold them back to the rebels at a substantial profit – and an additional dreamlike quality was provided by the numbers of Irish who joined the English army, melting away or changing sides as the fancy took them.

Although Tyrone, more than any other Irish leader, had been able to unite and discipline his forces and arm them, at least in part, with pikes and other modern weapons, the English had, or should have had, the edge in superior organisation, technique and equipment. But soldiering in Ireland would always be a specialised affair, very different from continental war as understood by the professionals and demanding special talents and expertise which few professionals, had had the chance to develop. Certainly Essex, himself no more than an enthusiastic and occasionally lucky amateur, had never developed them and from the start he floundered hopelessly out of his depth.

It had been agreed in London that his first and most important operation must be to lead the army into Tyrone's Ulster power-base and there seek to destroy the rebellion at its source. But on arrival in Dublin, the Lord Lieutenant allowed the Council of Ireland to persuade him to postpone the march north until later in the season and deal first with the troubles in Leinster and Munster, where the rebels had recently been reinforced by Tyrone. Accordingly, early in May, he set off on a circular tour of the south, penetrating as far as Limerick. 'This people against whom we fight hath able bodies, good use of the arms they carry, boldness enough to attempt, and quickness in apprehending any advantage they see offered them', he reported to the Privy Council from Kilkenny, where he had been welcomed by the townsfolk with speeches and rush-strewn streets. 'The advantage we have is more horse, which will command all champaigns; in our order, which these savages have not; and in the extraordinary courage and spirit of our men of quality. But, to meet with these helps, the rebels fight in woods and bogs, where horse are utterly unserviceable; they use the advantage of lightness and swiftness in going off, when they find our order too strong for them to encounter; and, as for the last advantage, I protest to your lordships it doth as much trouble me as help me. For my remembering how unequal a wager it is to adventure the lives of noblemen and gentlemen against rogues and naked beggars, makes me take more care to contain our best men than to use their courages against the rebels.'

Essex returned to Dublin on 11 July, with nothing to show for his southern jaunt but the loss of a third of his army and the waste of two months' valuable time. He expected blame and wrote defensively to London, still harping on his old theme of the enemies waiting to stab him in the back and who would now, in the dark, give him wound upon wound. The Queen was not impressed by this sort of talk, she had heard it all too often before; nor was she impressed by her general's performance in the field and on 19 July she despatched the first of a series of stinging rebukes.

'If you compare the time that is run on', complained her Majesty, 'and the excessive charges that is spent, with the effect of anything wrought by this voyage . . . you needs must think that we, that have the eyes of foreign Princes upon our actions, and have the hearts of people to comfort and cherish, who groan under the burden of continual levies and impositions, which are occasioned by these late actions, can little please ourselves hitherto with anything that hath been effected . . . Whereunto we will add this one thing, that doth more displease us than any charge or expense that happens, which is, that it must be the Queen of England's fortune (who hath held down the greatest enemy she had), to make a base bush kern to be accounted so famous a rebel, as to be a person against whom so many thousands of foot and horse, besides the force of all the nobility of that kingdom must be thought too little to be employed.'

This, of course, was the heart of the matter and Essex's failure to go north and confront Tyrone was rousing Elizabeth to a fury of frustration. 'When we call to mind . . . the scandal it would be to our honour to leave that proud rebel unassailed . . . we must now plainly charge you, according to the duty you owe us, so to unite soundness of judgement to the zeal you have to do us service, and with all speed to pass thither in such order, as the axe may be put to the root of that tree.'

The Queen was angry that Essex, in direct disobedience to her orders, had made Southampton General of the Horse and she was going to be even angrier when she discovered how many knighthoods he had conferred, but she remained rigidly determined to hold him to the Ulster expedition. 'You know right well', she reminded him, 'when we yielded to this excessive charge it was laid upon no other foundation than that to which yourself did ever advise us as much as any, which was to assail the Northern Traitor, and to plant garrisons in his country, it being ever your firm opinion, amongst others of our Council, to conclude that all that was done in other kind in Ireland, was but waste and consumption'.

The Earl had been confident that he alone could deal with Tyrone and Elizabeth was not going to let him forget it, pointing out that he'd been given ample facilities to do the job as well as power and authority 'more ample than ever any had, or ever shall have'. So, concluded her Majesty, it was more than time that he stopped breaking the soldiers' hearts and wasting his strength on 'inferior rebels' and did something to justify the large promises made at his departure, 'to the intent that all these six months' charges prove not fruitless'. To ram the point home (and perhaps to insure against any rash impulse on his lordship's part), she revoked his licence to return. He was now on no account to leave his post until he had 'reduced things in the north', and even then not without prior permission.

To the unhappy Essex who, like others before him, was learning how very different Ireland looked from Dublin than it did from London, the Queen's reproaches were hammer blows on an already bruised ego. He had staked his whole future on his ability to succeed where others had failed only to find himself failing more dismally than the rest. In the present disease-ridden and demoralised state of the army he knew that any attempt to confront Tyrone must end in still further humiliation, but the Queen's attitude made it plain that she was in no mood to listen to excuses and all the time the Cecil influence at Court would be growing stronger. It was a desperate situation which seemed to call for a desperate solution and wild schemes were flitting through his head for taking two or three thousand men, landing in Wales, where he could count on a following, and then marching on London to remove his enemies from the Council by force of arms.

The Lord Lieutenant discussed this plan with his two most intimate cronies, Southampton and Christopher Blount, who, so they later deposed, did everything they could to dissuade him, suggesting that he should instead seek a private interview with the Queen, taking with him no more than 'a competent number' of hand-picked supporters for his personal protection. First, though, he must make at least a token appearance in Ulster.

Essex had already, by the middle of August, been in secret contact with Tyrone, who had sent messages via an intermediary that if the Queen's deputy would follow his lead, he would make him the greatest man that ever was in England. It was the first step on a slippery path but, when Essex led the remnants of his army north at the beginning of September, he probably had no real treasonable intent in mind – his only thought being somehow to find a way out of his present intolerable predicament.

The armies met at Ardee in Louth, where Tyrone paraded his forces just out of range in a nicely calculated display of strength. He then sent to suggest a parley, offering his 'submission' and, after some public huffing and puffing by Essex, the two leaders met at the ford of Bellaclynth. They talked alone together for half an hour and it seems more than likely that Essex poured out his grievances and received offers of support – upon conditions. Tyrone outlined his peace terms, which amounted to little short of Irish autonomy, and Essex promised to deliver them to the Queen. At a second meeting, held on the following day with commissioners from both sides present, a six week truce was agreed, renewable for periods of six weeks until May 1600. The rebels would remain in possession of all the territory they held on the date of this agreement and the English undertook to establish no more forts or garrisons.

The Irish leader then retired into 'the heart of his country' with every reason to feel satisfied with the summer's work. He had made the Queen of England's great army dance to his piping and the Queen's most famous general look uncommonly foolish at negligible cost to himself. He was confidently expecting Spanish reinforcements to arrive before the spring and had gained all the time he needed. Essex, on the other hand, had gained nothing – it would be difficult to disguise his arrangement with Tyrone as anything but abject surrender, and his unwitnessed conversation with a notorious traitor would obviously be capable of the worst possible interpretations.

When the Queen heard what was going on, she wrote: 'We that trust you with a kingdom are far from mistrusting you with a traitor, yet both for comeliness, example, and your own discharge, we marvel you would carry it no better.' Essex had not yet dared to tell her about the terms of the truce, so that her Majesty, as she tartly pointed out, could not tell 'but by divination' what to think of the issue of his proceedings. She was sure of only one thing, 'that you have prospered so ill for us by your warfare, as we cannot but be very jealous lest you should be as well overtaken by the treaty'. 'To trust this traitor upon oath', she went on, 'is to trust a devil upon his religion. To trust him upon pledges is a mere illusory. . . . And, therefore, whatever order you take with him, yet unless he yield to have garrisons planted in his own country to master him . . . and to come over to us personally here, we shall doubt you do but piece up a hollow peace, and so the end prove worse than the beginning.'

Whether or not Essex actually received this letter, written on 17 September, seems doubtful, but in any case he had already made up his mind. He must see the Queen and make her understand how impossible it all was. He could not – would not – stay in Ireland another week. On the twenty-fourth he handed over or, more accurately, flung his responsibilities to Archbishop Loftus and the Earl of Ormonde and, taking the Earl of Southampton and a small group of kindred spirits, set off on a mad dash for home. After reaching England the little party rode hard down through the Midlands and by the early hours of Friday, 28 September, were clattering through the streets of Westminster. The Court was at Nonesuch, which meant crossing the river by the Lambeth ferry and more riding through the Surrey lanes, muddy from a wet autumn.

If Essex had a plan in his head, it was to take the Queen by surprise and this time to get his story in first, and to begin with it looked as if his crazy gamble might be going to succeed. 'Upon Michaelmas Eve, about ten o'clock in the morning, my Lord of Essex lighted at Court Gate in post, and made all haste up to the Presence, and so to the Privy Chamber, and stayed not till he came to the Queen's bedchamber, where he found the Queen newly up, the hair about her face; he kneeled unto her, kissed her hands, and had some private speech with her, which seemed to give him great contentment; for coming from her Majesty to go shift himself in his chamber, he was very pleasant, and thanked God, though he had suffered much trouble and storms abroad, he found a sweet calm at home. 'Tis much wondered at here, that he went so boldly to her Majesty's presence, she not being ready, and he so full of dirt and mire, that his very face was full of it.'

Thus Rowland Whyte's account of this famous confrontation between the gaunt, haggard old woman, the scanty white hair, usually so carefully concealed, hanging in wisps over her unpainted face, and the sweaty, mud-spattered man kneeling breathless at her feet. News of the Earl's approach had, in fact, preceded him by about fifteen minutes, but it had not reached the Queen and she therefore had no means of knowing whether or not he had brought his army with him, whether the palace might already be in his hands, her own handful of largely ornamental guards overwhelmed and she herself a prisoner. It was a nasty moment, not made any easier by the fact that she had been caught unawares, half-dressed and without her wig, but Elizabeth showed no signs of discomposure. Thinking on her feet, she smiled kindly on her unwelcome visitor, spoke to him soothingly and got rid of him as soon as she could by suggesting that he should wash and change before they talked again. Within an hour he was back and stayed with her until dinner-time. Still all seemed to be well and Essex went down to dinner flanked by his friends the Earls of Worcester and Rutland, and the Lords Mountjoy and Rich, while the ladies and gentlemen, avid with curiosity over this unexpected development, clustered round to hear his traveller's tales of Ireland. Only Mr Secretary, with Walter Raleigh, the Lords Grey and Cobham, the Earl of Shrewsbury, the Lord Admiral and Lord Thomas Howard remained aloof. Clearly some kind of showdown was imminent and all those whose careers and livelihoods depended on keeping in with the right people were sniffing the air like dogs. 'As God help me', wrote Rowland Whyte on that dramatic Friday, 'it is a very dangerous time here; for the heads of both factions being here, a man cannot tell how to govern himself towards them.'

In the afternoon Essex went to the Queen again, 'but found her much changed in that small time, for she began to call him to question for his return, and was not satisfied in the manner of his coming away; and leaving all things at so great hazard'. By this time, of course, Elizabeth had been able to take stock of the situation and to realise that this was not, after all, the armed coup she had feared. On the contrary, the great man had, in effect, run home to mother and was still apparently relying on her indulgence, or her dependence, to save him from the consequences of his gross mismanagement of her affairs and betrayal of her trust. But the days when Essex could sweet talk his way back into the Queen's good graces were long past. For nearly ten years she had put up with his tantrums, his bad manners, his arrogance and his broken promises, at the same time jealously watching his power and his prestige increase. Now that he had presented her with the long awaited opportunity to cut him down to size she meant to make full use of it. But she was still feeling her way in a highly volatile atmosphere, and when she finally dismissed him with a curt command to confer with her Council she can have had no idea that she would never see him again.

Only four members of the Council were actually present at Nonesuch and Essex spent an hour trying unsuccessfully to justify his actions to them. Meanwhile messengers were sent riding urgently to summon the rest and, late that evening, the Court heard that my Lord of Essex had been ordered to keep his chamber. Next day the full Council assembled and sat in conclave all morning before calling the Earl to appear before them. The clerks were sent out and behind closed doors Robert Cecil proceeded to read out the list of his crimes. He had contemptuously disobeyed the Queen's instructions by returning to England; many of his letters from Ireland had been presumptuous; his proceedings in Ireland had been contrary to what was agreed before he left; his coming away had been rash; he had been over-bold in going to her Majesty's presence in her bedchamber, and he had made too many idle knights. Significantly, there was no mention of his incautious dealings with Tyrone and outsiders heard that never man answered 'with more gravity or discretion to these matters laid to his charge'. After three hours' grilling he was released and returned to his quarters, while the Council deliberated for only fifteen minutes before going to make their report to the Queen. She listened without comment and told them she would think it over.

Some time during the weekend Essex received a visit from his old friend and mentor Francis Bacon, who said consolingly (and surprisingly for such a normally percipient individual) that he thought this present trouble was only a mist which would soon clear away. But he went on to urge his lordship not to try and pretend that the truce with Tyrone was anything but an inglorious shuffling up of 'a prosecution which was not very fortunate', not to let the Queen think she would be obliged to send him back to Ireland and, above all, to continue to seek access to her, 'seriously, sportingly, every way'. This might have been good advice in different circumstances but neither Francis Bacon nor anyone else, except perhaps Robert Cecil, had yet begun to grasp the real nature of the Queen's resentment against her former favourite, or the bitterness of her fury over the Irish debacle. By Monday morning she had made up her mind about the Earl's immediate future and Essex was informed that he was to be committed to the custody of the Lord Keeper at York House, there to remain during her Majesty's pleasure.

It was a decision clearly intended to make her displeasure manifest and, at the same time, to take the heat out of the situation. A period of house arrest, which no one expected to last more than a few weeks,

in the charge of a man well known to be his friend, was not likely
to rouse even the most fervent Essex man to drastic action, but
London was already filling up with a riff-raff of deserters from Ireland, 'all sorts of knights, captains, officers and soldiers', whose presence increased the risk of disturbance and also, incidentally, added
fresh fuel to the Queen's simmering rage.

John Harington, who was among those who had followed their
general home and was besides a recipient of an Irish knighthood,
soon discovered this to be one of the occasions when her Majesty's
demeanour 'left no doubtings whose daughter she was'. His first
encounter with his godmother was not auspicious. 'What, did the
fool bring you too?' she snorted. 'Go back to your business!' 'She
chafed much', Harington was to recall some years later, 'walked
fastly to and fro, looked with discomposure in her visage; and, I
remember, she catched my girdle when I kneeled to her, and swore,
"By God's Son I am no Queen; that *man* is above me. Who gave him
command to come here so soon? I did send him on other business." '
Elizabeth then insisted on seeing the diary which her godson had
kept during the Irish campaign and swore again, 'by God's Son, we
were all idle knaves, and the Lord Deputy worse, for wasting our time
and her commands in such wise.' Harington did his best to explain
about the peculiar difficulties and problems to be met with in Ireland,
but found it impossible to make her listen, 'for her choler did outrun
all reason'. However, after some four or five days, he received a
summons to Whitehall and the Queen, in calmer mood, put him
through a searching interrogation. 'Until I come to heaven', wrote Sir
John, 'I shall never come before a statelier judge again, nor one that
can temper majesty, wisdom, learning, choler, and favour, better than
her Highness did at that time.' All the same, when he was bid 'Go
home', he did not stay to be bidden twice. 'If all the Irish rebels had
been at my heels, I should not have had better speed, for I did now
flee from one whom I both loved and feared too.'

Meanwhile, the prisoner at York House had fallen sick, suffering
from nervous collapse aggravated by dysentery, 'the Irish flux',
which he had brought back with him from Dublin. 'He is grown very
ill and weak by Grief', reported Rowland Whyte, 'and craves nothing
more than that he may quickly know what her Majesty will do with
him; he eats little, sleeps less, and only sustains life by continual
drinking, which increases the Rheum.' There seems no reason to
doubt that on this occasion Essex's mental and physical distress was
genuine enough and, as the weeks went by with no hint of any
softening in the Queen's attitude, sympathy for his plight increased.

No official explanation of his mysterious disgrace had yet been given out and the Londoners, whose special favourite he was, were naturally growing restive, the more so since rumour had it that all the Lords of the Council had spoken in favour of his release. All the usual indicators as to the state of public opinion – ale-house talk, sermons and broadsheets – were pointing to storm and obviously it was high time the Queen took some action to justify herself.

At the end of the legal term it was customary for the Lord Keeper to deliver an exhortation to the people in the Court of Star Chamber – this being the Privy Council wearing its judicial hat – and, after some hesitation, Elizabeth made up her mind to use this opportunity to issue a statement listing the Earl's offences. Francis Bacon thought she was making a mistake and warned that such a one-sided proceeding would lead to complaints 'that my lord was wounded upon his back, and that justice had her balance taken from her, which ever consisted of an accusation and defence'. At the same time, Bacon came out strongly against any form of open trial, pointing out that Essex was an eloquent, well-spoken man who would also enjoy the advantage of overwhelming public sympathy; that, in short, the Queen was likely to come off worst in a public examination of the matter, and he therefore advised her to find some way of wrapping it up privately.

To be told that she stood in danger of losing a popularity contest with Essex confirmed the Queen's deepest fears and did nothing to improve her temper. Nevertheless, she stuck to her decision and, indeed, it is not easy to see what else she could have done at this juncture. To have climbed down and restored Essex to his former attendance 'with some addition of honour to take away discontent', as Bacon suggested, would not merely have been a stupendous sacrifice of pride but, more seriously, would undoubtedly have been taken by the Essex faction as a confession of weakness to be seized on and exploited. On the other hand, the time for a trial was not yet. Elizabeth knew as well as anyone that if and when that time arrived, the government must be in a position to present a cast-iron case.

Accordingly, on 29 November, all the privy councillors and judges assembled in the Star Chamber to make a public declaration 'for the satisfaction of the world' of the Earl of Essex's imprisonment, and 'for the reformation of divers abuses offered to her Majesty and her Council . . . by many dangerous libels cast abroad in Court, city and country, as also by table and alehouse talk abroad, both in city and country, to the great scandal of her Majesty and her Council.' There were many seditious people spread abroad to breed rebellion, declared Lord Keeper Egerton sternly, who had been uttering false and slanderous speeches against the Queen and her advisers concerning 'the marshalling of the affairs and state of Ireland'. Such people were no better than traitors, and he straightly charged all judges, justices and other officers to make stringent efforts to bring them to book.

Egerton then went on to deal with Irish affairs in detail. Far from being unreasonable or neglectful, the Queen, he said, had shown her special care for the government and good of her subjects in Ireland by sending her most famous commander against the rebels 'with so large a commission as never had any before . . . and that for the doing of this service, there was such an army, and such provision in every way, as the Earl himself could ask or thought fit'. But the plain facts were that my lord had acted 'clean contrary' to the plan of campaign he himself had helped to formulate. He had 'frivolously spent and consumed her Majesty's treasure, victuals and munition, and lost most part of his army'. He had conferred privately with the enemy and discussed a peace on such unfavourable terms 'as was not fit for any Prince to grant'. Lastly, he had deserted his post in disobedience to her Majesty's express commands given under her own hand. The Lord Treasurer, Lord Buckhurst, took up the story to spell out the ruinous cost of the Irish operation – three hundred thousand pounds between April and September; and the Lord Admiral added his voice, remarking scornfully that with such an army Essex might have gone all through Spain.

One of those present grumbled that the throng was so great and some of the lords spoke so softly that he could scarcely hear what was being said – Robert Cecil made a long and largely inaudible speech confirming that the Queen had written forbidding Essex to return to England – but on the whole the main object of the exercise seems to have been achieved. Although feeling continued to run high and scurrilous graffiti directed against Cecil appeared even on the palace walls, at least the more responsible sections of the community were now aware that the Queen had substantial grounds for her displeasure.

Despite persistent rumours that the Earl was to be committed to the Tower, nothing had been said about his future but, by the first week of December, it began to look as if the problem might be going to resolve itself in a particularly final manner. Essex was said to be critically ill and Elizabeth ordered eight leading physicians to examine the patient and advise her on his case. Their prognosis was not hopeful, for they found his liver 'stopped and perished', his guts and entrails exulcerated and could only suggest gentle glisters to keep him clean within. Looking rather pensive, the Queen sent one of her own doctors to York House with some of her special broth and a message that his lordship should comfort himself, adding that if she might with honour come to visit him, she would do so. This looked a hopeful sign but most people feared it had come too late, for Essex was now so weak that he had to be lifted on a sheet when his bed was made and scoured of all black matter, 'as if the strength of nature were quite gone'.

Since his condition had become so serious he had been moved, by royal command, into the Lord Keeper's own bed-chamber and his wife was allowed to go to him. Frances Essex cannot have known much happiness in her married life, but she appears always to have accepted her husband's neglect and his not infrequent infidelities in a proper spirit of Christian resignation, and to have stood staunchly by him in his disgrace. Although only just risen from her latest childbed, she had done her best to plead his cause, haunting the ante-rooms of power dressed in unrelieved black and, once leave had been granted, dutifully spent every day from six in the morning till seven at night – the permitted visiting hours – at his bedside. The fallen favourite was being publicly prayed for in the city churches and a few days before Christmas, when a rumour got around that he was dead, the bells tolled for him. But Essex was not dead. He was, in fact, a little better and a week or so later was able to sit up and to eat at a table.

As he recovered, the Queen's heart hardened again. She herself was in excellent health. The Court, which had moved out to Richmond, was crowded and gay for the Christmas holidays and her Majesty often to be seen relaxing in the Presence Chamber, playing cards with the Lord Treasurer and Mr Secretary or watching her ladies performing the new country dances – no doubt beating time to the music and calling out criticisms, as André de Maisse had reported was her habit. The year before she had danced with the Earl of Essex at the Twelfth Night festivities, but if she missed his company now she gave no sign of it.

VIII
The Madcaps All in Riot

Sweet England's pride is gone!
welladay! welladay!

Brave honour graced him still,
gallantly, gallantly;
He ne'er did deed of ill,
well it is known;
But Envy, that foul fiend,
whose malice ne'er did end,
Hath brought true virtue's friend
unto his thrall.

A new century had begun with England still at war with Spain – a war which had already lasted more than fifteen years – but the Queen had not given up hope of securing the 'safe honourable peace' which every sensible Englishman was longing for and there had been much conferring with the Dutch ambassador during the winter. In Spain, too, where a new king faced the problems of an empty treasury and a nation war-weary to the point of exhaustion, a negotiated settlement would have been welcomed thankfully. In October 1599, Archduke Albert of Austria who, with his wife, old Philip's favourite child the Infanta Isabella, now ruled the Spanish Netherlands, had sent an envoy secretly to London and in the spring of 1600 representatives of both sides met at Boulogne. But the talks broke down over a point of procedure and, in any case, the English remained firm in their insistence on satisfactory guarantees for the Dutch and on trading concessions in Spanish America.

The war at sea had now largely passed back into private hands. Individual privateers continued to cruise the sea lanes in search of prizes and in 1598 the Earl of Cumberland, succeeding where Drake and Hawkins had failed, captured Puerto Rico but took no treasure worth mentioning. In the summer of 1599 there had been another invasion scare, when a young Genoese adventurer in the Spanish service brought off a brilliant dash up the Channel and through the Dover Straits to Sluys with a fleet of six galleys. But there were to be no more major naval confrontations and the war was steadily losing momentum both by sea and land. The Anglo-Dutch victory at Nieuport in 1600 virtually settled the issue in the Netherlands and thereafter the English presence could safely be reduced to little more than the garrisons in Flushing and the other cautionary towns.

This was just as well, for in Ireland the situation was rapidly going from bad to catastrophic. Elizabeth had been forced to ratify Essex's infamous truce (which, needless to say, was already being broken) and the winter of 1599 saw Tyrone lording it unchallenged over the tribes. Aware that only bad weather and Spanish incapacity had so far prevented active intervention from that quarter, the Queen reverted to her original plan of appointing Lord Mountjoy as her Lord Deputy. Mountjoy at first protested. He was not strong and feared, so he said, that the Irish climate would be the death of him. He was also worried about Essex. The previous summer he had taken it on himself to get in touch with King James to assure him that 'my lord of Essex was free from those ambitious conceits which some of his enemies had sought to possess the world withal', that his lordship fully supported James's claim to be recognised as the heir apparent, and to propose that some joint action should now be discussed with a view to persuading the Queen to reconsider her stubborn refusal to make the recognition official.

Mountjoy, it was said later, had been motivated principally by his affection for Essex 'who by loss of her Majesty was like to run a dangerous course unless he took a course to strengthen himself by that means' (in other words, sought protection from James), and by an honest conviction that only the formal declaration of a Protestant successor would serve to safeguard the country against the machinations of undesirable pretenders. Ever since the death of Mary Queen of Scots, the Spanish royal family had been making the most of their dash of Plantagenet blood – the Infanta Isabella being the most favoured replacement for Queen Elizabeth in extreme Catholic circles.

Lord Mountjoy may have been guilty of nothing worse than officiousness in the summer of 1599, but once his appointment as Lord

Deputy was confirmed he began to be drawn into new schemes for using the army in Ireland as an instrument of coercion at home. Having sworn an oath to defend the Queen to the uttermost during her lifetime, and taken the precaution of extracting a similar solemn undertaking from the Earl of Southampton, the army's commander agreed to send another letter to James, suggesting that a contingent of four or five thousand of his men, acting in conjunction with the Scots, might be brought over to support 'the party that my lord of Essex would make head withal' in a show of force impressive enough to compel Elizabeth to name the King as her heir, restore Essex to favour and dismiss Robert Cecil.

Such a plan, if attempted, must have had disastrous consequences, but luckily for all concerned, by the time the messenger, who had been closely shadowed by Cecil's spies, returned from the north bringing a friendly but carefully non-committal answer from James, Mountjoy had left for Ireland. Once in Dublin, removed from the influence of the Essex wild men and, perhaps even more important, from Penelope Rich, a strong-minded lady devoted to her brother, he was able to see things in a clearer light. When Southampton joined him towards the end of April, bearing a letter from Essex and eager for action, he was absorbed in the challenge of his new job and no longer interested in playing with fire. His friend was clearly out of immediate danger and Mountjoy who, left to himself, possessed a good deal of common sense, flatly refused to have anything to do with an enterprise intended merely to restore the Earl's fortunes and satisfy his private ambitions.

The secret had been well kept, but even so Robert Cecil and the Queen already knew something and no doubt guessed a lot more about the activities of the Essex party in Scotland and elsewhere. In spite of this, Essex had not been committed to the Tower. On the contrary, his position had improved a little. On 20 March, to the intense relief of the Lord Keeper, he had at last been allowed to return to Essex House, empty now and stripped of its paraphernalia of power. The busy staff of secretaries, the secret agents coming and going on their mysterious errands, the jostling queues of petitioners and place-seekers, the visiting dignitaries, the courtiers and captains and hangers-on who had once filled it with bustle and the illusion of greatness had vanished. Even Lady Essex, the Earl's mother and sisters and Lady Southampton were required to find alternative accommodation before he was installed with only a bare handful of servants and a government-appointed custodian to keep him company.

The problem of his future remained unsolved. The Queen had

wanted to bring him to trial in the Star Chamber not, so she said, to destroy him, but to make him know himself and his duty towards her. Elizabeth was becoming increasingly worried by the bad publicity she had been getting over the Essex affair and was especially anxious to refute the charge that the Earl had been condemned unheard; but Robert Cecil, like Francis Bacon, strongly opposed any form of public proceeding at this stage and instead persuaded her Majesty to accept a letter of humble submission.

Walter Raleigh, evidently afraid that Cecil was going soft over Essex, wrote to warn him that 'if you take it for good counsel to relent towards this tyrant, you will repent when it shall be too late. His malice is fixed and will not evaporate by any your mild courses ... The less you make him, the less he shall be able to harm you and yours; and if her Majesty's favour fail him, he will again decline into a common person ... Lose not your advantage. If you do, I read your destiny.' This advice was almost certainly unnecessary. Cecil harboured no more illusions than Walter Raleigh about the fixity of Essex's malice, and could read his own destiny just as clearly if he lost his present advantage. But Mr Secretary, who had borne the brunt of the odium resulting from the Earl's disgrace, who commanded no popular following and depended entirely on the support of an ageing Queen, was understandably reluctant to pass the point of no return until he could feel a hundred per cent certain of his ground. The Star Chamber trial, which had been set for early February, was cancelled and another four months passed before a satisfactory compromise had been hammered out.

On 5 June 1600 Essex was summoned to appear before a special tribunal of Privy Councillors and judges sitting at York House under the chairmanship of the Lord Keeper to hear the charges against him, to give his answer and receive judgement. No witnesses would be called, no formal record kept and, as a further concession to the prisoner's special status, her Majesty had been graciously pleased to allow the proceedings to be held in a private place. However, since the tribunal's primary purpose was that of a public relations exercise, an invited audience of two hundred persons, carefully chosen for their standing and influence in the community, was present to see justice done.

The government's case opened with a reminder of the Queen's generosity. She had not only forgiven Essex ten thousand pounds worth of his debts to her before he left for Ireland, but had given him nearly as much again to buy horses and outfit himself for the campaign and was even now – despite the ingratitude with which her bounty had been repaid – unwilling to subject him to the rigours of an ordinary criminal trial. She had therefore directed that his misdeeds should receive 'before a great, honourable and selected council, a full and deliberate, and yet in respect a private, mild and gracious hearing'.

The Attorney General then rehearsed the Earl's various sins of commission and omission in Ireland: his appointment of Southampton as General of the Horse in defiance of the Queen's veto; his useless journey into Leinster and Munster which had ruined any chance of success in Ulster; his indiscriminate making of knights, again in disobedience to orders; his dishonourable and dangerous conference with the arch-rebel Tyrone; and his contemptuous leaving of his post contrary to her Majesty's absolute mandate. Edward Coke spoke in his usual hectoring style and could not resist the jibe that 'before my lord went into Ireland he vaunted and boasted that he would fight with none but Tyrone himself . . . But when he came thither, then no such matter, for he goes another way; it appeareth plainly he meant nothing less than to *fight* with Tyrone!'

The Solicitor General followed with a dissertation on the parlous state of Ireland since his lordship's return, which only went to show how little he had achieved, for Tyrone had now become more insolent than ever. Last, and perhaps most significant, Francis Bacon, as one of the Queen's learned counsel, rose to complete the case for the prosecution. After expressing the hope that all present would realise that any bond of duty he owed to the Earl had been temporarily laid aside, Bacon also described the unmitigated hash which his former patron had made of the Irish command. He went on to introduce two other matters – Essex's indiscreet letter to Thomas Egerton at the time of the ear-boxing row two years previously, and his patronage of Dr Hayward's tactless *History of Henry IV* – both of which had demonstrated undutifulness and disrespect.

When at last it came to Essex's turn, he spoke with becoming humility of the great sorrow and affliction which had fallen on him, and of the depth of his inner remorse. Since the Queen had been gracious enough to spare him the humiliation of a Star Chamber trial, he had resolved to give up all thought of attempting to justify his actions, he said. Instead, he would freely acknowledge, with grief and contrition, whatever faults of error, negligence or rashness it pleased her Majesty to impute to him. But the Attorney General had seemed to call his loyalty in question, and he would be doing God and his conscience a great wrong if he did not justify himself as an honest man. Speaking with passion and every appearance of sincerity, his lordship cried out that he would tear the heart out of his breast with his own hands if ever a disloyal idea had entered it.

Aware that the audience was showing ominous signs of responding to this display of eloquence, Lord Keeper Egerton hurriedly intervened to point out that no one had accused my lord of Essex of disloyalty, he was charged merely with contempt and disobedience and such affecting protestations were therefore irrelevant. His bubble pricked, Essex subsided, contenting himself with a pathetic plea that his former colleagues would make a just and honourable report of the disordered speeches which were the best an aching head and weakened body could utter. One by one the eighteen members of the tribunal then proceeded to give their opinion of the case, all agreeing that the Earl had been guilty of grave dereliction of duty, that he should be suspended from his various offices and remain under house arrest until such time as the Queen was pleased to release him.

Although many of the spectators shed tears to see 'him that was the mignon of Fortune now unworthy of the least honour', and Rowland Whyte heard that it had been 'a most pitiful and lamentable sight', the charade at York House had gone a long way towards destroying Essex's credibility as a public figure in the eyes of sensible men. Even more valuable from the government's point of view was the news coming in from Ireland, where Lord Mountjoy, ably assisted by Sir George Carew, was already beginning to make headway against the rebels; proving that with patience, persistence and determination – prosaic qualities notably lacking in the Earl of Essex – the Irish problem was not after all so insoluble as everyone had been led to believe.

It was widely expected that having made her point and taught Essex a lesson not even he could misunderstand, the Queen would soon relent, at least to the extent of restoring his freedom of movement, but what would happen after that was still anybody's guess. One thing, though, was certain. Unless he was eventually allowed to return to Court, his lordship's career was finished. Elizabeth might drop hints that once she was fully satisfied as to the sincerity of his repentance she would consider using his services again, but few people in a position to know anything of the inside story could bring themselves to believe that the Earl would ever again be trusted with a responsible office. Equally, it was hard to visualise him retiring unprotesting into private life.

If Elizabeth was worried about the situation, she rarely showed it. She seemed as active as ever, going briskly about her usual routine of work and pleasure, watching the bear baiting, a French tight-rope artist, taking long walks in Greenwich Park and dining with friends. All the same, Essex was obviously very much on her mind. Ten days after the tribunal had sat at York House, she was present at the social event of the season – the wedding at Blackfriars of Anne Russell, one of her favourite maids of honour, to Lord Herbert, the Earl of Worcester's heir. One of the entertainments provided at the marriage feast was a masque performed by eight ladies of the Court and when one of them, Mary Fitton, went to the Queen and wooed her to dance, her Majesty asked what character she represented. 'Affection', answered the girl. 'Affection', said Elizabeth sourly, 'affection is false', but she rose and joined the dancing.

During the previous summer some rather sinister rumours had been going about that the Queen was ailing, but this August Rowland Whyte told Robert Sidney that her Majesty was in very good health and went abroad every day to ride and hunt. Plans for a long progress were being discussed and when some of the older members of the household grumbled (progresses could be pretty uncomfortable affairs for those who no longer found it amusing to sleep in a tent), Elizabeth, who would be sixty-seven in September, snapped that the old could stay behind and the young and able go with her. In the end, though, she had second thoughts and went no further than Surrey, to Nonesuch, best-loved of her country houses, and Oatlands where the Court was given over to hunting and sports and the Queen said to be 'very merry and well'.

It was, perhaps, wiser to stay close to the centre. Essex, as anticipated, had now been relieved of his keeper and on 26 August was at last told he was free to go where he liked – except to Court. He announced that he meant to live quietly in the country, but his plea to be allowed the consolation of coming to kiss her Majesty's 'fair correcting hand' before retiring into solitude went unheeded. Outwardly the Earl was behaving with exemplary patience. There had been no tantrums, no outbursts of petulance, and his letters to the Queen positively crawled with penitence. But though Elizabeth sometimes sighed over them, she was not convinced and she was right – affection and contrition were both false.

Essex had not yet given up hope of Mountjoy and had already sent Sir Charles Danvers, another of his cronies, back to Ireland to remind the Lord Deputy of former promises and ask for his support in a bid to unseat Robert Cecil. Danvers went, not very optimistically, and found Mountjoy unsympathetic. Charles Blount, always hitherto overshadowed by the Devereux family, was enjoying his first experience of independent power (though this did not prevent him from complaining that he was not appreciated at home), and was discovering in himself an unexpected talent for command. He was, therefore, less and less inclined to put a promising career at risk by becoming involved in crack-brained schemes for rehabilitating my lord of Essex. He told Danvers that my lord must be content to 'recover again by ordinary means the Queen's ordinary favour'. When he came home he would naturally do what he could for him in the way of friendship, but in the mean time strongly advised him not to do anything rash.

Baulked, Essex turned again to Scotland and another messenger was sent north to warn James that unless he took steps to insist on his right to be named as the Queen's heir without further delay, he might find himself displaced by the Spanish princess, whose claim was favoured by one of the Queen's principal councillors – Cecil again. The Earl had 'infallible proof' that Cecil, in his anxiety for peace at any price, was plotting to hand England over to the Spaniards: he had been heard to say he could prove the Infanta's title to be better than that of any other competitor to the Crown; the Catholics, especially the Jesuits, were being treated with suspicious lenience; and the country was now almost entirely in the hands of Cecil supporters. Walter Raleigh was Captain of Jersey and commanded the whole of the West Country, Kent and the Cinque Ports were controlled by Lord Cobham and in Ireland, Munster, the province which of all others was 'fittest for the Spaniards' designs', had already been procured for Sir George Carew. As well as this, 'the treasure, the sinews of action, and the navy, the walls of this realm', were commanded by the Lord Treasurer and the Lord Admiral, two great officers of state well known to be 'principally loved by the principal Secretary'. The King of Scots, in short, had better realise that the Earl of Essex was his only friend and Essex urged him to send a reliable ambassador with whom his lordship could safely confer and decide on a joint plan of action. The cautious James was sufficiently alarmed by these scaremongering tactics to commit himself to a few lines of 'disguised' writing which Essex carried about with him in a little black bag hung round his neck, but by the time the reliable ambassador reached London, the Earl was no longer in a position to make use of their services.

Autumn was now approaching and still no one knew for certain whether the Queen meant to forgive Essex or not. His friends were still hopeful, finding it difficult to believe that any creature of flesh and blood could go on resisting the heartrending appeals of her humblest, faithfulest and more than most devoted vassal, the pining, languishing, despairing Essex. Other people took a more detached view, but everyone was watching to see what would happen at Michaelmas, when the Earl's 'farm' or monopoly of the duties on imported sweet wines fell due for renewal – or otherwise.

Many of Essex's past troubles, and a great deal of his present desperation, stemmed from his chronic financial problems which had always left him heavily dependent on the Queen's generosity. A man in his position, living precariously on an enormous overdraft of good-will, quite simply could not afford to retire into private life and wait patiently until such time as it might please her Majesty to notice him again. If the farm of sweet wines, which represented a major source of his income, were to be withheld, the big shiny bubble of confidence on which his career and his ostentatious lifestyle had been balanced for so long would be seen to have burst, and his creditors would close in to strip him naked.

Elizabeth knew this as well as anyone. She told Francis Bacon that my lord of Essex had written her some very dutiful letters, and she had been moved by them; but what she had taken to be the abundance of his heart, she now found was merely a preparation for a suit for the renewing of his farm. Bacon, as the Queen no doubt also knew, had helped to draft some of these moving letters. Despite his appearance at York House, the canny Francis was still keeping a foot in the Essex camp and, according to his own testimony, begging her Majesty 'not utterly to extinguish my lord's desire to do her service'. Her Majesty remained unresponsive. Michaelmas came and went and nothing was said. Essex had returned to town, living very quietly and keeping his gates closed to visitors, but there was no summons to Court, no suggestion that he was considered to have served his sentence. On 18 October he made one last attempt to soften the Queen. 'My soul cries out unto your Majesty for grace', he wrote, 'for access, and for an end of this exile. If your Majesty grant this suit, you are most gracious, whatsoever else you deny or take away. If this cannot be obtained, I must doubt whether that the means to preserve life, and the granted liberty, have been favours or punishments; for till I may appear in your gracious presence, and kiss your Majesty's fair correcting hand, time itself is a perpetual night, and the whole world but a sepulchre unto your Majesty's humblest vassal.'

Still nothing, and then, at the end of the month, came the announcement that the farm of sweet wines would not be renewed and would for the present be kept in the Queen's own hands. On the face of it, this was fair enough. It was now more than a year since the Earl of Essex had taken any part in affairs of state, and the state had, after all, managed quite well without him. In some ways it had managed rather better. The business of government had not been disrupted by any explosions of umbrage and in Ireland the troops had at last got their tails up. They were actually fighting and winning battles, and 'beating the rebels from their bogs'. In the circumstances, there was really no reason why his lordship should continue to be rewarded out of public funds – indeed, he might think himself lucky to have escaped the heavy fine and imprisonment in the Tower which, as the Lord Keeper had told him bluntly, would undoubtedly have followed a Star Chamber trial.

Essex, of course, being Essex could only see that he had been rejected, cast out and accursed; that he had humbled himself into the dust to no purpose, while his arch-enemy watched and gloated. Ahead lay nothing but ruin and disgrace, and as hope died, self-control frayed and finally snapped. Sir John Harington, who ventured to visit the Earl about this time, gave it as his opinion that 'ambition thwarted in its career doth speedily lead on to madness' – a conviction strengthened by the alarming manner in which Essex had shifted from sorrow and repentance to rage and rebellion, so suddenly 'as well proveth him devoid of good reason and right mind'. During their conversation, he began to talk so wildly that Sir John, who had once before nearly been wrecked on the Essex coast as he put it, hurriedly made his excuses and left. 'Thank heaven I am safe at home', he wrote, 'and if I go in such troubles again, I deserve the gallows for a meddling fool! His speeches of the Queen becometh no man who hath *mens sana in corpore sano*'. This may perhaps have been the occasion of the venomous remark always attributed to Essex that the Queen's mind had become as crooked as her carcase. Certainly he said something of the sort and, according to Harington, 'the man's soul seemeth tossed to and fro, like the waves of a troubled sea'.

Christmas approached and the Court settled down at Whitehall for the holiday season. Sir Robert Cecil invited the Queen to dinner, preparing to receive her 'with all fine and exquisite curiosity', and on Twelfth Night her Majesty feasted the Muscovy ambassador. The Orsini Duke of Bracciano, cousin of the new French Queen Marie de Medici, was also over on a private visit and being 'very graciously' entertained by Elizabeth, who danced measures and galliards before him 'to show that she is not so old as some would have her'. Everything seemed very much as usual. The musicians played, the children of the Chapel Royal sang as sweetly as ever, the trumpets sounded and the scarlet-coated yeomen of the guard performed their stately dinner-time ritual with the gold plate; while at the centre of the stage the Queen smiled and danced and made elegant small-talk with her distinguished guests, apparently unconcerned by the knowledge that less than a mile from the Palace a handful of angry, embittered men were plotting to overthrow her government.

Having abruptly abandoned his role of penitent and recluse, the Earl of Essex had now opened his doors to anyone who cared to enter, and a varied assortment of old friends and new were availing themselves of the opportunity to make common cause with the people's Robert. They ranged from wild young bucks like the Earls of Rutland and Southampton to militant young Catholics like Robert Catesby and Francis Tresham; from veterans of Essex campaigns like Christopher Blount, Sir John Davies, Sir Charles Danvers and the Governor of Plymouth Sir Ferdinando Gorges, to the Earl's secretary, Greek scholar Henry Cuffe, and included a rabble of impoverished lords and gentlemen who had all, for one reason or another, lost out in the harshly competitive Elizabethan rat-race. Pushing in behind the nobility and gentry came the bully boys and hoodlums, the discharged soldiers and unemployed captains, the petty criminals and professional trouble-seekers – 'swordsmen, bold confident fellows, men of broken fortunes, discontented persons, and such as saucily used their tongues in railing against all men' – every one of them ready for mischief and united, from earl to cutpurse, by their penury, their sense of grievance and their greed.

The general ambition of this promising assemblage was simple enough: to divert as much as possible of the life-giving stream of profit and perquisite flowing from the Crown into their own pockets, or to seize the Queen and become their own carvers, as the coarser element put it. But while they were strong on threats, when it came down to the actual ways and means of toppling a strong and widely popular regime, the would-be demagogues of Essex House became noticeably less self-confident. Detailed plans for taking over the Court, thus enabling Essex 'to present himself to the Queen' and enforce his demands – the dismissal of Robert Cecil, Raleigh, Cobham et al, their replacement by his own nominees and the calling of a Parliament to punish all enemies of the people – were discussed at a meeting chaired by the Earl of Southampton, but no firm decision was reached. The whole enterprise might yet have fizzled out in talk had not a small group of firebrands, impatient for some sort of action, brought matters to a head by bribing the reluctant company at the Globe Theatre to put on a special performance of Master Shakespeare's Tragedy of King Richard the Second.

For Essex's followers to demand to be entertained by the spectacle

of a king being deposed and murdered – bearing in mind the comparison which had already been drawn between the Earl and Henry
Bolingbroke – could only be construed as deliberate provocation, and
the Queen and Robert Cecil, who had been keeping a close watch
over the comings and goings at Essex House during the past three
months, were left with no option but to take up the challenge. The
same evening – it was Saturday, 7 February – the Privy Council met
in emergency session to consider how best to deal with a potentially
explosive situation.

The so-called Essex Rebellion is sometimes shrugged off as the
grotesque bungling of a desperate man, half-crazed with disappointment, and hardly to be taken seriously. But it is always easy to be
wise after the event and no one sitting round the Council table that
Saturday evening felt in the least amused. Whitehall was virtually
undefended and was, in any case, a rambling rabbit warren of a place
almost impossible to secure. It would be highly vulnerable to a surprise attack, and there were some dangerous and determined charac-
ters among the mob now gathered a bare twenty minutes march
away. If once they got into the precincts of the Palace, no one could
say with certainty whether all the courtiers could be relied on to
remain loyal; nor was it absolutely certain how the City would react.
Essex, after all, was still Essex, the darling of the Londoners.

However, it was decided not to over-react and the Lords of the
Council agreed to try and nip trouble in the bud by sending for Essex
to appear before them forthwith. But their emissary, Secretary John
Herbert, returned alone bringing word that the Earl had positively
refused to come. He was not well, he said, and besides had been
warned that the summons was a trap and Raleigh and Cobham were
planning to murder him. This sounded ominous, as did Herbert's
report of the scene at Essex House. So, first thing next morning, a
warning was sent to the Lord Mayor to be ready for possible disturbances, while a final effort was made to bring Essex to his senses.

At ten o'clock an impressive deputation consisting of Lord Keeper
Egerton, Lord Chief Justice Popham, the Earl of Worcester and Sir
William Knollys arrived at the gates of Essex House demanding
admission in the Queen's name. They found the courtyard 'full of
men assembled together in very tumultuous sort' and Essex himself
surrounded by his sidekicks, Southampton and Rutland, the Lords
Sandys and Mounteagle, Christopher Blount, Charles Danvers and
'many other knights and gentlemen and other persons unknown'.
Trying to make himself heard over the general hubbub, Egerton told
the Earl that they had come from her Majesty to 'understand the

cause of this their assembly, and to let them know that if they had any particular cause of grief against any persons whatsoever, it should be heard, and they should have justice'. Hereupon, according to Egerton's own account, 'the Earl of Essex, with a very loud voice, declared that his life was sought, and that he should have been murdered in his bed; that he had been perfidiously dealt with; that his hand had been counterfeited, and letters written in his name; and that therefore they were assembled there to defend their lives, with much other speech to like effect.'

Although Essex had pretty plainly passed beyond any appeal to reason, the Lord Keeper persisted bravely, repeatedly asking his lordship to let them understand his griefs in private, and commanding the jeering, jostling, cat-calling mob on their allegiance to lay down their weapons and depart. At last, Essex turned to go into the house and the deputation followed, pursued by insults and yells of 'Kill them! Kill them!' and 'Cast the Great Seal out of the window!' But once inside, instead of the private interview they had been hoping for, the Queen's representatives found themselves rudely locked up in a back chamber, the Earl telling them to be patient while he went into London 'to take order with the Mayor and Sheriffs for the City'.

The rest of the events of that Sunday – Essex's wild impromptu dash through the city streets, shouting hysterically that a plot was laid for his life and England was sold to the Spaniards, while the people came out to stare in open-mouthed amazement at the extraordinary sight of the hero of Cadiz running sweating and sobbing past their doors; his ignominious failure to win support or even credulity for his 'cause' and the final scrambling retreat to Essex House to find that his hostages had been released – all these are too familiar to need further repetition here. Nothing now remained for the Earl, stranded among the ruins of his lurid fantasy world, but to barricade his doors, burn his private papers and prepare to sell his life dearly. In the end, though, there wasn't even a heroic last stand. Soon after ten o'clock that night Essex and Southampton surrendered tamely enough to a force commanded by the Lord Admiral, and the Queen, who had sworn not to sleep until she knew they had been taken, was able to go to bed. The rebellion had lasted exactly twelve hours.

The rest of the Essex story is soon told. He and Southampton were arraigned together at Westminster Hall on 19 February before a jury of their peers, charged with conspiring with others to deprive and depose the Queen's majesty from her royal state and dignity, to procure her death and destruction and subvert the government of the realm; with having refused to disperse their disorderly company when called upon to do so by her Majesty's Privy Councillors, with imprisoning the said Councillors, and issuing into the City of London with a number of armed men with intent to persuade the citizens to join with them. Both the accused pleaded not guilty and defended themselves resolutely. Essex's 'boldness' was especially remarked on and, according to the letter-writer John Chamberlain, 'a man might easily perceive that as he had ever lived popularly, so his chief care was to leave a good opinion in the people's minds now at parting.' But the trial itself, like all treason trials of the period, was little more than a formal exercise, notable chiefly for the reappearance of the agile Francis Bacon among counsel for the prosecution and a dramatic confrontation between Essex and Robert Cecil.

Robert Cecil had put up with a good deal from Essex over the years, patiently enduring a long and spiteful campaign of smears and sneers and insults, but now he was determined to nail the nastiest slander of them all – that he had been deliberately plotting to sell England out to Spain. So, when his lordship repeated in open court that he had heard it reported how 'Mr. Secretary should say that the Infanta's title to the crown (after her Majesty) was as good as any other', Mr Secretary suddenly emerged from the hidden corner where he had been following the proceedings and, falling on his knees before the presiding judge, challenged Essex to name his sources for 'so false and foul an accusation'. Essex hedged and squirmed and passed the buck to the Earl of Southampton, but Cecil persisted and eventually it came out that the whole of the 'England is sold to the Spaniards' bogey was based on a casual remark made some two years earlier to Sir William Knollys. He and the Secretary had been walking in the garden at Court one morning discussing among other things the treatise by R. Doleman (alias Robert Parsons) on the *Next Succession to the Crown of England,* and Cecil had observed that it was a strange impudence on the part of Doleman to give an equal right in the succession to the Infanta as any other. The Secretary of State had triumphantly vindicated his honour and made my lord of Essex look both foolish and malevolent.

Indeed, from Cecil's point of view, everything was turning out very satisfactorily. He felt reasonably certain that he had got to the bottom of the conspiracy – the evidence of Sir John Davies, Christopher Blount, Charles Danvers and Ferdinando Gorges gave a clear picture of the discussions at Drury House and the plot to seize the Queen, and two days after his trial Essex, influenced by his favourite chaplain, had been seized with a desire to purge himself of guilt by telling all. In a long written statement he poured out every detail of his own and his friends' activities over the past eighteen months; he named names from Lord Mountjoy downwards and confessed himself to be 'the greatest, the most vilest and most unthankfullest traitor that ever was born'. This was very helpful and not only confirmed much that the government already knew or guessed, but added quite a lot of interesting new information. Fortunately, though, the Earl's impetuous eruption of 8 February had made it possible to suppress the most damaging of these revelations and Cecil could congratulate himself on a very smooth operation, handled without causing embarrassment to such public figures as Mountjoy and the King of Scots.

As for the Queen, she had shown all her usual cool confident courage on the day of the insurrection, remarking that God who had placed her in that seat would maintain her in it, and showing an alarming readiness to go out on the streets in person 'to see what any rebel of them all durst do against her'. But after the crisis came reaction. John Harington, who seems to have had quite a talent for turning up at awkward moments, was at Court just as the madcaps were all in riot, and found her Majesty in a fractious mood – refusing to eat, not bothering to change her dress and making the household's life a misery.

'I must not say much, even by this trusty and sure messenger', wrote Harington to Sir Hugh Portman; 'but the many evil plots and designs have overcome all her Highness' sweet temper. She walks much in her privy chamber, and stamps with her feet at ill news, and thrusts her rusty sword at times into the arras in great rage.' The sight of Harington reminded Elizabeth of his Irish knighthood, still a sore point, and she sent him packing with a sharp message delivered by Lord Buckhurst: 'Go tell that witty fellow, my godson, to get home; it is no season now to fool it here.' Sir John knew better than to argue and hurriedly took to his boots and returned to the plough in bad weather.

The Queen typically concealed her unease under a royal display of bad temper, 'swearing at those that cause her griefs in such wise, to the no small discomfort of all about her'; but the anxieties of the early months of 1601 had undoubtedly taken their toll – visiting Robert Sidney at Penshurst she called for a stick and 'seemed much wearied in walking about the house'. It wasn't only Essex's final and fatal defiance – that had, after all, been expected in some form or other. Far more disturbing was the knowledge that a man like Mountjoy had actually contemplated leading his army against her and that even such an old friend as Peregrine Bertie, Lord Willoughby, now Governor of Berwick, had helped the Earl's messengers on their way into

Scotland. It was a sign of the changing times that 'now the wit of the fox is everywhere on foot, so as hardly one faithful or virtuous man may be found'; but worse still, it was a sign that Gloriana's old magic was beginning to lose its potency.

It seems likely that it was reflections of this kind rather than personal grief for Essex which were responsible for Elizabeth's reportedly increasing tendency to mope by herself in a darkened room. Despite the various bogus romantic legends which grew up around the event, the Queen showed less reluctance than usual when it came to signing the Earl's death warrant, for though she might be saddened by the ignoble end of a once brilliant and beautiful young man, she never hesitated over its necessity. Essex had committed the two unforgivable sins – he would have touched her sceptre and he had tried to turn her own Londoners against her.

Elizabeth has often been blamed for her inept handling of Essex. At the time of his Irish fiasco, Francis Bacon thought she was making a mistake to criticise and discontent him as she did, and yet put so much military power into his hands. Robert Naunton, writing some thirty years later, commented on the 'violent indulgency of the Queen . . . towards this lord' as well as on 'a fault in the object of her grace, my lord himself, who drew in too fast, like a child sucking on an over-uberous nurse'. Naunton believed that 'had there been a more decent decorum observed in both, or either of those, without doubt the unity of their affections had been more permanent, and not so in and out as they were, like an instrument ill-tuned and lapsing into discord'.

Certainly, in the early and still unclouded years of their relationship, Elizabeth had over-indulged her pretty, red-headed boyfriend, allowing him to form an undesirably inflated idea of his own importance. It had also been a serious error of judgement to send him to Ireland as she did. But, at the same time, it is surely debatable whether any prodigies of tact or skill would have made any difference in the end in this classic case of hubris and nemesis. The conjunction of a young, essentially violent and unstable man, whose ambitions constantly outran his capabilities, and an ageing, autocratic woman, subject to the fears and stresses which afflict all ageing autocrats, can only have resulted in 'an instrument ill-tuned'. Essex's tragedy was that he could not be content with the position of domestical greatness which was his for the asking; Elizabeth's the bitter realisation that what she had to offer was not enough.

Essex paid the price of treason to the headsman on Ash Wednesday, 25 February 1601, acknowledging 'with thankfulness to God, that he was thus justly spewed out of the realm'. A few weeks later four of his fellow conspirators – his stepfather Christopher Blount, his secretary Henry Cuffe, his friend Charles Danvers and his steward Gilly Meyrick followed him into eternity, but these were the only members of his party to suffer the death penalty. Even the Earl of Southampton had his sentence commuted to imprisonment in the Tower and lived to become an ornament of a Court where he was far more at home. Francis Bacon, too, would gather the harvest of his patient pragmatism in the next reign, but his crippled brother Anthony did not survive to share it. Faithful to his former patron to the end, he died that spring in debt and obscurity.

Essex was gone, and with him went the last flicker of the old, turbulent, baronial England, in which an over-mighty subject could challenge the central power of the state, even the throne itself, and hope to win. Essex was gone, though his memory lived on and the people mourned their dead hero in sentimental ballads which were heard even around the Court. 'Sweet England's pride is gone', they sang, but they and England and England's Queen were all very much better off without him.

One result of his disappearance from the political arena was a dramatic improvement in Anglo-Scottish relations. The ambassadors who were to have conferred with the Earl of Essex on the best means of enforcing James's demand for immediate recognition as heir apparent arrived in London in March, in nice time to congratulate the Queen on her lucky escape from the Essex conspiracy. Being sensible men, who could see how the land lay, they approached Robert Cecil instead and Cecil quickly seized the opportunity to reassure them of his impeccable devotion to their master, for it was time to start thinking seriously about the future.

The succession had been a major cause of anxiety and dissension in the past – Elizabeth's inflexible refusal to name her heir or even to allow the subject to be discussed had raised a series of storms in Parliament and elsewhere – but since the death of Mary Queen of Scots the problem had lost much of its immediacy. The exiled Catholic community and its allies might continue to discuss it with feverish intensity among themselves, but the majority of Englishmen had gradually grown accustomed to the idea that Mary's son James, who was after all doubly descended from Henry VII, the first Tudor king, would in due time come to occupy his great-grandfather's throne. Indeed, he had no serious competitor, with the possible exception of his first cousin Lady Arbella Stuart. Her claim was dynastically inferior but it could be argued in her favour that she had been born in the realm, while James was technically a foreigner.

There were those who might have been prepared to support her. Not everyone fancied the idea of a Scottish king, especially the son of that well-known Jezebel Mary Stuart, and Lady Arbella had from time to time been an object of interest to the Catholics as a possibly useful pawn in their endless convoluted intrigues to unseat Queen Elizabeth. But the Queen had never given her any sign of encouragement and, apart from a brief visit to Court as a child, Arbella had spent virtually all her life in the wilds of Derbyshire under the eye of her maternal grandmother, the formidable Dowager Countess of Shrewsbury, better known as Bess of Hardwick. In fact, it would probably be true to say that outside Court and political circles, few people were even aware of her existence and Robert Cecil meant to ensure that it stayed that way, for Robert Cecil was about to stake his political career on stage-managing a smooth transference of power when the time came.

Obviously the first thing was to win James's confidence and endeavour to undo the damage of years of Essex mischief-making, and Cecil therefore embarked on a correspondence with the King which he took elaborate precautions to keep secret from everyone, including and especially the Queen lest, as he put it, her 'age and orbity, joined to the jealousy of her sex, might have moved her to think ill of that which helped to preserve her'. There can be no doubt but that Elizabeth had always regarded James as her rightful heir, witness her care to safeguard his position at the time of his mother's execution, and she no doubt guessed quite accurately what her Secretary was up to, but so long as the matter remained an official 'secret', she was content. She trusted Cecil, in the circumstances she had to trust him, and he did not betray her. Here, at least, was one faithful and virtuous man, for despite the bad press he has consistently received from historians dazzled by Essex's spurious glamour and despite the fact that he was not quite the man his father had been, Robert Cecil served the Queen loyally at a time when she would have been most vulnerable to deceit.

He soon had James eating out of his hand, and once that notoriously jumpy individual was convinced that he had at last acquired a competent and trustworthy friend at the English Court, his flirtations with the Catholic powers stopped abruptly. The fact that Cecil was able to negotiate an increase in his pension also helped. He also stopped pestering for recognition, assuring the Secretary that henceforward he would be content to wait for God's good time, rather than hazard the breaking of his neck 'by climbing of hedges and ditches for pulling of unripe fruit'. The fact that 'little Cecil' received cheering promises of favours to come, 'quhen it shall please God that the king shall succiede to his richt', did not alter the other fact that his tactful management of James protected Elizabeth's last years from unnecessary alarms and ensured a peaceful hand-over to the new branch of the family business.

IX
A Taper
of True Virgin Wax

An aged princess; many days shall see her,
And yet no day without a deed to crown it.
Would I had known no more! but she must die,
She must, the saints must have her, yet a virgin;
A most unspotted lily shall she pass
To the ground, and all the world shall mourn her.

By the summer of 1601 the Queen appeared to have recovered from the traumas of the Essex rebellion and was once more immersed in her usual round of activities. At the beginning of August Sir William Browne, deputy Governor of Flushing, came over to report on the situation in the Netherlands, where Ostend was currently being besieged by Archduke Albert. Elizabeth gave him an audience on Sunday morning after church, while walking in Sir William Clark's garden, and was at her most affable. 'I had no sooner kissed her sacred hands', wrote Browne, 'but that she presently made me stand up, and spoke somewhat loud, and said, Come hither, Browne; and pronounced that she held me for an old faithful servant of hers, and said, I must give content to Browne, or some such speeches. And then the train following her, she said, Stand, stand back, will you not let us speak but you will be hearers? And then walked a turn or two, protesting her most gracious opinion of myself . . . She called for a stool which was set under a tree, and I began to kneel, but she would not suffer me; in so much as that after two or three denials which I made to kneel, still she was pleased to say that she would not speak with me unless I stood up.'

These preliminaries disposed of, her Majesty 'discoursed of many things' and Browne found her to be remarkably well informed. She complained about lack of support from the Dutch, and when Browne attempted to defend them: 'Tush! Browne, saith she, I know more than thou dost. When I heard, said she, that they were at the first with their army as high as Nymegen, I knew then that no good would be done . . . I looked they should have come down nearer Ostend, or have taken some town in the part of Brabant or Flanders that might have startled the enemy. And that they promised me, or else I would not have let them have so many men.' She went on to talk of the French king and the support he had promised to the Dutch. Browne answered that 'the French king rather marvelled at their foolish boldness in venturing their army so far, than that he ever gave them any assurance to join with them'. But the Queen would not have it. 'Tush! Browne, said she, do not I know that Bucenval was written to, and written to again, to move the army to go that way and that then he would help them.' Browne answered slyly that if it were so, then her Majesty must think it was but a French promise. The conversation ranged over other topics, Browne could not remember 'all the discourses we had', but the end was that he 'received perfect joy by being so favoured of her Majesty, as that I shall think of it during life'.

Elizabeth gave unalloyed pleasure to another faithful subject that month, when she received the learned antiquarian and lawyer William Lambarde in the privy chamber at Greenwich. Lambarde, in his capacity of Keeper of the Records at the Tower of London, had compiled an inventory, or Pandecta, of the documents in his charge and had intended to present it to the Queen by the Countess of Warwick, but her Majesty would have none of that – if a subject of hers did her a service, then she would thankfully accept it from his own hands. She opened the book, read the epistle and title aloud, and at once began to ask intelligent questions about the meaning of certain technical terms, saying she would be a scholar in her age, and thought it no scorn to learn during her life. But when she reached the reign of Richard the Second, she was unfortunately reminded of recent events and exclaimed 'I am Richard. Know ye not that?' 'Such a wicked imagination', answered Lambarde, 'was determined and attempted by a most unkind gentleman – the most adorned creature that ever your Majesty made.' 'He that will forget God', observed her Majesty piously, 'will also forget his benefactors.'

Elizabeth went all through Lambarde's work, with obvious interest, and finally commended the gratified author 'not only for the pains therein taken, but also for that she had not received, since her first coming to the crown, any one thing that brought therewith so great a delectation to her; and so', he recorded, 'being called away to prayer, she put the book in her bosom, having forbidden me from the first to fall on my knee before her, concluding, "Farewell, good and honest Lambarde!" '

The Queen's summer progress that year took her to Reading and then on into Hampshire, where she stayed for nearly a fortnight at Basing as the guest of the Marquis of Winchester and entertained a grand embassy from France, headed by the Duc de Biron, which had been put up at The Vine, the stately home of Lord Sandys. The Vine was hastily embellished with extra plate, hangings and furniture borrowed from the Tower and Hampton Court. There was an exchange of visits, with hunting and feasting, and Elizabeth was able to boast 'that she had done more than any of her ancestors had ever done, or any other prince in Christendom was able to do – namely, in her Hampshire progress this year, entertained a royal ambassador royally in her subjects' houses'.

The party broke up on 19 September and Elizabeth started back towards Windsor, preoccupied by ominous news from Ireland. Early in the month a fleet of thirty-three ships, great and small, had set sail from Lisbon carrying nearly five thousand troops, a battery of siege guns and a quantity of spare arms and ammunition under the command of Don Juan de Aguila, the same who had once established the Spanish foothold in Brittany and master-minded the raid on Mousehole. This fleet was the long-heralded assistance for Tyrone and the Irish rebels, and on 23 September the Spaniards were disembarking at Kinsale to the west of Cork.

The Irish situation in general had eased considerably since Sir Henry Docwra had succeeded in establishing himself with a small independent force at Derry at the head of Lough Foyle in the heart of rebel territory; but this latest development put all the hard-won gains of the past eighteen months in jeopardy, for if de Aguila once joined forces with Tyrone the English would be hopelessly outnumbered. 'If we beat them', Mountjoy told Robert Cecil as soon as news of the landing reached him, 'let it not trouble you though you hear all Ireland doth revolt . . . if we do not, all providence bestowed on any other place is vain.' Clearly the next few weeks would see the

turning point of the war in Ireland and perhaps the turning point of
the whole long, bitter struggle. In London extra reinforcements were
being hastily levied and a squadron of the fleet under Sir Richard
Leveson was ordered to the coast of Munster, while the Queen wrote
to her Lord Deputy in her own hand: 'Tell our army from us . . . that
every hundred of them will beat a thousand, and every thousand
theirs doubled. I am the bolder to pronounce it in His name, that hath
ever protected my righteous cause, in which I bless them all. And
putting you in the first place, I end, scribbling in haste, Your loving
sovereign, E.R.'

Mountjoy had marched on Kinsale with the minimum of delay, for
although it might be beyond his powers to dislodge the invaders by
a direct assault, it was vitally important to prevent their breaking out
of the bridgehead and making contact with the rebel army. Fortunately, with the threat of the English force at Derry in his rear
preying on his mind and hampering his freedom of movement, Tyrone was slow in arriving. Mountjoy and George Carew were therefore able to get into position around Kinsale and, as autumn drew on,
the campaign developed into a grim race to bombard the Spaniards
out before the Irish came up.

Meanwhile, at Westminster, the Queen was meeting Parliament
for the thirteenth and last time. As usual, the government was in
urgent need of money. It was a year since the final instalment of the
treble subsidy granted in 1597–98 had been collected and, but for the
uproar caused by the Essex affair, the members would no doubt have
been summoned sooner. Elizabeth was still selling land and even
jewellery but, despite all her frugal housekeeping, the state was now
sliding inexorably towards bankruptcy, a slide which the huge additional expense of the Irish war was doing nothing to halt.

The session began badly. Owing to some official blunder a number
of MPs were shut out of the Lords and so missed the Lord Keeper's
opening address, and there was another awkward moment, due to
more bad management, when the Queen was jostled in the crowd of
Commoners as she came out of the Upper House. 'She moved her
hand to have more room; whereupon one of the gentlemen ushers
said openly: "Back, masters, make room." And one answered stoutly
behind: "If you will hang us, we can make no more room." Which
the Queen seemed not to hear, though she heaved up her head, and
looked that way towards him that spake.'

This was the first Parliament since old Lord Burghley's death and
his skill and experience in handling government affairs were soon
missed, as a first-class row blew up in the Commons over the so-

called monopolies. These, like Essex's farm of sweet wines, were
patents issued by the Crown granting to individuals the sole right to
manufacture, import or export certain commodities ranging from
starch to leather, from playing cards to glass and salt, and had long
been a source of grievance. From the Crown's point of view, of
course, they offered a temptingly easy and inexpensive way of re-
warding deserving cases or placating importunate suitors; but they
led naturally to all sorts of irritating abuses, to artificial shortages,
inflated prices and the curtailment of freedom of choice and private
enterprise. Probably, though, the greatest single cause of aggravation
was the fact that corrupt or oppressive patent-holders could not be
proceeded against in the courts. One member described the system
as ending only in beggary and bondage to the subject, another attacked the monopolists as 'these bloodsuckers of the Commonwealth', yet another was to enquire sarcastically when bread would
be added to the list and answered himself by declaring that if action
were not taken now, bread would be there by the next Parliament.

The issue soon resolved itself into a matter of principle, for the
monopolies were not a simple question of bad law which could be
reformed by legislation. They were personal grants made by the
Queen of her own authority and could only be revoked or withdrawn
by her. They came, in short, within the royal prerogative which she
guarded so jealously. The Commons knew they were on dangerous
ground; nevertheless they proceeded to appoint a committee to discuss the subject. One faction urged the passing of a private member's
bill entitled 'An Act for Explanation of the Common Law in certain
cases of Letters Patent' – in other words what amounted to a direct
attack on the prerogative; while another, more moderate, suggested
petitioning the Queen to revoke all monopolies grievous to the subject and to permit the passage of an Act withdrawing such patents
from the protection of the prerogative, so that their validity might be
tested at Common Law.

No decision was reached but the agitation was growing and, as in
the case of the Puritan campaigns of the past, had begun to show
ominous signs of spreading beyond the confines of the Palace of
Westminster. Propaganda sheets were being circulated and non-par-
liamentary supporters of the bill crowded in to lobby the members,
declaring that they were Commonwealth men who desired the House
'to take compassion of their griefs, they being spoiled, imprisoned
and robbed by monopolists'.

It was clear that the Commons had now fairly got their teeth into
the monopolies and were not to be shaken loose by promises – they

had been given promises before. Nor were they to be bullied. Cecil tried this and made matters worse. Worst of all from the government's point of view was the fact that the reading of the vital subsidy bill was being delayed. The holding up of supplies was a familiar weapon in the Commons' armoury, but in present circumstances it was an irresistible one. With the Spaniards on Irish soil, this was no time for a trial of strength, especially on such a doubtful moral issue. The Queen would have to yield, and on 24 November she yielded. On the following day the Speaker rose to inform the House that her Majesty, having learned to her surprise and distress that divers patents were proving grievous to her subjects, intended to take present order for the reformation of anything evil. Robert Cecil then spoke to confirm the royal message. He assured the House that a proclamation giving effect to the promised reformation would be issued without delay and went on to review those monopolies which were to be revoked at once. Every man, in future, would have salt as cheap as he could make or buy it and be able to eat his meat 'more savourly'. Those with weak stomachs would find vinegar set at liberty, and cold stomachs acqua vitae. Those who desired 'to go sprucely in their ruffs' would find starch cheaper, and so on through a long list. When Elizabeth gave way, she always did so handsomely. All the same, when the proclamation duly appeared two days later, it contained a clause re-affirming the power and validity of the prerogative royal and warned the lieges of the penalties which still awaited those who 'seditiously or contemptuously' presumed to call it in question. This was a face-saver, but it also made it plain that the Queen had not given way on principle. The proclamation was a device forced upon her by the necessity of the moment, and was intended to deflect Parliament from attempting to extend its legislative powers into forbidden territory. It was emphatically not a licence to do so.

But the Commons, rapturously welcoming so notable an instance of royal magnanimity, were in no mood for looking gift horses in the mouth. Some wept for joy and all were eager to show their loyal gratitude by giving the subsidy bill its first reading at once. Others wanted to do more, and on the afternoon of Monday, 30 September, a deputation of some hundred and fifty members headed by the Speaker filled the Council Chamber at Whitehall to offer their most humble and hearty thanks in person.

The Queen's reply has become known to history as her 'Golden Speech' and, famous though it is, it still deserves quoting as a classic example of the way in which Elizabeth fished for men's souls, using so sweet a bait that no one could escape her network. 'I do assure you', she told her audience on this occasion, 'there is no prince that loves his subjects better, or whose love can countervail our love. There is no jewel, be it of never so rich a price, which I set before this jewel: I mean your love. For I do esteem it more than any treasure or riches; for that we know how to prize, but love and thanks I count unvaluable. And, though God hath raised me high, yet this I count the glory of my crown, that I have reigned with your loves . . . Therefore, I have cause to wish nothing more than to content the subject; and that is a duty which I owe. Neither do I desire to live longer days than I may see your prosperity; and that is my only desire.'

The Queen went on to thank the Commons for the taxes they were voting her and then told the kneeling deputation to stand up, for she would yet trouble them with longer speech. She touched again on the subject of the monopolies, expressing pious gratitude to those of the Lower House who had brought the matter to her attention. 'For, had I not received a knowledge from you, I might have fallen into the lapse of an error, only for lack of true information . . . That my grants should be grievous to my people and oppressions privileged under colour of our patents, our kingly dignity shall not suffer it. Yea, when I heard it, I could give no rest unto my thoughts until I had reformed it.'

Elizabeth had ever been used to set the Last Judgement Day before her eyes, and she went on: 'I know the title of a King is a glorious title; but assure yourself that the shining glory of princely authority hath not so dazzled the eyes of our understanding, but that we well know and remember that we also are to yield an account of our actions before the great Judge. To be a King and wear a crown is a thing more glorious to them that see it, than it is pleasant to them that bear it. For myself, I was never so much enticed with the glorious name of a King or royal authority of a Queen, as delighted that God hath made me His instrument to maintain His truth and glory, and to defend this Kingdom from peril, dishonour, tyranny and oppression.

'There will never Queen sit in my seat with more zeal to my country, care for my subjects, and that will sooner with willingness venture her life for your good and safety, than myself. For it is my desire to live nor reign no longer than my life and reign shall be for your good. And though you have had and may have many princes more mighty and wise sitting in this seat, yet you never had nor shall have any that will be more careful and loving.'

And she ended: 'This, Mr. Speaker, I pray you deliver unto the

House, to whom heartily recommend me. And so I commit you all to your best fortunes and further counsels. And I pray you, Mr. Comptroller, Mr. Secretary, and you of my Council, that before these gentlemen go into their countries, you bring them all to kiss my hand.'

After this splendidly emotional occasion, the rest of the session passed relatively uneventfully, and an unprecedented quadruple subsidy was granted without too much grumbling. Between two and three o'clock in the afternoon of 19 December the Queen came down to the Lords to dissolve what she evidently believed would be her last Parliament, and after the ceremony of the royal assent she rose unexpectedly to make her valedictory address.

'Before your going down at the end of the Parliament', she said, 'I thought good to deliver unto you certain notes for your observation, that serve aptly for the present time, to be imparted afterward where you shall come abroad – to this end, that you by me, and other by you, may understand to what prince, and how affected to the good of this estate, you have declared yourselves so loving subjects.'

As far as home affairs were concerned, she believed 'yourselves can witness that I never entered into the examination of any cause without advisement, carrying ever a single eye to justice and truth; for, though I were content to hear matters argued and debated pro and contra, as all princes must that will understand what is right, yet I look ever as it were upon a plain table wherein is written neither partiality nor prejudice. My care was ever by proceeding justly and uprightly to conserve my people's love, which I account a gift of God.' When it came to the gloomy subject of finance: 'Beside your dutiful supplies for defence of the public . . . I have diminished my own revenue that I might add to your security, and been content to be a taper of true virgin wax, to waste myself and spend my life that I might give light and comfort to those that live under me.'

Elizabeth then referred briefly to Spanish aggression. 'The strange devices, practices and stratagems, never heard of nor written of before – that have been attempted, not only against my own person . . . but by invasion of the State itself, by those that did not only threaten to come, but came at the last in very deed, with their whole fleet – have been in number many, and by preparation dangerous; though it hath pleased God by many hard escapes and hazards . . . to make me an instrument of His holy will in delivering the State from danger and myself from dishonour. All that I challenge to myself is that I have been studious and industrious, in confidence of His grace and goodness, as a careful head to defend the body.'

Turning at last to 'foreign courses', the Queen took God to witness 'that I never gave just cause of war to any Prince . . . nor had any greater ambition than to maintain my own State in security and peace', and she went on to trace in some detail the origins of the war in the Netherlands and justify her own eventual intervention. At the same time, Elizabeth wanted her subjects to know 'that my care is neither to continue war nor conclude a peace, but for your good; and that you may perceive how free your Queen is from any cause of these attempts that have been made on her, unless to save her people or defend her state be to be censured. This testimony', she declared, 'I would have you carry hence for the world to know: that your Sovereign is more careful of your conservation than of herself, and will daily crave of God that they that wish you best may never wish in vain.'

Elizabeth, great actress as she was, was taking her final curtain – the Bishop of Durham thought he had never heard her 'in better vein' – and rendering a solemn account of her stewardship to a body which had caused her a good deal of trouble over the years but which she had always dealt with honestly according to her lights. It was fitting that the long association between Queen and Parliament should have ended on this stately and graceful note, but it was perhaps just as well that it ended when it did.

The Queen, with her invincibly old-fashioned views on the sanctity of the prerogative royal, on the concept of the people guided and ruled for their own good by a wise, careful and loving sovereign, had never pretended to regard the noisy, self-opinionated assembly at Westminster as an auxiliary branch of government. Government was very definitely her business – undertaken with the advice and assistance of Councillors appointed by herself. The Commons were granted freedom of speech, within limits defined by established custom, and Elizabeth respected them as a representative sounding-board of public opinion, but she had never hesitated to scold them for wasting time in 'vain discourses and tedious orations', or for attempting to meddle with matters 'beyond the reach of a subject's brain to mention' – matters which had included such vital political issues as religion, her marriage and the succession. Nor did she ever hesitate to remind them of the undoubted fact that as she alone had the authority to summon Parliament, to continue it at her good pleasure and dissolve it when she thought good, so she also had the power 'to appoint unto them . . . what causes they were to treat of' and assent or dissent to anything decided by them. Parliament was the servant, albeit the valued servant, of the Crown but never its master, for it was unthinkable that the feet should direct the head.

This philosophy had led to some notable confrontations in the past, when an understandably nervous and sometimes dangerously fanatical House of Commons had fought to do their sovereign lady good against her will. But thanks in part to a deeply ingrained veneration for the mystique of kingship, in part to the shared perils of subversion from within and invasion from without which had drawn Queen and people together, and in part to Elizabeth's own peculiar brand of magic, confrontation had never developed into head-on collision. It was a state of affairs which could not have lasted. The delicately balanced special relationship with Parliament which the Queen had just, but only just, maintained to the end was doomed by the forces of history and not even a ruler of her genius could have maintained it for much longer.

The Commons was rapidly discovering its own strength and, more important, how to organise and direct that strength (some valuable lessons had been absorbed during the Puritan agitations of the eighties). Values were changing and an increasingly articulate and self-confident middle-class of lawyers and landed gentry was less inclined to accept the Tudor ideality of the paternalistic state, readier to question the God-given superiority of the sovereign. On a more practical level, it was realising the potency of that old, cold truth that he who pays the piper can, in the last resort, call the tune. The time was fast approaching, if indeed it had not already arrived, when the Crown could no longer 'live of its own', even in peacetime, when it would become dependent on the goodwill of Parliament for survival. The revolutionary concept of the sovereign Parliament was not yet openly acknowledged – if any member of the 1601 assembly had been told that within half a century it would have arrogated supreme power to itself and assisted at the judicial execution of the Lord's anointed, he would no doubt have been genuinely appalled – but the seeds of revolution had already lain some twenty years in the ground and would need only the warmth generated by righteous anger to germinate with frightening speed.

By the second week of January 1602 news came in from Ireland which did much to cheer the last full year of the Queen's life. Early in December the English naval squadron commanded by Sir Richard Leveson had distinguished itself by annihilating a Spanish fleet bringing reinforcements and supplies to de Aguila, and on the twenty-third Mountjoy's army won an overwhelming victory over Tyrone for the loss of one officer and a dozen men. Tyrone himself was wounded and it was the end of the by now thoroughly disenchanted Spaniards, who surrendered to the Lord Deputy in return for free passage home. It was the beginning of the end, too, for Tyrone and his dream of an independent Gaelic Ireland. It was also the beginning of the modern Irish problem, but this the Queen could hardly have been expected to foresee as she wrote her glowing thanks to Mountjoy, adding one of her scribbled postscripts to the official despatch: 'For yourself, we can but acknowledge your diligence, and dangerous adventure, and cherish and judge of you as your careful Sovereign.'

Relieved of her most immediate anxieties, Elizabeth was ready to authorise a small-scale naval expedition (the first for five years) in Spanish waters and by the end of March Richard Leveson and William Monson were at sea with a force of eight galleons and some smaller craft. It was Leveson who at long last actually encountered the fabled treasure fleet off the Azores, but with apparently only four warships with him at the time he could do little against sixteen heavily armed galleons of the Indian Guard. He did, however, succeed in cutting out one great carrack sheltering in the Lisbon river, and in London the Privy Council, with memories of bitter past experience, took every precaution to prevent her cargo from falling into the hands of the sharks at Plymouth. 'Here is order taken', wrote John Chamberlain, 'that no goldsmiths or jewellers shall go into the west countrie', and Fulk Greville was sent down with instructions to have the prize brought round to Portsmouth for unloading.

Leveson and William Monson between them kept the sea till autumn, but the war was coming to an end now on all fronts. Elizabeth Tudor may not have been a great war-leader, but then she had never wanted to be. Her aims had always been essentially defensive – to save her people and defend her state. Nor was the emerging society she ruled as yet sufficiently well-organised or disciplined to see and seize all its opportunities in a type of naval warfare which was still very largely in the experimental stage. But some vital lessons had been learned and, although it had taken a quarter of a century of suffering and death, the war's great objective, the restoration of a balance of power in Europe, had been achieved. The French monarchy had been helped back on to its feet and freed from the fear of a Spanish take-over. In the Netherlands, the Dutch of Holland and Zeeland – an increasingly prosperous oligarchy soon to challenge their English allies for maritime supremacy – were no longer threatened by renewed Spanish hegemony. The predominantly Catholic southern provinces of Flanders and Brabant remained under Spanish and, later, Austrian rule, but that would protect them from a predatory France and it would be another hundred years before England would again have to fight to secure her frontiers across the North Sea. In Ireland, too, the vulnerable back door was once more locked and bolted, at least for the foreseeable future. Considering the resources at her disposal, the Queen had no reason to feel ashamed of her record, even as a reluctant commander-in-chief.

At home the great dearth of the mid-nineties was over, trade was reviving and new markets and new horizons were being eagerly explored in both the Old World and the New; while the programme of social and economic legislation undertaken during the last decade of the reign had laid the foundations of a system of poor relief which endured for centuries. For very many people the quality of life was showing a steady improvement for, despite increased taxation, the heaviest financial burden of the war had fallen on the Queen rather than her subjects. By the end Elizabeth had been forced to realise practically all the wealth which had accrued to the Crown by her father's nationalisation of Church property at the time of the Reformation. The monarchy was thus seriously weakened – as her successors were to discover – but Elizabeth had preserved her personal authority and safeguarded her realm and had considered the price worth paying.

The religious controversies which had overshadowed so much of the political life of the country for so many years of the Tudor century had now, at last, reached a kind of stalemate. Thanks to the work of churchmen like John Whitgift, Richard Bancroft, Bishop of London and the great Anglican polemicist Richard Hooker, the Church of England was probably in a healthier state than at any time since the Settlement of 1559. The aggressive Puritanism of the eighties had faded, and although Puritanism was by no means dead, it was no longer openly attacking the Established Church. In any case, the radicals cherished strong hopes of King James, who had after all been reared in the presbyterianism of the Church of Scotland, and were content to await developments. The Catholic revival, too, which had caused such a crescendo of alarm and fury in the early eighties, could no longer be represented as a serious threat to national unity. The suffering and sacrifice of the small devoted band of missionary priests trained in the seminaries of Douai and Rheims, and at the English College in Rome, had ensured that the Faith would survive, but they had come too late and too few to reverse the Protestant tide. By the nineties the sudden surge of spiritual fervour among the native Catholics, which had reached its zenith about the time of the famous mission of the Jesuit Fathers Campion and Parsons, was largely spent. A small percentage of the population still clung, and would continue to cling, to its convictions in the face of every discouragement from social ostracism to the death penalty. But constant pressure, a constant sense of insecurity and the wounding imputation of disloyalty to Queen and country were doing their work, and although the Catholics too had hopes of James (at least they would be relieved of the embarrassment of trying to reconcile obedience to the Pope with allegiance to an excommunicated sovereign), not even the most optimistic was expecting more than perhaps a measure of toleration for their diminishing numbers.

For Elizabeth the fact that an actively anti-Jesuit, anti-Spanish faction had now begun to emerge from the ranks of the English Catholics could be taken as a satisfying vindication of her policy of refusal to countenance religious persecution on anything resembling the Continental model. She would not, and could not of course, ever have granted her Catholic subjects freedom of worship, but she who had always refused to make windows into men's souls had never demanded more than outward compliance with her laws, and could never be persuaded that Englishmen who happened to be Catholics must also necessarily be traitors. It was a position which had needed courage to maintain in the menacing atmosphere of the early 1580s, but the Queen had never wavered from it. As always, once she had made up her mind on a matter of principle, she was immovable. The exact nature of her own religious principles has often been debated, but she herself summed it up neatly enough when she remarked to André de Maisse in 1597 that there was only one Jesus Christ and one faith, and all the rest was a dispute about trifles or, she might have added, about power.

There can have been few people living in that second year of the new century who knew more about the exercise of power than the old Queen of England. 'She only is a King! She only knows how to rule!' her former sparring partner the King of France had exclaimed in unfeigned admiration after the Essex revolt; and the King's astute Minister of Finance, the Duc de Sully, who came on a private mission to London in the summer of 1601, was deeply impressed by her Majesty's grasp of affairs and of political realities. 'She drew me aside', he was to recall in his Memoirs, 'that she might speak to me with the greatest freedom on the present state of affairs in Europe; and this she did with such strength and clearness, beginning from the Treaty of Vervins, that I was convinced this great Queen was truly worthy of that high reputation she had acquired.'

Elizabeth referred to the necessity of containing the power of the

House of Hapsburg within just bounds and went on to outline her views on the way in which the other European powers ought to combine, 'so that none of them might be capable of giving umbrage to the rest'. 'These were not the only reflections made by the Queen of England', wrote Sully; 'she said many other things, which appeared to me so just and sensible, that I was filled with astonishment and admiration. It is not unusual to behold princes form great designs; their sphere of action so forcibly inclines them to this . . . but to be able to distinguish and form only such as are reasonable; wisely to regulate the conduct of them; to foresee and guard against all obstacles in such a manner, that when they happen, nothing more will be necessary than to apply the remedies prepared long before – this is what few princes are capable of.' And at the end of their conversation, Sully's verdict was little different from that reached by his compatriot de Maisse four years earlier. 'I cannot bestow praises upon the Queen of England that would be equal to the merit which I discovered in her in this short time, both as to the qualities of the heart and the understanding.'

Not merely was Elizabeth's intellect unimpaired by advancing age, physically she was still in astonishingly good shape. She danced with the Duc de Nevers, who visited her in April 1602, and in September another foreign nobleman reported catching a glimpse of her walking in her garden as briskly as an eighteen-year-old. There was no long progress that year but the Queen paid a round of visits in the London area, finishing up at Oatlands, and Robert Cecil noted that she had not been in better health for years, riding ten miles in a day and hunting without apparent ill-effects. In September the Earl of Worcester wrote to the Earl of Shrewsbury: 'We are frolic here at Court; much dancing in the Privy Chamber of country dances before the Queen's Majesty who is exceedingly pleased therewith.' Later in the month, when Elizabeth had entered her seventieth year, another courtier remarked in a letter to the Countess of Shrewsbury: 'The best news I can yet write your ladyship is of the Queen's health and disposition of body, which I assure you is excellent good. And I have not seen her every way better disposed these many years.'

Like her father, Elizabeth had been fortunate in inheriting the splendid constitution of their Yorkist forebears, but unlike him had never abused it. She had always been fastidious in matters of personal hygiene; had always taken plenty of fresh air and exercise, and was noticeably abstemious over food and drink. She had also, wisely, avoided the ministrations of the royal physicians whenever possible. Probably, though, the real reason for her continued well-being was the fact that she had been lucky enough to spend her life doing work she enjoyed and was supremely good at.

It was true that during her last months she suffered from occasional fits of melancholy. In June she told the French ambassador that 'she was a-weary of life' and went on with a sigh to speak of Essex; while someone told one of King James's friends that 'our Queen is troubled with a rheum in her arm which vexeth her very much . . . She sleepeth not so much by day as she used, neither taketh rest by night.' And he added, for good measure, that her delight was to sit in the dark and sometimes with shedding tears, to bewail Essex. Well, naturally, the great days were over, and Elizabeth knew it. Without an Essex to attract the young men the Court was no longer such a brilliant social centre, and despite the Queen's refusal even now to permit any public mention of her successor, some of the younger element had already begun to turn their eyes northward – Sir John Harington found some less mindful of what they were soon to lose, than of what they might perchance hereafter get.

All the same, it was quite a gay autumn. Queen's Day, the forty-fourth anniversary of her accession, passed with 'the ordinary solemnity'. There were many young runners at the tilting and the Court fool, who appeared on a pony no bigger than a bull mastiff, 'had good audience of her Majesty and made her very merry'. At the beginning of December she was present at a house-warming party at Robert Cecil's and seemed to enjoy herself. Lord Hunsdon gave a grand dinner later in the month, and on the twenty-second the Lord Admiral entertained his sovereign at Arundel House. Christmas was spent at Whitehall and, thanks to the efforts of the new Comptroller Sir Edward Wotton, it was more cheerful than anyone had expected. Indeed, John Chamberlain reported that 'the Court hath flourished more than ordinary' with dancing, bear-baiting and plays.

But not even Elizabeth was immortal – though to James of Scotland it must sometimes have seemed as if she might be – and John Harington, who had come to town for the Christmas season, was shocked at the change he saw in her. 'Our dear Queen, my royal godmother and this state's most natural mother', he wrote to his wife down in Somerset, 'doth now bear show of human infirmity, too fast for that evil which we shall get by her death, and too slow for that good which she shall get by her releasement from pains and misery.'

Harington found the Queen 'in most pitiable state'. Unfortunately, the sight of her godson always brought a vivid reminder of Essex and the Irish disaster and she at once brought the subject up, 'dropped a tear and smote her bosom'. Sir John tried to divert her by reading her some of his witty verses. 'Whereat she smiled once, and was pleased to say: "When thou dost feel creeping time at thy gate, these fooleries will please thee less; I am past my relish for such matters." ' She was eating hardly anything now and for the first time there were signs that her memory was beginning to fail. 'But who', wrote Harington sadly, 'shall say that "your Highness hath forgotten"?'

But he must have seen her on a bad day, for she rallied again and in January was said to be 'very well'. She was still in harness, still dealing with mopping-up operations in Ireland and negotiating the conditions for Tyrone's surrender. There was talk of sending another fleet to blockade the Spanish ports that summer, and plans were being discussed for raising an auxiliary fleet of private ships to guard commerce in the Channel from Spanish privateers and the Dunkirk pirates.

On 21 January the Court moved down to Richmond. The weather had turned very cold, but Elizabeth insisted on wearing 'summer-like garments' and on 6 February she received Giovanni Scaramelli – the first Venetian ambassador appointed to her Court since her accession – resplendently dressed in white and silver, her hair 'of a light colour never made by nature' and apparently in good spirits. She addressed Scaramelli in his own language, and said at the end of the audience: 'I do not know if I have spoken Italian well; still I think so, for I learnt it when a child and believe I have not forgotten it.'

Then, towards the end of February, she lost her cousin and closest woman friend, the Countess of Nottingham, granddaughter of her aunt Mary Boleyn. Elizabeth's mood of wretchedness returned and this time she did not throw it off. Early in March, Lady Nottingham's brother, Robert Carey, came down to Richmond and found the Queen in one of her withdrawing chambers, sitting huddled on a pile of cushions. 'I kissed her hand', he recorded in his Memoirs, 'and told her it was my chiefest happiness to see her in safety, and in health, which I wished might long continue. She took me by the hand, and wrung it hard, and said, "No, Robin, I am not well", and then discoursed with me of her indisposition, and that her heart had been sad and heavy for ten or twelve days; and in her discourse, she fetched not so few as forty or fifty great sighs. I was grieved at the first to see her in this plight; for in all my lifetime before, I never knew her fetch a sigh, but when the Queen of Scots was beheaded.'

Carey did what he could 'to persuade her from this melancholy humour', but found it was too deeply rooted in her heart and hardly to be removed. This was on a Saturday evening. Next day the Queen was not well enough to go to church and heard the service lying on cushions in her privy chamber. 'From that day forwards', says Carey, 'she grew worse and worse. She remained upon her cushions four days and nights at the least. All about her could not persuade her, either to take any sustenance, or go to bed.'

The French ambassador told his master on 19 March that 'Queen Elizabeth had been very much indisposed for the last fourteen days, having scarcely slept at all during that period, and eaten much less than usual, being seized with such a restlessness that, though she had no decided fever, she felt a great heat in her stomach, and a continual thirst, which obliged her every moment to take something to abate it, and to prevent the phlegm, with which she was sometimes oppressed, from choking her.'

The immediate physical cause of the Queen's last illness seems to have been an ulcerated throat which made swallowing difficult and painful, but evidently some form of bronchitis or pneumonia soon set in. Still no one could persuade her to go to bed until, at last, the Lord Admiral, who had left the Court in mourning for his wife, was fetched back and, partly by persuasion, partly by force, he succeeded in getting her off her cushions and into bed. There, temporarily, she felt a little better. An abscess in her throat had burst and she was able to take some broth, but 'there was no hope of her recovery, because she refused all remedies'.

Elizabeth had said repeatedly that she had no desire to live longer than would be for her subjects' good, and now it seemed as if she felt her task was done. She had outlived her century, outlived nearly all her friends, outlived her usefulness to her beloved country and she was very tired. Recently the coronation ring, outward and visible token of her symbolic marriage with the people of England which for nearly forty-five years had never left her finger, had grown into the flesh and had to be cut away. It was an omen. 'The Queen grew worse and worse', said Robert Carey significantly, 'because she would be so.' She lay speechless and semi-conscious, her eyes open, one finger in her mouth, the power flowing out of her, the great golden dangerous world in which she had played so valiant a part fading into darkness.

But there was still one last important duty to be performed, and about six o'clock in the evening of Wednesday, 23 March she made signs asking for the Archbishop of Canterbury and her chaplains to be summoned. Robert Carey was among the company in the bed-chamber and sat upon his knees, full of tears to see that heavy sight. 'Her Majesty', he remembered, 'lay upon her back, with one hand in the bed, and the other without. The Bishop kneeled down by her, and examined her first of her faith; and she so punctually answered all his several questions, by lifting up her eyes, and holding up her hand, as it was a comfort to all the beholders. Then the good man told her plainly what she was, and what she was come to; and though she had been long a great Queen here upon earth, yet shortly she was to yield an account of her stewardship to the King of Kings. After this he began to pray, and all that were by did answer him.'

Old John Whitgift prayed till his knees were weary and then blessed the dying woman and made to rise and leave her. But she would not let him go, making a sign with her hand which Lady Scrope interpreted as a desire that he would pray still. After another 'long half hour' he tried again to leave, and again 'she made a sign to have him continue in prayer. He did so for half-an-hour more, with earnest cries to God for her soul's health, which he uttered with that fervency of spirit, as the Queen, to all our sight, much rejoiced thereat, and gave testimony to us all of her Christian and comfortable end. By this time it grew late, and every one departed, all but her women that attended her.'

'This that I heard with my ears, and did see with my eyes', says Robert Carey, 'I thought it my duty to set down and to affirm it for a truth, upon the faith of a Christian, because I know there have been many false lies reported of the end and death of that good lady.'

Elizabeth slipped away between two and three o'clock on the morning of 24 March, 'mildly like a lamb, easily like a ripe apple from the tree', and Carey, who had been standing by with a horse ready saddled, set out in pouring rain on the first stage of his wild ride north to tell the King of Scotland that the long wait was over – that the last English sovereign of the English nation was at peace.

Epilogue
Queen Elizabeth
of Famous Memory

No oblivion shall ever bury the glory of her
name. For her happy and renowned memory
still liveth and shall for ever live in the minds of men.

The belief that one of Queen Elizabeth's last conscious acts had been to indicate her wish to be succeeded by the King of Scots was current within a few days of her death. Robert Carey repeats the story, but does not say he witnessed the occasion, and the French ambassador reported that, while he already knew the Council intended to proclaim James at once, Elizabeth herself had named no successor. It seems more likely that she who had always dreaded the prospect of being 'buried alive' had remained silent to the end, and that all the convenient tales of death-bed recognition were no more than precautionary propaganda circulated by a prudent government.

In fact, they proved unnecessary. King James's proclamation was duly read on the morning of 24 March at the gates of Whitehall and in Cheapside and the people listened quietly, with great expectation but 'no great shouting'. 'I think the sorrow for her Majesty's departure was so deep in many hearts', wrote the diarist John Manning-

ham, 'they could not so suddenly show any great joy.' Watch was
kept at every gate and street 'to prevent garboils', but there was no
tumult, no contradiction, no hint of disorder in the city. During the
winter Arbella Stuart had made a desperate last-minute attempt to
draw attention to herself, but the poor woman was no match for
Robert Cecil and the transference of power had been accomplished
without a hitch. There was no mention of Lady Arbella, not a whis-
per of the Spanish claim. Bonfires were lit and church bells rung to
celebrate the new reign and 'every man went about his business as
readily, as peaceably, as securely as though there had been no change,
nor any news ever heard of competitors'. For those who could remember the hag-ridden days of the seventies and early eighties, this
peaceful transition provided a final vindication of Elizabeth's policy
over the succession; for those who still mourned the Earl of Essex it
was a vindication of the trust she had reposed in Robert Cecil, but
for very many of her contemporaries England would never be the
same again.

The Queen was carried to her tomb in Westminster Abbey on 28
April, at which time, John Stow recorded in his Annals, 'the City of
Westminster was surcharged with multitudes of all sorts of people,
in the streets, houses, windows, leads, and gutters, who came to see
the obsequy. And when they beheld her statue or effigy, lying on the
coffin, set forth in royal robes, having a crown upon the head thereof,
and a ball and sceptre in either hand, there was such a general sighing,
groaning and weeping, as the like hath not been seen or known in
the memory of man – neither doth any history mention any people,
time or state, to make like lamentation for the death of their sovereign.'

What sort of woman was she, this great Queen, and how can her
achievement best be summed up? Among her surviving friends, John
Harington, who both loved and feared her, blessed her memory for
all her goodness to himself and his family. 'I never did find greater
show of understanding and learning than she was blessed with', he
wrote after her death. Robert Cecil, who had served her declining
years, remembered her as 'more than a man and, in troth, sometimes
less than a woman'; but although he was to prosper under the new
regime, he would always remember her too as 'our blessed Queen'.
'I wish I waited now in her Presence Chamber, with ease at my foot,
and rest in my bed', he was to write to Harington. Lord Burghley,
who of all the Elizabethans is surely best qualified to give an opinion,
said of her that she 'was the wisest woman that ever was, for she
understood the interests and dispositions of all the princes in her

time, and was so perfect in the knowledge of her own realm, that no councillor she had could tell her anything she did not know before'.

That the Queen's greatest strength lay in her matchless skill in promoting and exploiting her unique relationship with the people of England can scarcely be disputed. Their love affair had begun in the first months of the reign and to the end of her life she never forgot its importance – never made the mistake of taking it for granted. Once, 'in merry sort', she asked her godson's wife how she kept her husband's good will and love, and when Mary Harington replied that she always sought to persuade him of her own affection, 'and in so doing did command his', the Queen exclaimed: 'Go to, go to, mistress, you are wisely bent I find; after such sort do I keep the good will of all my husbands, my good people; for if they did not rest assured of some special love toward them, they would not readily yield me such good obedience.' Three years after her death, in a letter to his cousin Markham, Harington himself recalled that: 'Her speech did win all affections, and her subjects did try to show all love to her commands; for she would say, "her state did require her to command what she knew her people would willingly do from their own love to her." Herewith did she show her wisdom fully: for who did choose to lose her confidence; or who would withhold a show of love and obedience, when their Sovereign said it was their own choice, and not her compulsion?'

Like her father and her Yorkist grandfather before her, Elizabeth knew all about the truth of the somewhat cynical maxim that 'the common people oftentimes more esteem and take for greater kindness a little courtesy, than a great benefit'. Of course she traded on her charm – stories of the Queen's 'condescension' to the 'meaner sort' of her subjects are legion – and of course much of it was done for effect. Of course there was self-interest on both sides. But that there was also sincerity is not in question – a love affair does not stand the test of over forty years nourished on self-interest alone. Beneath all the bad poetry, the heavily allegorical pageants, the painstaking Latin orations and the romantic extravaganzas of the Gloriana cult, there lay a solid sub-stratum of mutual need, affection and respect.

The Queen, observed Bishop Mandell Creighton, one of the more percipient of her nineteenth century biographers, 'represented England as no other ruler ever did. For the greater part of her long reign the fortunes of England absolutely depended upon her life, and not only the fortunes of England, but those of Europe as well . . . In asking England to rally round her, Elizabeth knew that she could not de-

mand any great sacrifices on her behalf. By cultivating personal loyalty, by demanding it in exaggerated form, she was not merely feeding her personal vanity; she was creating a habit which was necessary
for the maintenance of her government.' And he goes on: 'Elizabeth's
imperishable claim to greatness lies in her instinctive sympathy with
her people.'

The contemporary historian and schoolmaster, William Camden,
would have agreed with the Victorian Bishop in this assessment of
the Queen. 'Though beset by divers nations, her mortal enemies', he
wrote, 'she held the most stout and warlike nation of the English four
and forty years and upwards, not only in awe and duty, but even in
peace also. Insomuch as, in all England, for so many years, never any
mortal man heard the trumpet sound the charge to battle.'

As far as her own people were concerned, this was undoubtedly
the Queen's greatest achievement – that she had so satisfactorily
defied the might of Spain and of Antichrist, while at the same time
keeping the war out of English territory. And given the passions of
the times, it was a very great achievement indeed. 'She found herself
a sane woman in a universe of violent maniacs', wrote Lytton Strachey in his *Elizabeth and Essex*, 'between contending forces of terrific
intensity – the rival nationalisms of France and Spain, the rival reli-
gions of Rome and Calvin; for years it had seemed inevitable that she
should be crushed by one or other of them, and she had survived
because she had been able to meet the extremes around her with her
own extremes of cunning and prevarication. It so happened that the
subtlety of her intellect was exactly adapted to the complexities of
her environment. The balance of power between France and Spain,
the balance of factions in France and Scotland, the swaying fortunes
of the Netherlands, gave scope for a tortuosity of diplomacy which
has never been completely unravelled to this day . . . Religious
persons at the time were distressed by her conduct, and imperialist
historians have wrung their hands over her since. Why could she not
suppress her hesitations and chicaneries and take a noble risk? Why
did she not step forth, boldly and frankly, as the leader of Protestant
Europe, accept the sovereignty of Holland, and fight the good fight
to destroy Catholicism and transfer the Spanish Empire to the rule
of England? The answer is that she cared for none of these things.
She understood her true nature and her true mission better than her
critics.'

In the field of foreign policy Elizabeth has frequently been accused
of tergiversation, indecision, faint-heartedness and plain dishonesty,
but behind the baffling pallisade which she deliberately erected to

conceal her real intentions it is now possible to see that her underlying purpose was paradoxically not only extremely simple but unwavering in its aim – to keep her people, her kingdom and her throne peaceful, prosperous and secure. In order to achieve that aim and stay dryshod in the quicksand of European politics, the Queen was prepared to shift her ground as often as seemed necessary, for the more confusion and uncertainty she could create in the minds of others, the more freedom of action she retained for herself.

The diplomatic poker game as played by Elizabeth Tudor demanded strong nerves and unremitting concentration. The fact that it also demanded subtlety, subterfuge and a high degree of histrionic ability only added to its zest. There can be no doubt that Elizabeth enjoyed the game for its own sake – certainly her skill as a player has never been equalled. Its justification is that it paid off. Throughout the bloody wars which tore sixteenth century Europe apart no foot of English countryside was laid waste – except, of course, the unlucky village of Mousehole. No English farmstead was burned down, no English town looted or put to the sword, no Englishman, woman or child slaughtered by an invading army. This was Elizabeth's objective, and if her methods of gaining it have laid her open to charges of selfishness and deceit she would have thought it cheap at the price.

The fact that the war was building the foundations of English sea-power and thus of so much of her future greatness scarcely concerned the Queen. She knew all about the importance of sea-power as it affected the struggle with Spain, but she was no visionary and if she cherished no dreams of empire, neither, it should be remembered, did the majority of those doughty entrepreneurs sailing uncharted oceans in vessels in which nowadays one would hesitate to cross the English Channel. They, like their Queen, were preoccupied with the purely practical considerations of trade and profit.

Elizabeth was, above all, an immensely shrewd and successful practical politician, completely at home in the arcane mysteries of her craft, but she was no political theorist. Partly through pressure of circumstances and partly from natural inclination, she was content to live from day to day, dealing with problems as they arose. It is arguable that if she had been readier to move with the times, to look ahead and to recognise the necessity of admitting Parliament at least to junior partnership, the history of the seventeenth century might have taken a different course. But that was not Elizabeth's way and, in any case, she would have regarded any such action as a gross betrayal of everything she stood for. For nearly forty-five years it had been her sacred trust to maintain intact the power, authority and prestige of the Crown, and she had done just that.

To what extent she realised that the system she had so stoutly upheld was crumbling beneath her feet; that the system of government which had been accepted as the natural order of things since Saxon times was doomed, must be a matter for speculation. But that was not Elizabeth's concern. She had held the breach. By sheer force of will she had kept the future at bay and was handing on her inheritance undiminished. The future would be for her successors, for the sickly baby in Scotland and the four-year-old son of Robert and Elizabeth Cromwell of Huntingdon.

Notes on Sources

These notes, like those appended to the individual chapters, are intended only as a guide for the general reader to the more easily accessible source material and are very far from being an exhaustive catalogue. Anyone wishing to dig more deeply into the vast mass of material which does exist should refer in the first instance to the *Bibliography of British History: Tudor Period, 1485–1603*, ed. Conyers Read, 2nd edn (London, 1959).

E. P. Cheyney's two-volume *History of England* (New York, 1914–26) remains the standard modern survey of the post-Armada period and is good on political institutions, if somewhat marred by a strong anti-Elizabeth bias.

Other helpful modern works include: A. L. Rowse, *The Expansion of Elizabethan England* (London, 1955); the second volume of J. E. Neale's definitive *Queen Elizabeth and Her Parliaments* (London, 1957); two classics by the great naval historian J. S. Corbett, *Drake and the Tudor Navy*, 2 vols (London, 1898–9) and *The Successors of Drake* (London, 1900); M. A. S. Hume, *Treason and Plot* (London, 1901); Patrick McGrath, *Papists and Puritans under Elizabeth I* (London, 1967); and Roy Strong, *The Cult of Elizabeth* (London, 1977).

Biographies of Elizabeth continue to proliferate, but J. E. Neale's *Queen Elizabeth I*, first published in 1934 and reprinted many times since, is still the best to my mind. Of the older lives, Mandell Creighton's *Queen Elizabeth* (London, 1896) is the most perceptive; and, for an excellent recent one, Paul Johnson's *Elizabeth I: A Study in Power and Intellect* (London, 1974).

Other biographies covering this period are generally rather thin on the ground. There is, for example (and surprisingly), no satisfactory life of Robert Cecil. For Essex we have two volumes of W. B. Devereux's *Lives and Letters of the Devereux, Earls of Essex* (London, 1853), which are chiefly useful for the documents they print. Lytton Strachey's classic *Elizabeth and Essex* (London, 1928) is perhaps better regarded as literature than as history. More recent, and the most scholarly, is G. B. Harrison's *The Life and Death of Robert Devereux, Earl of Essex* (London, 1937). The most recent, Robert Lacey's *Robert, Earl of Essex: An Elizabethan Icarus* (London, 1971), makes a good. read and a good introduction to its subject, but I found it disappointingly thin. Daphne du Maurier's *Golden Lads* (London, 1975) is a fascinating study of the Bacon brothers, especially of the little-known Anthony. For Francis there is also James Spedding's *The Letters and Life of Francis Bacon,* 2 vols (London, 1890), which prints a lot of useful material relating to his relationship with Essex.

Of contemporary printed sources the following are basic. *Annals of Queen Elizabeth* by William Camden, master at Westminster School and a friend of Lord Burghley; originally written in Latin, the best English translation is by H. Norton (London, 1688). Thomas Birch, *Memoirs of the Reign of Queen Elizabeth,* 2 vols (London, 1754), drawn chiefly from the Bacon manuscripts in Lambeth Palace Library. *The Sidney Papers,* ed. Arthur Collins, 2 vols (London, 1746), which contain the letters written to Robert Sidney during his governorship of Flushing by his agent at Court, Rowland Whyte, and are particularly valuable regarding the downfall of Essex. *The Letters of John Chamberlain,* ed. N. E. McClure, 2 vols (Philadelphia, Pa., 1939), gives most of the gossip for the final years of the reign, and John Harington's *Nugae Antiquae,* ed. Thomas Park, 2 vols (London, 1804), prints the letters, miscellaneous papers and jottings of the Queen's merry godson.

Other source collections include: Robert Naunton's *Fragmenta Regalia: or Observations on the Late Queen Elizabeth, Her Times and Her Favourites,* reprinted by Edward Arber (London, 1895); John Nichols, *The Progresses and Public Processions of Queen Elizabeth,* 3 vols (London, 1823); Thomas Wright, *Queen Elizabeth and Her Times* (London, 1838); and E. Lodge, *Illustrations of British History,* 3 vols (London, 1838).

The Calendar of State Papers, Spanish, Elizabeth vol. IV (London, 1899), and *The Calendar of State Papers, Venetian,* vols. VIII and IX, (London, 1894, 1898), all contain relevant material, with especial reference to the Armadas of the 1590s. Although there was no official Venetian ambassador accredited to London until the very end of Elizabeth's reign, the Venetians always took a close and informed interest in the Anglo-Spanish conflict.

PROLOGUE

The best modern account of the Armada is Garrett Mattingly, *The Defeat of the Spanish Armada,* Cape, 1959, but see also Michael Lewis; *The Spanish Armada,* Batsford, 1960 and A.M. Hadfield, *Time to Finish the Game,* J. M. Dent, 1964. Most of the documents are printed in J.K. Laughton, *The Defeat of the Spanish Armada,* 2 vols., Navy Record Society, 1894.

For a description of the visit to Tilbury, see J. Nichols, *The Progresses of Queen Elizabeth,* vol. II.

CHAPTER I.　A MOST RENOWNED VIRGIN QUEEN

The fullest description of the procession to St Paul's is to be found in Nichols's *Progresses and Processions of Queen Elizabeth,* vol. II. Another account appears in Emanuel van Meteren's narrative of the defeat of the Spanish Armada printed in Richard Hakluyt, *Principal Navigations,* Everyman's Library, vol. vi; and there is also a reference in Camden's *Annals.*

Harington's *Nugae Antiquae* is the best single source for personal descriptions of Elizabeth in later life, but there are also, of course, numerous other references scattered through the memoirs and correspondence of the period; for example, John Clapham's *Observations Concerning the Life and Reign of Queen Elizabeth,* ed. E. P. and Conyers Read (Philadelphia, Pa., 1951), and letters in Lodge's *Illustrations of British History,* vol. ii.

For the Earl of Leicester's death, see *Calendar of State Papers, Spanish, Elizabeth (C.S.P. Span. Elizabeth),* vol. iv, pp. 420–1 and 431. For the rise of Essex, see Naunton's *Fragmenta Regalia* and Devereux, *Lives and Letters of the Devereux, Earls of Essex,* vol. i.

The aftermath of the attempted Spanish invasion of 1588 and European reaction to its failure can be followed in *C.S.P. Span. Elizabeth,* vol. iv and *Calendar of State Papers, Venetian (C.S.P. Ven.),* vol. viii. The Venetian despatches are especially valuable, being usually well informed and unbiased.

For a detailed, modern and scholarly account of the great Portugal expedition of 1589, R. B. Wernham's two articles, 'Queen Elizabeth and the Portugal Expedition', *English Historical Review,* vol. lxvi (Jan. and April 1951), are of the greatest value. See also Corbett's *Drake and the Tudor Navy;* Cheyney's *History of England,* vol. i; William Monson's *Naval Tracts,* ed. M. Oppenheim, vol. i (Navy Records Society, 1902); and *Acts of the Privy Council,* ed. J. R. Dasent, vol. xvii. Other sources include: Devereux, *Earls of Essex;* Lodge, *Illustrations of British History; C.S.P. Ven.,* vol. viii; Birch, *Memoirs of the Reign of Queen Elizabeth,* vol. i; and Anthony Wingfield's narrative in Hakluyt, *Principal Navigations,* vol. vi.

CHAPTER II.   GOD'S HANDMAIDEN

The aftermath of the Portugal voyage can be followed in Anthony Wingfield's narrative; in Monson's *Naval Tracts,* vol. i; in the despatches of the Venetian ambassador in Madrid, *C.S.P. Ven.,* vol. viii; and in *Acts of the Privy Council,* vol. xviii.

For a general account of the activities of the privateers, see Rowse, *Expansion of Elizabethan England;* also, of course, references in Hakluyt's *Principal Navigations,* and in Monson's *Naval Tracts,* vol. i, which contains an account of Frobisher's and Hawkins's 1590 expedition.

For Anglo-French affairs in 1589, see Cheyney, *History of England,* vol. i, and Conyers Read, *Lord Burghley and Queen Elizabeth* (London, 1960). *Acts of the Privy Council,* vol. xviii, contains a lot of detail regarding the organisation of the 1589 expeditionary force; and Lady Georgiana Bertie's *Five Generations of a Loyal House* (London, 1845) contains Lord Willoughby's journal of the campaign itself. Lord Burghley's letter to the Earl of Shrewsbury is printed in Lodge, *Illustrations of British History,* vol. ii.

For the Parliament of 1589 and all other parliamentary proceedings, see Neale's invaluable *Queen Elizabeth and Her Parliaments* – in this case, vol. II.

There is a considerable literature on the growth of the Puritan and Presbyterian movements in England, but McGrath's *Papists and Puritans under Elizabeth I* provides a lucid general introduction to a highly complicated subject and contains notes and a full bibliography.

Roy Strong's *The Cult of Elizabeth* contains an illuminating account of both the Accession Day celebrations and the Accession Day tilts, but see also J. E. Neale's *Essays in Elizabethan History* (London, 1958), and E. C. Wilson's scholarly survey, *England's Eliza* (Cambridge, Mass., 1939). George Peele describes the 1590 tilt in his *Polyhymnia: Works*, ed. A. H. Bullen (London, 1888), vol. II.

CHAPTER III.   FAIR STOOD THE WIND FOR FRANCE

For a general survey of the European situation in the early 1590s, see Cheyney, *History of England*, vol. I; and, for an account of the Brittany campaign in particular, Thomas Churchyard, *Service of Sir John Norris in Brittany in 1591* (London, 1602).

The main sources for the operations in Normandy in 1591–2 are: Birch, *Memoirs of the Reign of Queen Elizabeth*, vol. I; *The Correspondence of Sir Henry Unton* (Roxburghe Club, 1847); 'Journal of the Siege of Rouen,' in *Camden Society Miscellany*, vol. I (1847); and *English Historical Review*, vol. XVII. Essex's letters are to be found in Devereux, *Earls of Essex*, vol. I; and see also *Letters of Queen Elizabeth*, ed. G. B. Harrison (London, 1935). For a valuable modern account of the campaign, see the article by R. B. Wernham, 'Queen Elizabeth and the Siege of Rouen', in *Transactions of the Royal Historical Society*, 4th series, vol. XV.

The classic description of the last fight of the *Revenge* was written by Sir Walter Raleigh shortly after the event, and is printed in *Somers Tracts*, vol. I (1809), in Edward Arber's *English Reprints* (1871), and in Hakluyt's *Principal Navigations* (1903 ed.), vol. VII. But see also Monson's *Naval Tracts*, vol. I, and A. L. Rowse, *Sir Richard Grenville of the 'Revenge'* (London, 1937).

For the *Madre de Dios* affair: Monson's *Naval Tracts*, vol. I; Rowse, *Expansion of Elizabethan England*; and letters printed in Wright's *Queen Elizabeth and Her Times*, vol. II.

For the genesis of the Essex–Cecil feud, see Read, *Burghley and Queen Elizabeth*, and also Essex's correspondence in Devereux, *Earls of Essex*, vol. I. Much of Anthony Bacon's correspondence is printed in Birch, *Memoirs of the Reign of Queen Elizabeth*. See also Spedding, *Letters and Life of Francis Bacon*, vol. I, and Daphne du Maurier's penetrating study, *Golden Lads*.

For the Parliament of 1593, see Neale, *Elizabeth and Her Parliaments*, vol. II.

CHAPTER IV.   A MAID IN AN ISLAND

For the Queen's journeyings of 1591 and 1592, see Nichols, *Progresses of Queen Elizabeth,* vol. III.

The story of the struggle to get the Attorneyship for Francis can be found in Spedding, *Letters and Life of Francis Bacon,* vol. I, and in Birch, *Memoirs of the Reign of Queen Elizabeth,* vol. I; but see also Devereux, *Earls of Essex,* vol. I, and Harrison, *Robert Devereux.*

The main sources for the Lopez affair are Birch, *Memoirs of the Reign of Queen Elizabeth,* vol. I, and Hume, *Treason and Plot;* but see also *C.S.P. Span. Elizabeth,* vol. IV, and Arthur Dimock, 'The Conspiracy of Dr Lopez', in *English Historical Review,* July 1894.

The 'Device' presented by Essex at the Accession Day tilts of 1595 is printed in Spedding, *Letters and Life of Francis Bacon,* and also described by Rowland Whyte in *Sidney Papers,* vol. I.

For a general account of the political situation in France following the King's conversion, see Cheyney, *History of England,* vol. I. For a more detailed view of Anglo-French diplomatic relations from 1592 onwards, see Thomas Birch, *An Historical View of the Negotiations between the Courts of England, France and Brussels . . . Extracted from the State Papers of Sir Thomas Edmondes,* and G. G. Butler, *The Edmondes Papers* (Roxburghe Club, 1973). The last expedition to Brittany in 1594–5 is described in Monson, *Naval Tracts,* vol. I.

The Drake–Hawkins voyage of 1595 is also covered in Monson, *Naval Tracts,* vol. I, and a contemporary account by one of the participants is Thomas Maynarde's *Sir Francis Drake His Voyage, 1595,* ed. W. D. Cooley, Hakluyt Society, vol. IV (1849). See also, of course, Corbett's classic *Drake and the Tudor Navy.*

For the fall of Calais, the negotiations leading to the Treaty of Greenwich, and the preparatory stages of the great expedition of 1596, see: Cheyney, *History of England,* vol. II; Read, *Burghley and Queen Elizabeth;* Birch, *Memoirs of the Reign of Queen Elizabeth,* vols. I and II; *Sidney Papers,* vol. I; Devereux, *Earls of Essex,* vol. I; Harrison, *Robert Devereux;* and Monson, *Naval Tracts,* vol. I.

CHAPTER V.   GREAT ELIZA'S GLORIOUS NAME

For an authoritative modern account of the Cadiz voyage, see Corbett, *Successors of Drake.* Other sources include: Monson, *Naval Tracts,* vols. I and II; Hakluyt's *Principal Navigations;* Sir Walter Raleigh's *Relation of the Cadiz Action,* printed in *Works,* 8 vols (Oxford, 1829), vol. VIII; and Sir William Slingsby, *The Voyage to Calis,* Navy Record Society, vol. XX (1902). See also L. W. Henry, 'The Earl of Essex as Strategist and Military Organiser (1596–97)', in *English Historical Review,* vol. LXVIII (1953).

For the aftermath of Cadiz, see: *Acts of the Privy Council,* vol. XXVI; Birch, *Memoirs of the Reign of Queen Elizabeth,* vol. II; and Devereux, *Earls of Essex,* vol. I.

Francis Bacon's famous letter of advice to his patron is printed in Birch, *Memoirs of the Reign of Queen Elizabeth,* vol. II, in Devereux, *Earls of Essex,* vol. I, and in Spedding, *Letters and Life of Francis Bacon,* vol. II.

For the Armada of 1596, see: Birch, *Memoirs of the Reign of Queen Elizabeth,* vol. II; Monson, *Naval Tracts,* vol. II; Corbett, *Successors of Drake;* Hume, *Treason and Plot;* and, of course, *C.S.P. Ven.,* vol. IX, and *C.S.P. Span. Elizabeth,* vol. IV.

The episode of swearing in the Lord Keeper in 1596 is described in Read, *Burghley and Queen Elizabeth,* and in Joel Hurstfield, *Elizabeth I and the Unity of England* (London, 1960).

For foreign impressions of the Queen in the early 1590s, see W. B. Rye, *England as Seen by Foreigners* (London, 1865), and Victor von Klarwill, *Queen Elizabeth and Some Foreigners,* trans. T. N. Nash (London, 1928).

For the great dearth of 1594–7, see: William Camden's and John Stow's respective *Annals; Acts of the Privy Council,* vol. XXVI; and also the general account in Cheyney, *History of England,* vol. II.

The manoeuvrings at Court during 1596–7 are described in the splendidly gossipy letters of Rowland Whyte, Robert Sidney's agent, and printed in *Sidney Papers,* vol. II. See also Birch, *Memoirs of the Reign of Queen Elizabeth,* vol. II; Devereux, *Earls of Essex,* vol. I; and Harrison, *Robert Devereux.*

For the Islands Voyage and the 1597 Armada, the main sources are: Corbett, *Successors of Drake;* Monson, *Naval Tracts,* vol. II; Hakluyt, *Principal Navigations;* Devereux, *Earls of Essex,* vol. I; Hume, *Treason and Plot;* and *C.S.P. Ven.* and *Span., Elizabeth.*

CHAPTER VI.   A VERY GREAT PRINCESS

The row which resulted from Charles Howard's promotion is described by Rowland Whyte in his letters to Robert Sidney (*Sidney Papers,* vol. II), but see also: Birch, *Memoirs of the Reign of Queen Elizabeth,* vol. II; Devereux, *Earls of Essex,* vol. I; and Harrison, *Robert Devereux.*

For André de Maisse's mission and his impressions of the Queen and the Court, see his *Journal,* trans. and with an introduction by G. B. Harrison and R. A. Jones (London, 1931).

For Cecil's precautions before leaving for France and also the 'reconciliation' with Lady Leicester, see *Sidney Papers,* vol. II.

Paul Hentzner's account of his visit to England is printed in Nichols, *Progresses of Queen Elizabeth,* vol. III, and also in Rye, *England as Seen by Foreigners.*

For a general account of the intrigues being carried on by King James with the European powers during the 1590s, see Hume, *Treason and Plot.*

Essex's *Apology* concerning his reasons for wishing to continue the war with Spain is printed in Devereux, *Earls of Essex,* vol. I, and the prayer-book incident is described by Camden in his *Annals.*

The great face-slapping row is also related by Camden, and the correspondence which followed is printed in Birch, Devereux and Harrison.

For Burghley's last letter, see Wright, *Queen Elizabeth and Her Times*, vol. II; and, for the Queen's reaction to his death, see William Knollys's letter to Essex printed in Birch, *Memoirs of the Reign of Queen Elizabeth*, vol. II, p. 390, and also Harington, *Nugae Antiquae*, vol. I, pp. 173 and 244.

For Essex's return to Court after the Yellow Ford disaster, see Birch, Harrison and Devereux. His appearance at Lord Burghley's funeral is described in *Letters of John Chamberlain*, vol. I; and Bacon's letter is printed in Spedding, *Letters and Life of Francis Bacon*, vol. II.

CHAPTER VII.   THE GENERAL OF OUR GRACIOUS EMPRESS

The history of Elizabethan Ireland is, like all Irish history, exceedingly complicated and there is in consequence a voluminous literature on the subject. For a catalogue of contemporary sources and later works up to 1959, see the section on Ireland in *Bibliography of British History: Tudor Period, 1485–1603*, ed. Read. The standard general survey, however, remains Richard Bagwell, *Ireland under the Tudors*, 3 vols (London, 1885). See also the illuminating chapters on Ireland in: Rowse, *Expansion of Elizabethan England;* R. Dudley Edwards, 'Ireland, Elizabeth I and the Counter-Reformation', in *Elizabethan Government and Society* (London, 1961); and Cyril Falls, *Elizabeth's Irish Wars* (London, 1950).

The build-up to Essex's appointment as Lord-Lieutenant may be followed in Camden's Annals, in Birch's *Memoirs of the Reign of Queen Elizabeth*, vol. II, in Harrison's *Robert Devereux* and, of course, in the relevant volumes of the *Calendar of State Papers, Ireland (C.S.P., Ireland)*. Robert Markham's and Essex's letters to John Harington can be found in Harington's *Nugae Antiquae*, vol. I, which also contains Harington's Irish journal.

Most of the correspondence between Essex and the Queen during his absence is printed in Devereux, *Earls of Essex*, vol. II, in Harrison's *Robert Devereux* and *Letters of Queen Elizabeth*, but see also *C.S.P. Ireland*.

For Essex's confabulations with Tyrone and his plans for a *coup d'état* in 1599, see the depositions printed as Additional Evidences in Spedding, *Letters and Life of Francis Bacon*, vol. II.

Rowland Whyte's letters to Robert Sidney, printed in *Sidney Papers*, vol. II, are a primary source for Essex's dramatic arrival at Nonesuch and for the events of the autumn, but see also Harington, *Nugae Antiquae*, vol. I, and Spedding, *Letters and Life of Francis Bacon*, vol. II.

CHAPTER VIII.   THE MADCAPS ALL IN RIOT

There are brief discussions of the peace negotiations with Spain in Rowse, *Expansion of Elizabethan England*, and Cheyney, *History of England*, vol. II, pp. 559–60; but see also *Calendar of State Papers, Domestic (C.S.P. Domestic)*, 1598–1601, and *Sidney Papers*, vol. II.

For the continuing war on sea and land, see: Rowse, *Expansion of Elizabethan England;* Corbett, *Successors of Drake;* and Clements R. Markham, *The Fighting Veres* (London, 1888).

For the appointment of Lord Mountjoy as Lord Deputy of Ireland, see *Sidney Papers,* vol. II, and Birch, *Memoirs of the Reign of Queen Elizabeth,* vol. II. His correspondence with King James is revealed in Charles Danvers's confession, printed in Spedding, *Letters and Life of Francis Bacon,* and the appendix of *Correspondence of King James of Scotland with Sir Robert Cecil,* ed. John Bruce (Camden Society, 1861).

For Essex's return to Essex House, see: *Sidney Papers,* vol. II; *Letters of John Chamberlain,* vol. I; and Devereux, *Earls of Essex,* vol. II. Walter Raleigh's letter to Cecil is printed in E. Edwards, *Life of Sir Walter Ralegh,* 2 vols (London, 1868), vol. II. Accounts of the proceedings at York House in June 1600 can be found in: *Sidney Papers,* vol. II; Birch, *Memoirs of the Reign of Queen Elizabeth,* vol. II; Spedding, *Letters and Life of Francis Bacon,* vol. II; and Devereux, *Earls of Essex.* See also Harrison, *Robert Devereux.*

See *Letters of John Chamberlain* and *Sidney Papers* for Elizabeth in the summer of 1600, and Devereux, *Earls of Essex,* for most of Essex's letters.

The plottings of the autumn and winter 1600–1 can be followed in the confessions printed in Spedding, *Letters and Life of Francis Bacon,* vol. II, and appendix to *Correspondence of King James and Robert Cecil.* See Devereux, *Earls of Essex,* for Essex's last letters to the Queen, and Harington, *Nugae Antiquae,* vol. I, for his attitude towards her.

For the rebellion itself, see: Camden's *Annals;* Devereux, *Earls of Essex,* vol. II; Birch, *Memoirs of the Reign of Queen Elizabeth,* vol. II; *Acts of the Privy Council;* and *C.S.P. Domestic.* There is an account of Essex's trial in D. Jardine, *Criminal Trials,* vol. I (1832), but see also: Spedding, *Letters and Life of Francis Bacon,* vol. II; Devereux, *Earls of Essex;* and Harrison, *Robert Devereux.* For the Queen's reaction, see Harington, *Nugae Antiquae;* and Robert Naunton's comments appear in his *Fragmenta Regalia.*

Cecil's correspondence with James is printed in the Camden Society's *Correspondence of King James and Robert Cecil.*

CHAPTER IX.   A TAPER OF TRUE VIRGIN WAX

The Queen's encounter with Sir William Browne is described by himself in *Sidney Papers,* vol. II, and an account of her interview with William Lambarde appears in Nichols's *Progresses of Queen Elizabeth,* vol. III.

For a general account of the Spanish landing at Kinsale, see the relevant chapters in Rowse, *Expansion of Elizabethan England,* and Corbett, *Successors of Drake.* For more detail: *C.S.P. Ireland;* Fynes Morison, *Itinerary* (Glasgow, 1907–8); and Falls, *Elizabeth's Irish Wars.* Some of Elizabeth's letters to Mountjoy are printed in *Letters of Queen Elizabeth.*

There is a lucid discussion of the monopolies in Cheyney, *History of England,* vol. II; but, for a detailed account of proceedings in the Parliament of 1601 and the definitive text of the Golden Speech, see Neale, *Queen Elizabeth and Her Parliaments*, vol. II.

For the end of the war in Ireland, see second paragraph above; and, for Leveson's and Monson's exploits at sea, Corbett's *Successors of Drake* and Monson's *Naval Tracts*, vol. II. For the closing stages of the war in general, see Corbett, *Successors of Drake;* Rowse, *Expansion of Elizabethan England;* and Markham, *Fighting Veres.*

There is a useful and detailed summary of the religious situation at the end of the reign in McGrath, *Papists and Puritans.*

For the Queen's journeyings in the summer of 1601, see Nichols, *Progresses of Queen Elizabeth,* vol. III; and, for Sully's impressions, *Memoirs of the Duc de Sully,* trans. Charlotte Lennox, vol. II (London, 1756).

Glimpses of the Queen in the last year of her life can be found in: *Letters of John Chamberlain;* Lodge, *Illustrations of British History,* vol. II; *Sidney Papers,* vol. II; Nichols, *Progresses of Queen Elizabeth,* vol. III; and Harington, *Nugae Antiquae.* See *C.S.P. Ven.,* 1592–1603, for her interview with Scaramelli.

The best and most reliable account of her last illness and death is printed in *Memoirs of the Life of Robert Carey,* ed. Sir Walter Scott (Edinburgh, 1808). The French ambassador's letters are printed in Birch, *Memoirs of the Reign of Queen Elizabeth,* vol. II; and see also *Letters of John Chamberlain,* and *The Diary of John Manningham,* ed. John Bruce (Camden Society, 1868).

Index